BARRON'S

MECHANICAL APTITUDE AND SPATIAL RELATIONS TESTS

2ND EDITION

Joel Wiesen, Ph.D.
Director, Applied Personnel Research

BARRON'S

Acknowledgments

I would like to heartily thank my good friends Charles Halbfinger and Cyd Josephy; a dear colleague, Laura Bradford; and my beloved and talented wife, Laura Wiesen, who provided many valuable suggestions while I was writing this book and helped edit and proof it.

© Copyright 2009 by Joel Wiesen
© Previous edition copyright 2003 by Joel Wiesen under the title *How to Prepare for the Mechanical Aptitude and Spatial Relations Tests*

All inquiries should be addressed to:
Barron's Educational Series, Inc.
250 Wireless Boulevard
Hauppauge, New York 11788
www.barronseduc.com

Request for Your Help
If you take a mechanical aptitude or spatial ability test that looks different from the tests in this book, please let the author of this book know by sending a letter describing the new test to the Editorial Department at Barron's Educational Series, Inc., 250 Wireless Boulevard, Hauppauge, New York 11788. **www.barronseduc.com**
Or e-mail the author directly at JWiesen@appliedpersonnelresearch.com

ISBN-13: 978-0-7641-4108-9
ISBN-10: 0-7641-4108-2

Library of Congress Catalog Card No. 2008941098

PRINTED IN THE UNITED STATES OF AMERICA
9 8 7 6 5 4 3 2

Contents

Introduction   v

1 The Streetwise Test Taker   1

2 How to Develop Your Mechanical Aptitude and Spatial Ability   9

3 General Mechanical Understanding   13

4 Gears   49

5 Pulleys   67

6 Tools   85

7 Map Reading   101

8 Line Following   121

9 Matching Shapes   127

10 Visual Comparison   135

11 Finding Rotated Shapes   141

12 Cut-Ups   149

13 Jigsaw Puzzles   161

14 Hole Punching   177

15 Hidden Blocks   189

16 Counting Touching Blocks   203

17 Making Rectangular Boxes   211

18 Paper Folding— Shape Known   223

19 Paper Folding— Shape Unknown   239

20 Parts Assembly   271

21 Practice Tests   283

General Mechanical Understanding   285
Gears   293
Pulleys   303
Tools   313
Map Reading   321

Line Following 333

Matching Shapes 339

Visual Comparison 349

Finding Rotated Shapes 357

Cut-Ups 365

Jigsaw Puzzles 373

Hole Punching 381

Hidden Blocks 389

Counting Touching Blocks 399

Making Rectangular Boxes 407

Paper Folding—Shape Known 415

Paper Folding—Shape Unknown 425

Parts Assembly 435

Appendix A: The Different Types of Computer-Based Tests 445

Appendix B: Taking a Video-Based Test 453

Index 465

Introduction

Welcome to the world of mechanical aptitude and spatial ability tests. Whether you have an hour, a day, a week, or a month or more to prepare, you can use this book to help you do your best on these tests.

Mechanical aptitude and spatial ability tests look very different but try to measure the same basic ability. People who do well on one of these tests tend to do well on the others. These tests are different from math and biology tests which most people take in school. Mechanical aptitude tests may ask about topics we learn about in school, but they also ask about topics we learn about outside of school as we play, cook, work, and live our lives. Spatial ability tests usually ask questions about topics that are not taught in school.

This chapter gives you some basic background to help you understand and do your best on these tests. It also answers these questions:

- What are mechanical aptitude tests?

- What are spatial ability tests?

- What jobs are these tests used for?

- How can I use this book?

TIP

Try several ways to learn what the test will cover. (See Chapter 2 for details.)

WHAT ARE MECHANICAL APTITUDE TESTS?

Mechanical aptitude tests measure your aptitude for, or ability to learn about, mechanical concepts (how things work). These tests measure your knowledge of some widely known and understood mechanical and scientific concepts. Often these tests use simple drawings to ask questions about practical, everyday situations. Mechanical aptitude tests usually ask only one or two questions about a topic, and cover many topics. This book will help you study the topics that are most often covered by this type of test.

Questions about gears, pulleys, and tools make up a large part of some tests. This book has a chapter on each of these topics, including short lessons in many of them. You might need to spend extra time studying and reviewing these chapters.

WHAT ARE SPATIAL ABILITY TESTS?

Spatial ability tests measure your ability to think about how flat and solid objects can be rotated, put together, turned over, and folded. Some tests ask about 2-D (flat) objects. Other tests ask about 3-D (three-dimensional) or solid objects. Other tests ask you to think about folding paper patterns into solid shapes. Some tests (such as those on hidden blocks and touching blocks) ask you to think about blocks that are hidden by other blocks. This book has a chapter on each of these types of questions.

WHAT JOBS ARE THESE TESTS USED FOR?

Employers and schools often use tests to help decide who to hire for trainee and entry-level jobs or who to accept as students. Each employer and school makes its own decisions on what tests to use. Some companies and schools ask applicants to take several different tests, such as reading, math, and mechanical aptitude. Employers often give mechanical aptitude and spatial ability tests to applicants in many fields and for many different jobs, such as the following:

Aerospace Engineer

Aircraft Maintenance Trainee

Aircraft Launch and Recovery
  Specialist

Airplane Pilot

Auto Mechanic Trainee

Automotive and Heavy Equipment
  Mechanic

CADD—Computer-Aided Design
  and Drafting

Communications Equipment
  Repairer

Drafter

Drafter's Assistant

Electrical Worker

Firefighter

Flight Engineer

Helicopter Pilot

Machine Tool Technologist

Machinist

Maintenance Worker

Manufacturing Technologist

Marine Engine Mechanic

Mechanic's Helper

Plumber and Pipe Fitter

Police Officer

Power Plant Operator

Powerhouse Mechanic

Precision Instrument Repairer

Production Worker

Ship Engineer

Skilled Trades Apprentice

  — mechanic

  — HVAC (heating/ventilation/
    air-conditioning)

  — toolmaker

  — instrumentation

  — other skilled trades

Transportation Maintenance Manager

Water and Sewage Treatment Plant
  Operator

Weapons Maintenance Technician

WHAT IS IN THIS BOOK?

This book covers what you need to learn and study to help you do your best on mechanical aptitude and spatial ability tests. This book includes chapters on

- The Streetwise Test Taker
  This has tips for finding out what is on the test, preparing for the test, and not losing points when you take the test. It also gives pointers on taking tests with short time limits.

HOW CAN I USE THIS BOOK?

How you use this book depends on how much time you have to prepare. If you have just an hour or two, look at the chapter or chapters that you think are most similar to the test you will be taking. If you have a little more time, also take some of the practice tests at the end of the book. If you have a day or more, read chapter 1 on being a streetwise test taker and do some of the things suggested in that chapter. If you have more time, spread out your preparation. It is better to study for an hour on many days than to study for many hours on one day. If you have a few weeks or more, read chapter 2 on how to develop your mechanical aptitude and spatial ability and do some of the things suggested in that chapter.

Good luck!

The Streetwise Test Taker

The streetwise test taker prepares in several ways to do his or her best on the test. This chapter gives you tips from some of the most experienced test experts in the world. These tips will help you:

- learn about the test(s) you will take

- get ready for the test

- avoid losing credit because of computer grading errors

- deal with time limits

- decide when to guess

- get comfortable with the test.

This chapter is divided into eight parts:

- How to Learn What the Tests Cover

- Before the Test

- What to Bring to the Test

- When You Get to the Test Location

- Filling Out the Answer Sheet

- Test Instructions

- Test-Taking Strategies (including time limits and guessing)

- When the Test Is Over

> **TIP**
>
> Talk to people who have taken the test.

These are must-reads for any test taker. The more you know about taking tests and about the tests you will be taking, the more prepared you will be, the more comfortable you will feel, and the better you will do.

HOW TO LEARN WHAT THE TESTS COVER

To learn what the tests cover,

- find out what topics or areas the tests you are taking will cover.

- learn as much as you can about the test topics.

Most schools do not offer courses in taking this type of test. Companies or other organizations choose and even make up their own tests. To help learn what the tests will cover, you could:

- read all the descriptions the organization may give you.

- talk to your contact person at the organization.

- talk to people who have taken the test you will be taking.

After you know what topics or types of topics will be covered on the test, use this book to become familiar with the tests and to practice taking them. In this book you can:

- learn any special rules for taking a certain type of test.

- learn about the topics covered in each type of test.

- take practice tests.

Learning about the tests in this way helps you become comfortable with the test material and do your best.

BEFORE THE TEST

You may be taking a test to try to get a job with a certain company. If so, call the company and ask to speak with the **human resources department**. Explain that you are applying for a job and have been told you will have to take a test. Very politely, ask the following questions:

- Will I receive a practice test beforehand? If so, when?

- How long will the testing session last?

- How many tests will I be taking?

- What subjects do each of the tests cover?

- Is there any preparation you recommend?

- Do you lose credit for guessing?

- How long are the individual tests?

- Will I be allowed to use a calculator on the test? (There is almost no math on these tests, but some people feel more comfortable with a calculator.)

Start practicing as soon as you can. Several months before the test is not too soon, but even the day before is not too late. Try not to leave it to the last few days. Practicing problems that are similar to the problems on the test will still help you improve your score in four ways. It will help you:

- become familiar with the test instructions and rules
- be comfortable when taking the test
- learn about the test topics
- improve your speed.

If the company gives you a practice test, go through it several times. Then find the chapters in this book that are closest to that practice test and study them.

The more you practice, the better. The best way to practice is to do a little work each day. You may feel ready to stop practicing after you get a few practice questions right. That is the time to keep studying. Your goal is to learn how to do these problems so well that doing them successfully becomes second nature. This will make it easier to do them correctly when you're under pressure on the day of the test.

The next chapter in this book gives suggestions of things you can do to develop your mechanical and spatial abilities. The chapters on the various types of test questions give suggestions of ways to practice and learn more.

The Week Before the Test

Make sure you know how to get to the test location and where to park if you are driving. If you are not sure where it is, make a practice trip a few days before the actual test day. You do not want to be late to the test. Some companies will not give you extra time if you are late, and other companies will not let you into the testing room if you are late.

The Day of the Test

Get an early start on the test day. You may need extra travel time in case of unexpected delays caused by traffic, parking, or finding the test room. Wear comfortable clothes and dress in layers. There is no way to predict the temperature of the testing room.

Eat moderately before the test. You won't want to be hungry or too full. It is distracting to hear your stomach rumbling during the test. It is also uncomfortable to have to leave the test for the bathroom, so make sure to go beforehand.

What to Bring to the Test

Make sure you have everything you will need on the test day. This may include such things as:

- directions to the test location
- your identification and admission letter

- a pen and No. 2 pencils with erasers (No. 1 pencils are too soft and may smudge. No. 3 pencils write too lightly.)

- a watch

- a calculator (if they are allowed).

Get a good night's sleep before the test day. It will help you be at your best.

When You Get to the Test Location

Here are a few helpful things for you to consider when you get to the test location.

GO TO THE BATHROOM

The testing session may be an hour or longer. (Part of this time will be spent filling out forms.) Some people need to use the bathroom when they get nervous. In any case, it is a good idea to use the restroom before the test starts.

GET A GOOD SEAT

If you can choose your seat, try to get one that is to your liking. Here are some things to think about when choosing a seat:

- lighting

- comfort of chair and desk

- the wall clock (Can you see it?)

- the front of the room (Can you hear and see the person giving the test?)

- heating or air-conditioning vents (Will you be in a draft?)

If you are assigned a seat, you can ask to have your seat changed if you have a good reason. If you want to change your seat, ask as soon as possible, and definitely before the test begins.

TURN OFF YOUR CELL PHONE

The person giving the test will ask you to turn off your cell phone. Even if you are not asked, turn it off. If it rings, you will lose time and be distracted. If you answer it, you may be suspected of cheating.

Filling Out the Answer Sheet

Most tests are computer graded. If you fill out the answer sheet wrong, the computer may mark you wrong. **You do not want to lose points this way**, so be careful and neat when filling out the answer sheet. Here are some tips for filling out the answer sheet:

- Keep track of what question you are on.

- Study the answer sheet before the test starts. See how the answers are numbered.

- Fill out the answer sheet very carefully.

- Fill in the bubbles completely and dark enough for a machine to notice.

- Don't let the machine think you gave two answers to one question. Erase fully if you erase.

- Fill in your name and ID number correctly.

- Write neatly.

- **DO NOT DOODLE** on the page. (Some answer sheets are scanned through, so that doodles on one side may be read as marks on the other side.)

Test Instructions

Use the time before the test starts to fully understand the instructions. Do not waste test time learning the instructions. If you are given written instructions, read them carefully at least twice. Sometimes there are changes from the written directions, so pay close attention to the person giving the test. If you have questions on the test instructions, raise your hand before the test starts. You will not get a chance to redo the test just because you did not understand the instructions. Pay careful attention to the time limit for the test.

SAMPLE QUESTIONS

Many tests have sample questions. Pay close attention to them. They will help you get a feel for the real questions and the answer sheet. Make sure to try to answer them and to fill in the corresponding circle on the answer sheet if there is one. Sample questions will not count toward your test score. Read the explanations of the answers. Ask the person giving the test to explain the sample questions if you don't understand them. Ask before the test begins, because often no questions are allowed during the test. Make sure you know how to use the answer sheet.

Test-Taking Strategies

Whether running a race, playing a game, or taking a test, strategies can help. We will suggest strategies in seven important areas:

- Cheating

- Time Limits

- Skipping Questions

- Guessing

- Marking the Answer Sheet

- Checking Your Answers

- Writing on the Test

CHEATING

Do not cheat. Do not copy from anyone else's answer sheet and do not let anyone copy from yours. Besides not being fair, if you are caught cheating you will suffer the consequences. Try to sit so others cannot copy from your answer sheet. Do not even look like you are looking at anyone else's answer sheet, because the person giving the test might think you are cheating. Do not talk during the test.

TIME LIMITS

Some tests have generous time limits and almost everyone finishes the whole test. Other tests have short time limits and no one finishes all the questions. Tests with long time limits are called **power tests**. Tests with very short time limits are called **speeded tests** or **speed tests**. Often the questions on speed tests are relatively easy, and most people get most of the questions right. Your score on these tests is based mainly on the number of questions you answer.

On a speed test you will not have time to go back and check your answers, so do not even think about it. If you are taking a power test, you should have time to go back and check your answers, so remember what questions you want to go back to and check.

Work as fast as you can without losing accuracy. Do not worry if you are not able to finish all the questions. Just do the best you can and try to give a reasonable answer to as many questions as you can.

SKIPPING QUESTIONS

You should plan to answer the questions in order. If you skip around, you will waste time. Usually the easy questions are at the beginning of a test. If you do skip a question, make sure to skip a line on your answer sheet.

You should know before the test begins if the test is speeded. If the test is speeded, do not spend too much time on any one question. Usually on speeded tests you are expected to answer two or more questions per minute, so definitely try not to spend more than a minute on each question. Also, you might think of skipping a question if it takes more than double the time of the previous one.

GUESSING

TIP
You get no credit for a blank answer, so guessing usually works in your favor.

You should guess whenever you have any idea which is the right answer or which answer or answers are wrong. If you know something about the right or wrong answers, do not leave the question blank.

Some tests have a penalty for guessing. On those tests you lose some credit for each question you get wrong. On this type of test, guess only if you have some idea about the right or wrong answers. Most speed tests have a penalty for guessing. Some power tests do also.

Many tests have *no* penalty for guessing. On these tests you should fill in an answer for every question.

If you do not know whether the test you are taking has a penalty for guessing, answer every question that you know something about.

The only penalty for leaving a question blank is that you do not get any credit for that question.

MARKING THE ANSWER SHEET

Check to see how the questions are numbered on the answer sheet. Be careful when you go from one column to another on the answer sheet or from one page to the next in the test booklet. **Make sure you are on the right number on the answer sheet!**

CHECKING YOUR ANSWERS

Check your answers whenever you have time. Check two things:

- Check your answer sheet. Be sure you have only one answer for each question.

- Check your answers. Be sure you did not mark the wrong answer by accident.

It is easy to make a silly mistake on the answer sheet, such as filling in two answers to one question and leaving the next question blank, or getting off by one question on the answer sheet. It is also easy to plan to choose B and to fill in the answer sheet for C instead. These types of errors are easy to make but they are also easy to fix. So check your answer sheet and answers so that your score is as high as possible.

WRITING ON THE TEST

Sometimes you will be allowed to write on the test booklet. If you are allowed, you can cross out wrong answers and draw lines or make notes as you try to figure out the answer to a question. If you are not allowed to write on the test booklet, don't worry about it. Just take the test as best you can.

WHEN THE TEST IS OVER

Right after the test, think about your test-taking experience. It might be important to you. You might need to take the test a second time. If you applied for a job and were not hired, the company may give tests again in a few months or a year. Also, other companies may give similar tests. Think about what you could do to get a better score next time. For example, ask yourself these questions:

- What did the test cover?

- What did the test not cover?

- Was there enough time to finish the test?

- How could I have been better prepared to take this test?

Do not be discouraged if you were not selected for a job based on a test. Often there are many people applying for each job opening. Companies often hire every few months, and you might do better the next time you apply. You can use the time to help improve your mechanical aptitude and spatial ability. The next chapter gives some suggestions for ways to do this.

CHAPTER 2

How to Develop Your Mechanical Aptitude and Spatial Ability

Runners get faster when they practice and exercise. To learn to play tennis, you need to practice with a tennis racquet. To learn a musical instrument you need to practice. You can get better, stronger, or faster in most areas with practice over time. The rest of the chapters in this book help you learn about many types of test questions and give you practice answering test questions. This chapter gives you hints and suggestions to help you develop your mechanical aptitude and spatial ability so you can do your best on any type of mechanical or spatial ability test.

There are five ways to go about developing your mechanical and spatial ability. They are:

- watching

- doing

- reading

- taking courses

- thinking.

WATCHING

Watching others doing mechanical work is a great way to learn how to use tools properly and safely and to see how mechanical things are put together and repaired. Here are some places and ways you can watch others doing mechanical work:

- Watch the TV program *Trading Places* (about remodeling a room in a house).

- Watch the TV program *This Old House* (about remodeling a house).

- Watch friends or relatives when they fix things around the house and ask them to explain what they are doing.

- Watch construction workers as they build a house or other building.

- Go to a hardware store and look at the tools in the hardware department.

- Ask a friend or relative who has a tool collection to explain the tools to you.

DOING

Doing is a wonderful way to learn about how mechanical things work and how they are put together and repaired. Here are three suggestions:

- When you or a friend buy something that has to be put together, you do it.

- When there is something that needs to be fixed, try to fix it.

- Use tools whenever you can.

You can also get practice with all sorts of spatial problems. Here are a few ideas:

- Borrow or buy and use inexpensive building toys. There are many of these, for example: blocks, and Erector Set®, and Legos®.

- Borrow or buy and use inexpensive puzzle toys such as Tangrams or Tangoes®.

- Search the Internet to find Web pages for puzzles, for example:

  http://strongmuseum.org/just_for_kids/tangrams.html

  http://tangrams.ca/weboog/weboog.htm

  http://aimsedu.org/Puzzle/Heart/heart2.html

  http://paperfolding.com/diagrams

- Find and do maze puzzles. (You might find books of puzzles at your local library.)

READING

- Use the Internet to find Web pages that explain how mechanical and electrical things work, for example:

  http://howstuffworks.com/

- Use the Internet to find amateur science Web pages, for example:

  http://kidscom.com/games/tangram/tangram.html

  http://amasci.com/amateur/coolsci.html

  http://amasci.com/amasci.html

  http://school-for-champions.com/science.htm

- Use the Internet to find puzzles involving shapes, for example: http://subhelp.com

- Read magazines on mechanics and science. Your local librarian can help you find these.

- Read magazines on home repair, such as *This Old House.*

- Read children's books on machines, tools, pulleys, and science. Books for elementary school kids are very helpful, and fun too. Your local library will have books like these. (If you are embarrassed, say you arc looking for a book to read with a younger relative.)

TAKING CLASSES

Many public schools offer courses both for their regular students and for adults. Try to take classes to help you develop your mechanical aptitude and spatial abilities, for example:

- appliance repair

- home repair

- car maintenance and repair

- bicycle maintenance and repair

- drafting (or CADD—computer-aided design and drafting)

- woodworking.

Some large hardware stores offer free mini-classes in home repair in the evenings and on weekends. For example, the classes might cover using power equipment, or installing cabinets and countertops.

THINKING

Think about how the things around you work, how they are put together, and why they are made the way they are. Why is the can opener shaped the way it is? Why is the handle the shape it is? What happens when I turn the handle? These are the types of questions you could ask yourself about many mechanical tools, toys, and other objects.

You may already be doing some of the things described in this chapter. If so, keep it up. The more you practice, the more you will improve.

WHAT ELSE CAN I DO TO PREPARE?

Reading the chapters in this book and doing the practice questions in each chapter and at the end of the book are very good ways to help develop your mechanical aptitude and spatial ability. Also, some of the chapters have ideas and suggestions for other things you can do to prepare for a particular type of test. Look for these at the end of each chapter, just before the practice questions.

General Mechanical Understanding

CHAPTER 3

IMPORTANT WORDS IN THIS CHAPTER

Belt Pulley	Lever
Closed Circuit	Open Circuit
Conductor	Parallel Circuit
Electrical Circuit	Pendulum
Electrical Load	Pivot Point
Electrical Path	Positive and Negative Poles
Electrical Switch	Power Source
Fuse	Series Circuit
Gear	Short Circuit
Horseshoe Magnet	Toggle Switch
Knife Switch	Weight Times Distance

These tests use diagrams of real-life objects and situations to measure your mechanical understanding and aptitude. The questions are usually easy to understand, even if it is not easy to get the right answer. The questions may ask about any of a wide range of objects. Sometimes they are objects you can see or learn about in your everyday life, such as a bicycle, a baby stroller, or a tree. Sometimes the objects are less common and are learned about only on the job or in school, such as parts of cars or machines. To answer this type of question, you usually have to figure out what is happening in the picture or what will happen.

WHAT DO THESE QUESTIONS ASK ABOUT?

You may be asked about any of many mechanical and physical principles or objects, such as what they do, how they move, and how they work.

WHAT DO THESE TESTS LOOK LIKE?

Usually this type of test has 50 or more multiple-choice questions, each containing one or two drawings. Most people are able to finish these questions within the time limit. The questions on these tests jump from one subject to another. This sample question is typical.

FACT

Small wheels go around more often than larger wheels, just as a child takes more steps than an adult.

Sample Question

Which wheel is turning faster?

(A) Wheel A
(B) Wheel B
(C) No difference

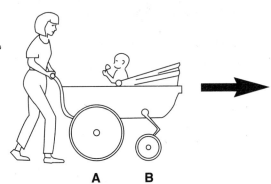

A   B

ANSWER AND EXPLANATION

The correct answer is B. Because wheel A is larger, it covers more ground in one turn, and it turns less often than wheel B when the carriage is pushed. You need to read the question carefully. The exact wording of the question is important. If the question asked which wheel is turning more slowly, the correct answer would be A.

The drawing is easy to understand. It is clear this is a baby carriage and wheel A is bigger than wheel B. The arrow shows that the carriage is being pushed and is moving to the right. Usually the diagrams in this type of question are easy to understand. It is your job to try to think about the mechanics of the situation and to figure out the correct answer to the question.

WHAT DO THESE QUESTIONS MEASURE?

These questions measure your mechanical knowledge by asking questions about many mechanical things and about different mechanical and physical principles. These tests usually cover a wide range of topics, including, for example,

- gears

- pulleys

- basic electricity

- gravity

- levers

- the mechanics and physics of everyday objects, such as
    how things work
    weight and strength of materials
    effects of heat and cold.

This is one of the most widely used types of test for measuring mechanical aptitude. It is also one of the hardest to study for because it covers so many areas. This chapter is long and has the most training material of all the chapters in this book. You may want to read this chapter several times to get the most out of it.

WHAT THIS CHAPTER COVERS

This chapter covers four main subjects:

- basic electricity

- gravity

- levers

- the mechanics and physics of everyday objects.

   Gears and pulleys are also important topics for this type of test, and they are covered in two separate chapters in this book.

- Gears (Chapter 4)

- Pulleys (Chapter 5)

Basic Electricity

Although electricity is a big topic, some basic facts will help you answer many questions. Mastering these will help you learn more about electricity. Places and ways to learn more are described later in this chapter and in Chapter 2 of this book.

> **FACT**
>
> Electricity travels in a circular path, or it does not travel at all.

THE PATH ELECTRICITY TAKES

Electricity travels through metal wire easily. We say that wire is a good conductor. A **conductor** is any material that allows electricity to pass through it. Wood and most nonmetals are poor conductors, letting little or no electricity pass. Also, if a wire is broken, the electricity will not get past that place in the wire. Because electricity travels easily in wire, we use wire to make paths for electricity to follow.

   When we use electricity, it travels in a circular path called a **circuit.** If only one end of a battery in a flashlight is connected, no electricity will flow. Electricity can flow only if both sides of the battery are connected, so the electricity can get from one end to the other. The same is true of electricity coming from an electrical outlet in the wall. If only one of the two prongs (or sides) of a plug is attached, no electricity will flow.

WHAT ARE THE PARTS OF AN ELECTRICAL CIRCUIT?

For a circuit to work, it needs these three parts:

- a **source** of electrical energy (such as a battery or a wall plug)

- a **path** for the electricity to follow (usually wires)

- a **load** (a lightbulb, buzzer, or other electrical device).

Usually there is a fourth part, a **switch,** which controls the flow of electricity. See if you can identify the four parts of a circuit in the next drawing.

TRY TO FIND THE FOUR PARTS IN THIS CIRCUIT

- Power source

- Load

- Path

- Switch

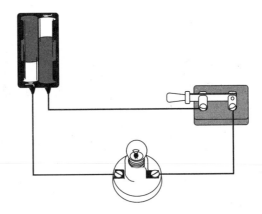

In this drawing, the two batteries are the source of electrical power. The electricity flows through wires, which are the path. When the switch is on, the electricity flows through the load, which in this case is the lightbulb. The parts of this circuit are labeled in the next drawing.

HERE ARE THE FOUR PARTS IN THIS CIRCUIT

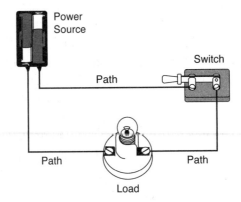

WHAT WILL THESE PARTS LOOK LIKE ON THE TEST?

HINT

Learn the symbols that go with the parts.

Some tests show pictures or realistic drawings, and other tests show simplified drawings or use symbols for parts. Now we will look at both pictures and symbols for parts you may find on the test. Seeing them now will help you recognize them when you take a test.

Electrical Hardware You May See on a Test

You may see batteries, switches, and bulbs in holders on these tests. Seeing them before the test will help you recognize them on exam day. Now we will look at some parts, one at a time. The symbol for the part is to the right of the picture.

LIGHTBULB IN A HOLDER

A lightbulb is screwed into this lightbulb holder. You can see two wires attached to the bottom of the holder. These wires can be attached to a battery to light the bulb.

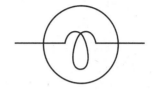

ON-OFF KNIFE SWITCH IN THE OPEN POSITION

This uncovered switch lets you see the metal pathway for the electricity. It is called a knife switch because a flat metal piece with a handle is used to close or open the switch. When the blade is up, the switch is in the open position. The open position does not allow electricity to flow. **The open position is off.**

ON-OFF KNIFE SWITCH IN THE CLOSED POSITION

Here the flat metal piece makes a path connecting the two wires. When the blade is down the switch is in the closed position. The closed position allows electricity to flow. **The closed position is on.**

FACT

When the blade of a knife switch is up, the switch is *off*.

ON-OFF TOGGLE SWITCH

This on-off switch has a black cover over the connections. You can see two wires attached to the bottom. These wires can be attached to control a circuit. The symbol is the same as for a knife switch.

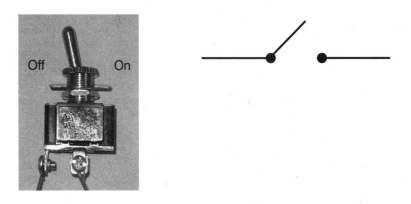

A 1½-VOLT BATTERY

The electrical contacts are at the left and right ends of this battery. This is a 1½-volt battery. The voltage is often printed right on the battery like this: 1.5 volts.

A 9-VOLT BATTERY

This battery has two places on the top to connect wires. It is a 9-volt battery. This is often written 9 v.

A 6-VOLT BATTERY

This battery has two places on the top to connect wires.

BATTERIES IN A HOLDER

You can see two wires on the left side of this battery holder. These wires can be used to power a circuit.

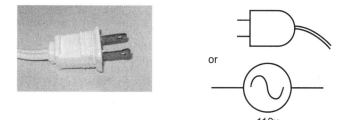

110-VOLT POWER

Sometimes a regular wall plug is used to power a circuit. Two ways to show 110-volt power are shown here. One shows a wall plug. The other is the symbol for an AC electric generator or another type of AC power supply.

WIRES THAT MAKE A CONNECTION

These show two wires crossing and making a connection.

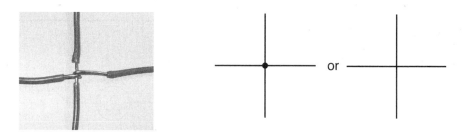

WIRES THAT DO NOT MAKE A CONNECTION

These show two wires crossing but not making an electrical connection.

FUSE

A fuse protects an electrical circuit against too much electricity flowing. Too much electricity can make electrical parts heat up and even burn. A fuse has a small wire inside. If too much electricity tries to flow through a fuse, the small wire inside gets hot and melts, which opens the circuit and stops the electricity. In this way the fuse protects the rest of the circuit. The picture to the left shows a fuse. The one to the right shows a fuse in a holder.

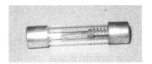  

PRACTICE READING A CIRCUIT USING SYMBOLS

The circuit here is the same as the one you saw earlier in this chapter, this time drawn with symbols. Sometimes the drawing of a circuit shows the parts in somewhat different places from the picture, which is fine as long as the electrical connections are the same. For example, in the picture on page 16 the switch is to the right and above the light. The circuit drawing shows the switch next to the light but not above it. From an electrical point of view, the two circuits (the picture and the drawing) are the same since the electrical connections are the same.

TRY TO FIND THE FOUR PARTS IN THIS CIRCUIT

- Power source
- Load
- Path
- Switch

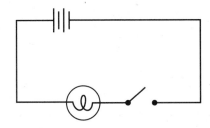

HERE ARE THE FOUR PARTS IN THIS CIRCUIT

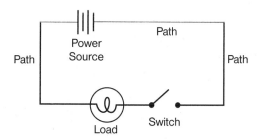

Now that we have learned about some electrical hardware and symbols, let's look at some questions about open and closed circuits.

ANOTHER WAY TO SHOW THIS CIRCUIT

Sometimes the drawing of a circuit will not show the full path. The two wires coming from the power source may be called hot and ground, or positive and negative, and their connection to the power source may not be shown. You will have to imagine the connection between hot and ground and the power source. Drawn this way, the circuit above might look like this:

What Are Closed and Open Circuits?

In a closed circuit all the parts of the circuit are connected. In an open circuit, at least one part is not connected. Electricity travels through a closed circuit, and never travels through an open circuit. The next question shows an open and a closed circuit.

Sample Question

TIP

Circuit diagrams show electrical connections and paths.

HELP YOURSELF

Try this with flashlight bulbs and batteries. Use paperclips as wires.

Which bulb will light up?

(A) Drawing A
(B) Drawing B
(C) Both

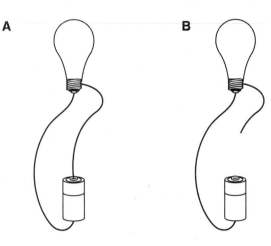

A   **B**

ANSWER AND EXPLANATION

The correct answer is A. In drawing A the path or circuit is closed, because there is a wire path the electricity can use: the path leaves the battery, goes through the bulb, and returns to the battery. In B the circuit is open because the wire does not touch the top of the battery. For that reason, the bulb in B will **not** light up. **An open circuit does not pass electricity.**

WHAT IS THE ELECTRICAL PATH INSIDE AN INCANDESCENT LIGHTBULB?

There is a simple electrical path inside the typical lightbulb. To see this, let's take a look at a drawing that shows the working parts inside a lightbulb.

THE ELECTRICAL PATH INSIDE A LIGHTBULB

Inside the typical incandescent lightbulb is a small wire, called the filament. When electricity is passing through it, the filament gets so hot it gives off light. Each side of the filament is connected to the base of the bulb in a way that allows the electricity to travel in a path from one part of the base, through the filament, and to the other part of the base.

Incandescent
Bulb

Filament

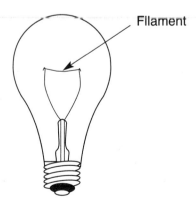

WHAT ARE THE TWO WAYS TO CONNECT TWO LIGHTBULBS?

We can think of many ways to connect two lightbulbs, but only two types of connections work, and they are called series and parallel circuits. First let's look at series circuits.

When you connect two lightbulbs in a series circuit, the electricity travels through a single electrical path that goes through both lightbulbs. Following is a drawing of two lightbulbs in a series circuit.

TWO LIGHTBULBS CONNECTED IN A SERIES CIRCUIT

Follow the electrical path from the top of the battery. You can see that the path goes through the lightbulb on the left, and then through the lightbulb on the right, and then back to the bottom of the battery, completing the circuit. The electricity here flows through both lightbulbs.

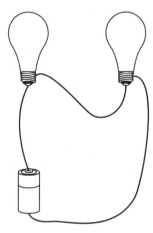

In a series circuit, the electricity goes through all parts of the circuit. If you take out any one part, the electrical path is broken.

A parallel circuit works a little differently. We will look at parallel circuits next.

PARALLEL CIRCUITS

A parallel circuit has more than one electrical path. In a parallel circuit with three bulbs, you can take out one bulb and the other two will stay lit. Let's look at a parallel circuit with three bulbs.

THREE LIGHTBULBS CONNECTED IN A PARALLEL CIRCUIT

Look at the diagram on the next page. Follow the electrical path from the battery holder. You can see that the path goes through the left side of all three lightbulbs, and then back to the battery holder from the right side of all three lightbulbs, completing the circuit. The electricity flows through all three lightbulbs.

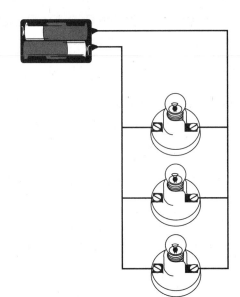

If any lightbulb is taken out of a parallel circuit, there will still be a complete circuit. The next picture shows what happens when you take away the middle bulb.

TAKE AWAY THE MIDDLE BULB

Taking away the middle lightbulb does not cause the other bulbs to go out. The electricity still can flow from the battery, through the two lightbulbs, and back to the battery.

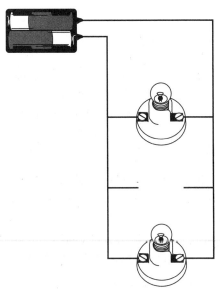

Now we will look at what happens when a part of a circuit is removed.

OPEN CIRCUITS

For electricity to flow, it has to be able to get from one connection on the battery to the other. If there is no path, you have an open circuit. **No electricity flows through an open circuit.** We will look at some examples of an open circuit.

Both of the drawings on the next page are open circuits, which can result if one of the bulbs is taken out of the series circuit shown on this page.

Two examples of an open circuit. The lightbulbs will not light up.

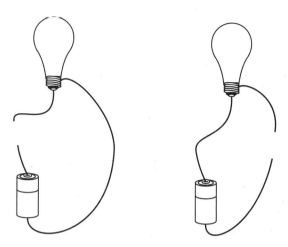

Both of these are open circuits because there is no complete path for the electricity to follow. The lightbulbs will not light up in either of these open circuits.

Series circuits do not all look the same. Here are three more questions that will teach you more about series circuits.

Sample Question

If you take away the bulb on the left, will the bulb on the right stay lit?

(A) Yes
(B) No
(C) Can't tell

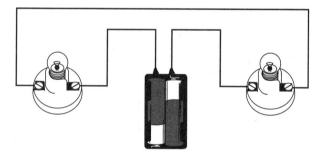

ANSWER AND EXPLANATION

The correct answer is B. The electrical path includes both bulbs. If either bulb is missing the path is broken and electricity will not flow.

Sample Question

Will this circuit let these lightbulbs light up?

(A) Yes
(B) No
(C) Can't tell

ANSWER AND EXPLANATION

The correct answer is A. This is a series circuit. An electrical path goes through both bulbs. Electricity can flow and the bulbs will light up.

Sample Question

If you take away the bulb on the left, will the bulb on the right go out?

(A) Yes
(B) No
(C) Can't tell

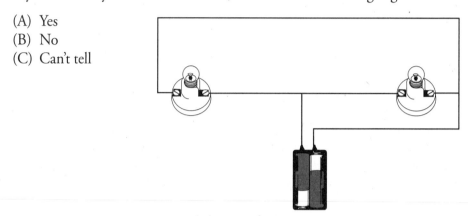

ANSWER AND EXPLANATION

The correct answer is B. This is a parallel circuit. The electrical path splits and goes through both bulbs. The next drawing shows the circuit without the bulb on the left.

WITH A BULB MISSING, WE HAVE A COMPLETE PATH

The electricity can still go from the battery through the lightbulb and back to the battery. So the bulb will light up.

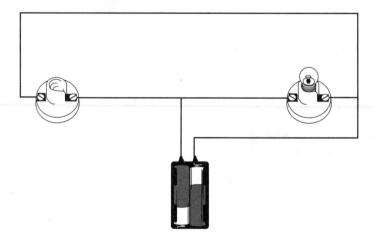

Some electrical circuits are combinations of series and parallel. We will see this in some of the sample questions on the following pages.

Now let's look at some sample questions using what we have learned.

Sample Question

If you take away bulb number 1, which bulbs will light up?

(A) Only bulb 2
(B) Only bulb 3
(C) Both bulbs 2 and 3
(D) None of the bulbs
will light up.

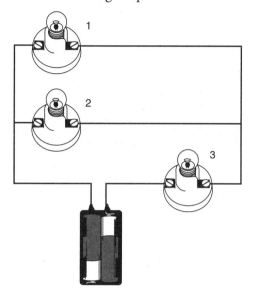

ANSWER AND EXPLANATION

The correct answer is C. When you take away bulb 1, what is left is a series circuit with an electrical path through bulbs 2 and 3. (Bulb 1 is wired in parallel with bulb 2.)

WHAT IS A SHORT CIRCUIT?

In a short circuit, the electricity flows without going through the load. If the load is a lightbulb, the bulb will not go on. This is because electricity tends to take the path of least resistance. If there are two paths, one through a wire (low resistance) and one through a lightbulb (higher resistance), the electricity will go through the wire and the lightbulb will not light up. A short circuit usually is unintended and often happens when a wire is in the wrong place. Short circuits are usually not useful because they do not work. Since a switch is low resistance, it can form a short circuit. We will see a short circuit in action in the next sample question.

FACT

A short circuit lets electricity flow without going through the load.

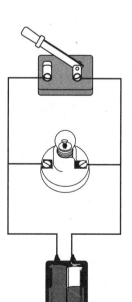

Sample Question

If you close this switch, will the lightbulb be lit?

(A) Yes
(B) No
(C) Can't tell

ANSWER AND EXPLANATION

The correct answer is B. If we close the switch, it will make an electrical connection between the two wires from the battery holder. It is easier for electricity to travel through wires than to go through a lightbulb, so if we close the switch, all the electricity will travel through the wire, and the lightbulb will not go on. (If you are not sure what a circuit is, reread pages 15–29 of this chapter.)

Usually a short circuit happens by accident when bare wires touch when they are supposed to be separate, or when a wire is added in the wrong place. Look at the next two drawings, each of which has an extra wire.

Sample Question

Which bulb will light up?

(A) Drawing A
(B) Drawing B
(C) Both

A 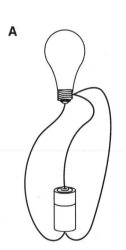 B

ANSWER AND EXPLANATION

The correct answer is B. Both drawings have an extra wire. But in drawing A the extra wire creates a new path that ends up connecting the top and bottom of the battery. In drawing B, the extra wire makes a second connection between one end of the battery and the side of the lightbulb. This is not a short circuit because the path still leads through the bulb. The short circuit is shown in drawing A. The drawing below shows the short circuit more clearly.

Following the path drawn with the thick lines, we see the electricity can go from the top of the battery to the bottom without going through the lightbulb. This is an example of a short circuit. The path touches one side of the base of the lightbulb, but the electricity does not have to go through the lightbulb. **In a short circuit, the electricity does not go through the load.**

The thicker wire is the short circuit.

The word *short* in *short circuit* needs some explanation because it can be confusing. A long wire may still cause a short circuit. Electricity, like water, tends to follow the path of least resistance. Electricity flows through a wire more easily than through a lightbulb, or any electrical load. So if there are two paths, the electricity will take the easier path. If the easier path does not include the lightbulb (or some other load), it is called a short circuit. In the next drawing, a long wire is causing a short circuit.

This long wire is causing a short circuit.

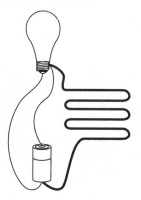

The electrical path drawn with the thick line is physically longer than the path drawn with the thin line, but it is still causing a short circuit. The term *short circuit* is used for any path the electricity can follow that allows it to go from the top of the battery to the bottom without going through the lightbulb.

USING TWO BATTERIES TOGETHER

You can connect two batteries in two ways that work and in several ways that do not work. Whether the two batteries work together or not depends on how you connect the positive and negative poles of the batteries. First we will look at the positive and negative poles of some batteries, and then we will look at connecting batteries together.

POSITIVE AND NEGATIVE POLES OF A 9-VOLT BATTERY

The positive contact sticking up on the left is labeled with a plus sign. The other contact is the negative one.

FACT
All batteries have a positive and a negative side or pole.

POSITIVE AND NEGATIVE ENDS OF A 1.5-VOLT BATTERY

The metal contact sticking up at the top is positive and is labeled with a plus sign. The metal contact at the bottom is negative.

POSITIVE AND NEGATIVE POLES OF A 12-VOLT CAR BATTERY

The contact sticking up at the left is positive. The one at the right is negative. The battery says 12 V, which means it is a 12-volt battery.

Now we will look at the two ways to connect batteries so they work.

CONNECTING BATTERIES IN SERIES

One way to connect batteries is by attaching the positive of one battery to the negative of the other, and then attaching the load to the other two battery contacts. This is called connecting batteries in series. The next question shows a series connection of two batteries.

Sample Question

Will this bulb light up?

(A) Yes
(B) No

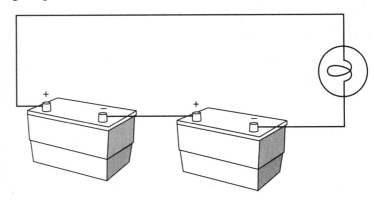

ANSWER AND EXPLANATION

The correct answer is A. These two batteries are correctly connected in series. The wires form a path for the electricity to leave the batteries, flow through the lightbulb, and then return to the batteries.

CONNECTING BATTERIES IN PARALLEL

Another way to connect two batteries is by connecting the positive poles of both batteries, connecting the negative poles of both batteries, and connecting the load to both the positive pair and the negative pair. This is called connecting batteries in parallel. The next question shows a parallel connection of two batteries.

Sample Question

Will this bulb light up?

(A) Yes
(B) No

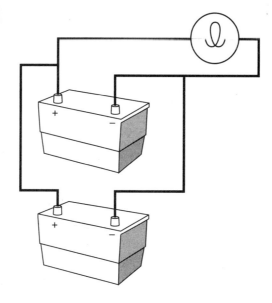

ANSWER AND EXPLANATION

The correct answer is A. These two batteries are correctly connected in parallel. The wires form a path for the electricity to leave the batteries, flow through the lightbulb, and then return to the batteries.

CONNECTING BATTERIES WRONG

If you connect batteries wrong, they will not work. Here are some sample questions that show wrong ways to connect batteries.

Sample Question

In which of these circuits will the bulb light up?

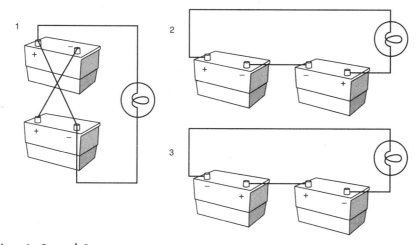

A.   1, 2, and 3
(B) Only 1 and 2
(C) Only 2 and 3
(D) Only 1 and 3
(E) None of the bulbs will light up.

ANSWER AND EXPLANATION

The correct answer is E.

- In circuit 1, all four poles are attached to each other. The bulb will not light up because the wires connect the positive and negative poles of the batteries, causing a short circuit.

- In circuit 2, the negatives are connected to each other. Because the circuit starts at a positive but does not end at a negative, electricity will not flow and the bulb will not light up.

- In circuit 3, the positives are connected to each other. Like in circuit 2, the circuit starts at a negative but does not end at a positive, so electricity will not flow and the bulb will not light up.

This material on electricity will be a big help for some of the questions you will find on this type of test.

Now we will switch topics and learn about gravity.

Gravity

Questions on this type of test sometimes ask about gravity. Gravity is the invisible force that makes things fall when we drop them. We will go over some sample questions based on important facts about gravity.

Sample Question

Which way will the fishing line hang when the rod is tilted?

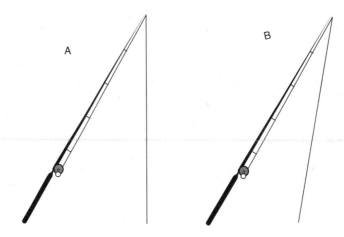

(A) Drawing A
(B) Drawing B
(C) Either

ANSWER AND EXPLANATION

The correct answer is A. There is one difference between these drawings. The fishing line is tilted in drawing B. This is incorrect. Even though the fishing rod is tilted, the fishing line will hang straight up and down. **Gravity always pulls in the same direction.**

Sample Question

If a car and a bowling ball fell off a 100-foot cliff at the same time, which would hit the ground first?

(A) Car
(B) Ball
(C) No difference

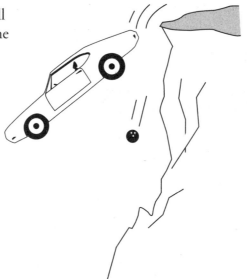

> **TIP**
>
> Read the pages, not only these tips.

ANSWER AND EXPLANATION

The correct answer is C. Even though the car is much heavier than the bowling ball, both will fall at the same rate. (The resistance of the air is not important here.) **The rate of fall is the same, no matter what the weight of the object.**

Sample Question

If a cannon fires a cannonball horizontally and you drop a cannonball at the same time, which will hit the ground first?

> **FACT**
>
> Forward speed does *not* affect the speed of falling.

(A) Drop
(B) Fire
(C) No difference

ANSWER AND EXPLANATION

The correct answer is C. Gravity pulls on both cannonballs equally and both have the same distance to fall before hitting ground. The fired cannonball will land far away, but it will land at the same time as the cannonball that is dropped. (Of course, if you fire the cannonball upward, it will take longer to come down.) The rule is, **Forward speed does not affect speed of falling.**

Gravity also makes a pendulum work. We will look at this next.

WHAT IS A PENDULUM?

A pendulum is a name used for a weight that swings from the end of a string. We will see pendulums and learn about them with the next two sample questions.

Sample Question

You tie a string to the ceiling and attach a weight to the end. You hold the weight next to your face but not touching it and then let go. The weight swings down and away from you and then starts swinging back toward you. If you do not move, will it hit you in the face?

(A) Yes
(B) No
(C) Can't tell

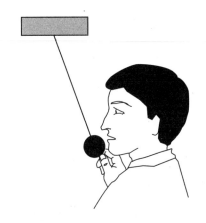

ANSWER AND EXPLANATION

The correct answer is B. **When a pendulum swings back, it does not go higher than the point where it started.**

Sample Question

You put the same amount of weight at the end of these two pendulums. If you let go of the two pendulums at the same time, which will swing faster?

(A) A
(B) B
(C) No difference

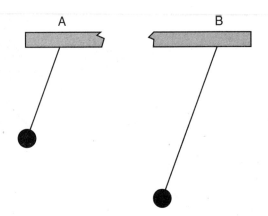

ANSWER AND EXPLANATION

The correct answer is A. When other things are equal, **a pendulum with a shorter string swings faster.** You can try this out for yourself with some string and a weight.

This material on gravity will be a big help for some of the questions you will find on this type of test.

Now we will switch topics and learn about a type of simple machine called the lever.

Levers

A lever is a simple machine. Often a lever is just a flat or round metal rod. Levers are used to help move heavy objects or apply force. There are levers all around us. Here are just a few of the things around us which are levers:

- seesaw
- scissors
- wheelbarrow
- nutcracker
- nail clippers

- stapler
- crowbar
- tweezers
- some can openers

We will use the seesaw, a familiar lever, to review two important facts about levers. Then we will look at some questions about levers.

- Equal weights balance only if they are equal distances from the place the seesaw pivots.
- Unequal weights balance only if the weights times distances from the pivot are equal.

Sample Question

These children weigh the same and are sitting the same distance from the middle of the seesaw. Will this seesaw balance?

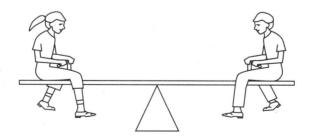

(A) Yes
(B) No
(C) Can't tell

ANSWER AND EXPLANATION

The answer is A. The two children are equal in weight and are equal distance from the center, so the seesaw will balance. Remember, equal weights balance only if they are equal distances from the center.

Sample Question

A mother weighs 100 pounds and her son weighs 50 pounds. If the son is sitting 6 feet from the pivot, the mother should sit _____ feet from the pivot to balance the seesaw.

HINT

Levers are all around us. Look for some at home or work today.

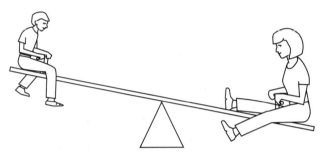

(A) 1
(B) 2
(C) 3
(D) 5
(E) 6

ANSWER AND EXPLANATION

The answer is C. The mother weighs twice as much as the son, so she has to sit half as far from the pivot to balance the seesaw. Remember, unequal weights balance only if weight times distance is equal. Let's do the math.

- For the mother, weight times distance is 100×3 or 300.

- For the son, weight times distance is 50×6 or 300.

Because weight times distance is 300 for both mother and son, the seesaw will balance.

A TEMPORARY LEVER

Unlike a seesaw, some levers are temporary. On the next page, a screwdriver is being used to help open a can. Unlike the seesaw, which has a fixed pivot point in the center, the pivot point here is the place the screwdriver rests on the rim of the can. The lid of the can is close to the pivot point, and the handle of the screwdriver is much farther from the pivot.

A Screwdriver Being Used as a Lever to Open a Can

Before

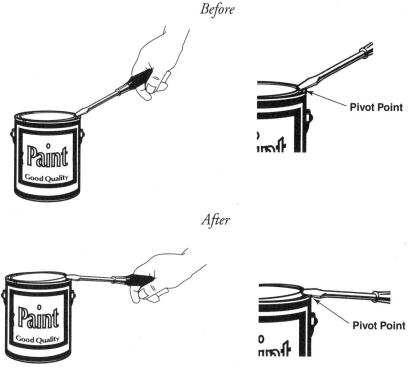

Pivot Point

After

Pivot Point

The handle of the screwdriver moves several inches and the tip of the screwdriver moves just a little bit, but it is enough to lift the lid of the can. Because the tip is much closer to the pivot point than the handle, you can push down on the handle with a small force and still lift a lid that is shut tight.

SCISSORS: ANOTHER TYPE OF LEVER

Scissors are a type of lever. The two parts of a pair of scissors are joined at the pivot point. Your hand always holds the scissors by the handle, so the distance from your hand to the pivot does not change. But you can put the paper in different places, so the distance from the paper to the pivot can change. It is easier to cut paper if you put it closer to the pivot point.

The pivot point for scissors is where they are joined.

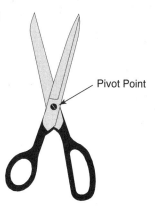

Pivot Point

Sample Question

How far should you open the scissors so it is easier to cut a piece of cardboard?

(A) A
(B) B
(C) No difference

A   B

ANSWER AND EXPLANATION

The correct answer is B. In picture A the scissors would cut near the tip, away from the pivot point. It is easier to cut cardboard that is closer to the pivot point.

Now we will switch topics and learn about belt pulleys.

Belt Pulleys

Gears, rope pulleys, and belt pulleys all can pass along motion. Gears and rope pulleys have their own chapters in this book. We'll look at belt pulleys here.

WHAT IS A BELT PULLEY?

A belt pulley is a wheel with a belt that goes around its edge. Often the pulley wheel has a groove that helps guide the belt and keep it in place. Belt pulleys are used to transfer or deliver turning motion from one place to another, and to change direction of motion from clockwise to counterclockwise or from horizontal to vertical. Here is a picture of two belt pulleys without a belt.

TWO SAMPLE BELT PULLEYS

These show the groove on the rim. The belt fits in the groove and does not slip off the wheel.

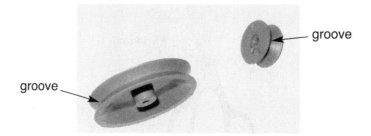

Pulleys are connected with a rubberlike belt that fits snugly and moves whenever the pulleys turn.

TWO SAMPLE PULLEYS WITH A BELT

Here are two pulleys with a rubber belt around them.

- When one of these pulleys moves, the other moves in the **same** direction.

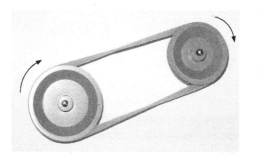

Here are some general rules about pulleys turned with a belt.

- Pulleys the same size turn at the same speed.
- Smaller pulleys turn faster than larger pulleys.

TWO SAMPLE PULLEYS WITH A TWISTED BELT

Here the belt around the pulleys is twisted.

- When one of these pulleys moves, the other moves in the **opposite** direction.

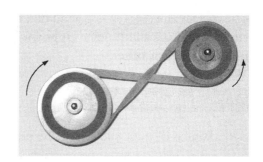

THREE SAMPLE PULLEYS

One belt links all the pulleys.

- When one of these pulleys moves, the others move in the **same** direction.
- The smallest pulley turns the fastest.

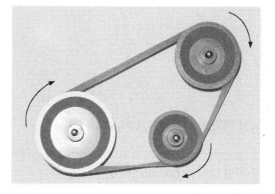

Pulleys are often used with ropes. Another chapter in this book is about pulleys used with ropes.

The last topic of this chapter will look at everyday objects of the type that appear on this kind of test.

Mechanics and Physics of Everyday Objects

Many of the things around us are mechanical or partly mechanical, including toys, cars, kitchen objects, furniture, sports equipment, office machines, hobby tools, gardening tools, and home appliances. We will learn some mechanics and physics of everyday objects in the following questions. You may find a question or two about these topics on your test.

Sample Question

Which of these pairs of magnets will stick together in the positions they are in?

(A) Drawing A
(B) Drawing B
(C) Both drawings

A | N   S | N   S |

B | S   N | N   S |

ANSWER AND EXPLANATION

The correct answer is A. One end of a magnet is called the north pole, and the other end is called the south pole. **Opposite poles of magnets attract each other. Same poles repel each other.**

Sample Question

Which of these show how the poles are arranged on horseshoe magnets?

(A) Drawing A
(B) Drawing B

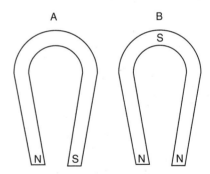

ANSWER AND EXPLANATION

The correct answer is A. Horseshoe magnets have both poles at the open end. The closed end is not magnetic.

Sample Question

Which ball would bounce higher if dropped from the same height?

(A) Ball A
(B) Ball B
(C) No difference

Wood

Rubber

A

B

ANSWER AND EXPLANATION

The correct answer is B. A rubber ball usually bounces more than a ball made out of wood.

In questions with two drawings the difference between the drawings usually is clear. In this example, the two balls are the same shape and height. The only difference is that one is made of wood and one of rubber. This difference is clear because the balls are labeled. In two-diagram questions, your job is to figure out whether the obvious difference is important to the action, and then to answer the question.

Sample Question

To the right is a drawing of a glass container holding water and oil. If you add more water what would it look like?

(A) A
(B) B
(C) C

Oil

Water

Oil
and
Water

Water

A

Water

Oil

Water

B

Oil

Water

C

ANSWER AND EXPLANATION

The correct answer is C. Since oil is lighter than water, the water will settle to the bottom and the oil will float on the top.

Sample Question

These stools are the same height. Which is more likely to tip over when an active child sits on it?

(A) Stool A
(B) Stool B
(C) No difference

A   B

ANSWER AND EXPLANATION

The correct answer is A. The legs on stool B are spread out. Its wider base makes stool B more steady and less likely to tip over.

Sample Question

FACT

Objects in motion stay in motion unless stopped by something.

If the shopping cart were moving in the direction of the big arrow and then you stopped it suddenly, which way would the milk carton fall?

(A) A
(B) B
(C) Can't tell

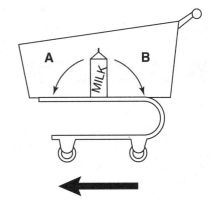

Answer and Explanation

The correct answer is A. This is because of two mechanical principles. First, objects in motion tend to stay in motion. The milk carton was moving in the direction of the big arrow, so it would tend to continue moving in that direction. It might slide in that direction, but its bottom is standing on the cart, and there is some friction that helps hold it where it is. So rather than slide, it falls over.

As you can see from the examples above, this type of test covers many topics. To get ready to take this type of test you need to learn as much as you can about how things work and move. Here are some suggestions to help you learn more. There are more suggestions in the second chapter of this book.

WHAT CAN I LEARN TO HELP MYSELF DO BETTER?

Unlike most tests of spatial ability, for this type of test you need to learn a lot about mechanics and physics that is not covered in this chapter. Even though this chapter is a good start, it helps to learn as much as you can about how all kinds of machines work, including, for example, cars, bicycles, airplanes, and rockets.

WHAT ELSE CAN I DO TO PREPARE?

There are many things you can do to help prepare for this type of test.

- Watch television programs like *This Old House* that show how to use tools properly and safely.

- Look at children's books and other easy books on machines, electricity, pulleys, gears, home repair, bicycle repair, auto repair, and how things work.

- Go to the library. Look at children's books and other easy books on many different science topics like: magnets, gravity, color, sound, siphons, electricity, mirrors, lenses, lasers, rockets, and airplanes.

- Take courses in home repair, auto repair, and appliance repair. (These are often offered by public schools as adult education courses.)

- Put together and repair things and use tools whenever you can.

- Watch others put things together and repair things and ask them to explain what they are doing.

- Read magazines and books about mechanics and home improvements. Your library probably has many of these.

TIPS

1. Read the questions carefully. One word might change the meaning of the question.
2. Look at the picture carefully. The largest, most obvious difference is usually the important difference.

TIME LIMIT

These tests tend to have long time limits, some as long as 30 minutes. Most people have enough time to finish all the questions without rushing.

HOW TO USE THE PRACTICE QUESTIONS

There are practice questions on this and the following pages and more at the end of this book.

- Do the practice questions in this chapter without any time limit.

- Time yourself when you do the practice questions at the end of the book, using the time limit shown there.

Practice Questions

1. How many switches do you have to close to light up just one bulb?

   (A) 0
   (B) 1
   (C) 2
   (D) 3
   (E) 4

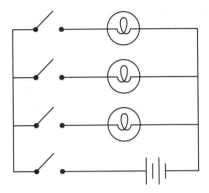

2. Which battery has the higher voltage?

   (A) Battery A
   (B) Battery B
   (C) There is no difference.
   (D) Can't tell

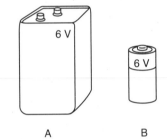

3. Which wheels are turning in the same direction as wheel 4?

   (A) 1, 2, and 3
   (B) 1, 2, and 5
   (C) 2 and 5
   (D) 1, 3, and 5

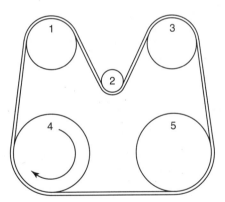

4. Which wrench will make it easier to tighten the bolt?

   (A) A
   (B) B
   (C) No difference
   (D) Can't tell

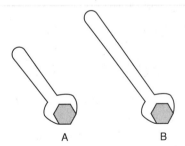

5. Lightning strikes at one end of a city. You are at the other end of the city. Would you hear the thunder or see the lightning first?

   (A) Hear the thunder
   (B) See the lightning
   (C) You will hear and see them at the same time.

6. Which slide will give the faster ride?

   (A) A
   (B) B
   (C) No difference

7. If you close both switches, how many bulbs will light up?

   (A) 0
   (B) 1
   (C) 2
   (D) Can't tell

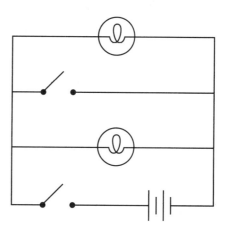

8. How many other pulleys are turning in the same direction as the largest pulley?

   (A) None
   (B) 1
   (C) 2
   (D) 3
   (E) 4
   (F) 5

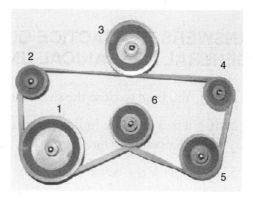

9. If you removed bulb 1 and closed the switch, how many bulbs would go on?

   (A) 0
   (B) 1
   (C) 2
   (D) 3
   (E) Can't tell

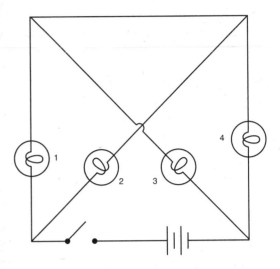

10. If you closed the switch, would the lightbulb go on?

    (A) Yes
    (B) No
    (C) Can't tell

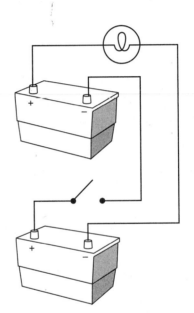

The answers to these questions follow.

ANSWERS TO PRACTICE QUESTIONS: GENERAL MECHANICAL UNDERSTANDING

1. (**C**) You need to close the switch attached to the battery and one other switch.

2. (**C**) The voltage is indicated on the battery. Batteries of different sizes can have the same voltage.

3. (**D**) Follow the belt around to see how the wheels move.

4. (**B**) The handle of the wrench is a lever. A longer lever makes it easier to tighten.

5. (**B**) Light travels faster than sound.

6. (**B**) Slide B begins with a steeper slope, so the child goes more quickly sooner.

7. (**A**) Closing both switches causes a short circuit from one side of the battery to the other. The electricity flows through the switch rather than through the lightbulbs.

8. (**E**) Pulley 1 is the largest pulley. Pulleys 2, 4, 5, and 6 will turn in the same direction as pulley 1.

9. (**D**) With the switch closed and bulb 1 removed, there is a path for the electricity that goes through bulb 2 and also through bulbs 3 and 4.

10. (**A**) With the switch closed the batteries are connected in series, since the negative of the top battery is connected to the positive of the bottom battery.

You will find more questions about general mechanical understanding at the end of this book.

Gears

CHAPTER 4

IMPORTANT WORDS IN THIS CHAPTER

Clockwise	Mating Gears
Counterclockwise	Miter Gear
Double Spur Gear	Spur Gear
Driver/follower	Square Gear
Gear	Teeth
Internal Gear	Worm Gear

Many tests ask at least a few questions about gears. Usually the questions are easy if you know some basic information. This chapter will give you that basic information. Some questions ask about unusual gears, and these questions are often hard. This chapter will introduce some unusual gears. Because there are thousands of different types and combinations of gears, it is impossible to learn them all. Your best approach is to learn the basics well so you will know the answers to the easy questions and can try to figure out the answers to unusual gear questions.

WHAT DO THESE QUESTIONS ASK ABOUT?

You will be shown a drawing of two or more gears. You will be asked about their direction or speed of movement.

WHAT DO THESE TESTS LOOK LIKE?

You will find gear questions on tests with questions on several different topics. It is not usual to have a test that asks only gear questions.

Most often the gears in these questions are simple gears like the ones following questions. Sometimes the questions ask about other types of gears, like ones covered later in this chapter.

In what direction will gear 2 turn?

(A) Clockwise
(B) Counterclockwise
(C) Can't tell

The answer to this sample question is A. A full explanation of the answer to the sample question is given on page 52.

Now we'll learn about different types of gears, starting with simple gears.

Pictures and Diagrams

Some tests use pictures or realistic drawings of gears; others use line diagrams. Here is an example of the sample question using a line diagram. We'll use both photos and diagrams in this chapter, and we'll use photos of different sizes and types of gears so you can see different ways these questions are asked.

Sample Question Using Diagrams

In what direction will gear 2 turn?

(A) Clockwise
(B) Counterclockwise
(C) Can't tell

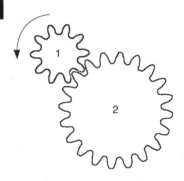

WHAT IS A GEAR?

A gear is a moving mechanical part with teeth. Teeth are evenly spaced, equal-size bumps along the outer edge or rim. Gears are made to work with one or more other gears. The teeth of one gear interlock with the teeth of at least one other gear. The teeth are there to stop the gears from slipping as they turn together. Here is a drawing of a gear that has 10 teeth.

This is a gear with 10 teeth.
A **spur gear** has straight teeth on the outside edge.

REMEMBER

The gear that pushes is the *driver.*

These
are called
teeth.

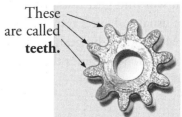

This is a pair of mating gears.
Pairs of gears with their teeth interlocking are called **mating gears.**

Mating gears move together because their teeth keep the gears from slipping.

When one gear turns, its teeth push the teeth of the other gear and make it turn. **The gear that does the pushing is called the driver** and the other can be called the **follower.**

Basic Facts About Gears

A few basic facts about gears will help you with gear questions.

WHAT ARE GEARS USED FOR?

Gears are often used to change the direction and speed of a circular movement.

HOW ARE GEARS HELD IN PLACE?

Two gears that work together are placed next to each other so their teeth mesh. A gear is often held in place with a metal shaft or axle, which goes through the center of the gear. The shafts can turn, so the gears can turn. The main thing to remember is **gears are attached so that they can turn.** The diagrams and pictures in this type of test usually show gears without the shafts. In case you see questions that include a shaft, the picture below shows what one type of shaft looks like.

Two Gears, Each on a Shaft

WHAT ARE GEARS MADE OF?

Gears are usually made of metal or plastic. The pictures in this chapter show both types. Metal and plastic gears work the same way.

DIRECTION OF GEARS

Questions about gears often ask the direction they will turn. Let's look more closely at the sample question that was on the first page of this chapter.

Sample Question

In what direction will gear 2 turn?

(A) Clockwise
(B) Counterclockwise
(C) Can't tell

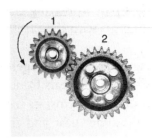

ANSWER AND EXPLANATION

The correct answer is A. If either of the two gears shown here turns, the other has to turn also because their teeth interlock. The key to understanding the direction of the turning is to look at the teeth that are touching. When the teeth that are touching are moving in an upward direction, gear 1 is turning counterclockwise and gear 2 is turning clockwise. Some gear questions will ask you to figure out the direction in which gears are turning. Remember that **two mating gears turn in opposite directions.**

WHAT IS COUNTERCLOCKWISE?

> **HINT**
>
> With an odd number of gears, the first and the last will move in the same direction.

The hands on a clock move clockwise. The opposite direction is counterclockwise.

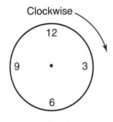

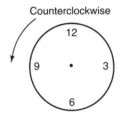

Direction switches with each gear in a row

Gears that are next to each other turn in opposite directions. That means every other gear turns in the same direction. From this we can learn that

1. with an odd number of gears, the first and last gears turn in the same direction.
2. with an even number of gears, the first and last gears turn in opposite directions.

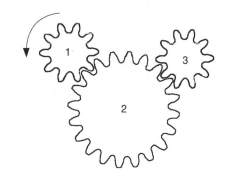

In what direction will gear 3 turn?

(A) Clockwise
(B) Counterclockwise

ANSWER AND EXPLANATION

When there are three gears, the last gear will turn in the same direction as the first. This is true for any odd number of gears. If you have an odd number of gears, the last gear turns in the same direction as the first gear. The correct answer is B.

SPEED OF GEARS

When two mated gears turn, we can tell which will turn faster by comparing the number of teeth in the two gears.

- Two mated **gears with an equal number of teeth will turn at the same speed.**

- When two mated gears have an unequal number of teeth, **the gear with fewer teeth will turn faster.**

- In a mated pair, **the larger gear will have more teeth than the smaller gear** because the teeth and the spaces between the teeth are the same size.

- **Count the number of teeth** to tell how much faster one gear turns compared with its mate.

Some questions ask about speed of turning. Here are a few examples.

Which gear will turn faster?

(A) Gear 1
(B) Gear 2
(C) They will turn at the same speed.

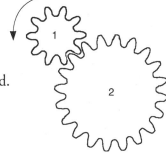

ANSWER AND EXPLANATION

The correct answer is A. Even without counting you can tell that gear 1 has fewer teeth than gear 2. If you count the teeth, you find that gear 1 has 10 teeth and gear 2 has 20 teeth. When gear 1 turns once, each of its 10 teeth push gear 2. But because gear 2 has 20 teeth, gear 2 will turn only halfway. So if gear 1 turns once every second, it will take two seconds for gear 2 to turn. Whenever a pair of mating gears has a smaller gear and a larger gear, **the smaller gear turns faster than the larger gear.**

Sample Question

Which gear will turn faster, gear 1 or gear 3?

(A) Gear 1
(B) Gear 3
(C) They will turn at the same speed.

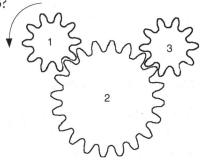

> **HINT**
>
> Counting the number of teeth will help you figure out how much faster a gear will turn compared to its mate.

ANSWER AND EXPLANATION

Gears 1 and 3 look like they have the same number of teeth. If you count, you will find that both have 10 teeth. Because they have the same number of teeth, they will turn at the same speed. Every time one gear moves one tooth, the other gears also move one tooth. Since gears 1 and 3 have the same number of teeth, they will turn at the same speed. **The number of teeth on the gear in the middle does not matter.** The correct answer is C.

Sample Question

If gear A turns 5 times, how many times will gear B turn?

(A) 1 time
(B) 5 times
(C) 10 times
(D) 15 times
(E) 20 times

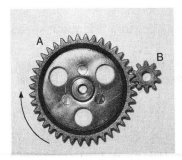

ANSWER AND EXPLANATION

Since gear A is bigger, you know gear B will turn faster. But you have to count the number of teeth on the gears to find out how much faster. Gear A has 40 teeth and Gear B has 10 teeth. So, every time gear A turns once, gear B turns 4 times. The question says gear A turns 5 times, so gear B must turn 4 times that much, or 20 times. The answer is E.

Sample Question

If gear B turns at the rate of 40 rotations per second, how fast will gear A turn?

(A) 1 rotation per second
(B) 5 rotations per second
(C) 10 rotations per second
(D) 20 rotations per second
(E) 40 rotations per second
(F) 50 rotations per second

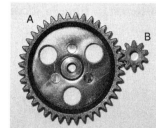

ANSWER AND EXPLANATION

Gear A has 40 teeth and gear B has 10 teeth. Each time gear B turns once, its 10 teeth push Gear A, which makes gear A move only one-quarter turn. So gear A turns one-fourth as fast as gear B. The question says gear B turns 40 times a second. So gear A will turn at 40 ÷ 4 or 10 times a second. The answer is C.

Sample Question

Every time A turns, B turns _____ times.

(A) ½
(B) 1
(C) 1½
(D) 2
(E) 2½

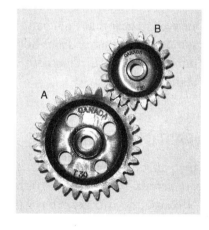

ANSWER AND EXPLANATION

By counting we can tell that gear A has 30 teeth and gear B has 20 teeth. So each time gear A turns, its 30 teeth make gear B turn one and a half times. To get the relative speed **divide the number of teeth on one gear by the number of teeth on the other**. In this case 30 ÷ 20 = 1½. The answer is C.

SPEED OF TURNING DOES NOT DEPEND ON THE NUMBER OR SIZE OF GEARS IN BETWEEN

The speed of turning of the two gears at each end of a row does not depend on the number or size of the gears in between. If the two gears are the same size, they will turn at the same speeds. Two examples will show this more clearly.

If A turns 10 times a second, C will too.

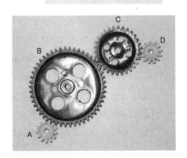

If A turns 10 times a second, D will too.

GEARS THAT CHANGE DIRECTION FROM HORIZONTAL TO VERTICAL

Gears can be used to change the direction of rotation to go around corners, or to go from horizontal to vertical rotation. We will look at two ways this is done. The first way is with miter gears.

A MITER GEAR

One type of gear that can change the direction of the turning movement, such as from horizontal to vertical, is called a miter or bevel gear. The **teeth of a miter gear are cut on a slant.**

A PAIR OF MITER GEARS

This pair of miter gears will change the rotating motion from vertical to almost horizontal.

Because the two gears have the same number of teeth, they will turn at the same speed.

MITER GEARS OF TWO SIZES

This pair of miter gears will change the rotating motion from vertical to horizontal.

Because the two gears have different numbers of teeth, they will turn at different speeds.

SPUR GEARS CAN ALSO BE USED TO CHANGE DIRECTION

This pair of spur gears will change the rotating motion from vertical to horizontal.

Because the two gears have the same number of teeth, they will turn at the same speed. This is true even though one is horizontal and one is vertical.

DOUBLE SPUR GEARS

There are thousands of different sizes, types and combinations of gears. We will look at a few in this chapter. Sometimes two spur gears are made from one piece of metal or plastic. We will call this type a double spur gear. Sometimes it is called a dual spur gear.

A DOUBLE SPUR GEAR

This spur gear is made out of one solid piece, but has two sets of teeth. The speed of rotation will depend on which set of teeth is used.

Here, the smaller set has 10 teeth and the larger set has 30 teeth.

Sample Question

Which gear will turn faster?

(A) Gear 1
(B) Gear 2
(C) They will turn at the same rate.

ANSWER AND EXPLANATION

In this pair the small set of teeth on gear 1 is mated with the large set of teeth on gear 2. Because the part of gear 1 that is being used has fewer teeth, gear 1 will turn faster.

More Complex Gear Arrangements

There are many possible ways to arrange gears. We will look at a few gear arrangements and learn some things about them.

Sample Question

Which gear will turn fastest?

(A) Gear A
(B) Gear B
(C) Gear C
(D) They will all turn at the same speed.
(E) None of the above

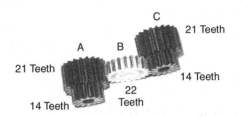

ANSWER AND EXPLANATION

This drawing shows two double spur gears with a regular spur gear in the middle. The double spur gears each have 21 and 14 teeth. Gear A is using 21 teeth. Gear C is using 14 teeth. The gear with the smallest number of teeth turns the fastest. Here the smallest number of teeth being used is 14 on gear C. So the correct answer is C.

Sample Question

In which direction will the gear at the right turn?

(A) Clockwise
(B) Counterclockwise

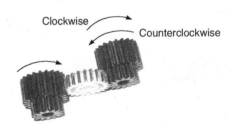

ANSWER AND EXPLANATION

This problem is similar to the ones we saw at the beginning of this chapter. When you have an odd number of gears, the last gear will turn in the same direction as the first. The correct answer is A.

GROUPINGS OF GEARS WITH BRANCHING

Sometimes you will see a question with many gears, and not all arranged in a row. Look at the example on the next page.

1. Which gear will turn fastest?

2. Which gear will turn slowest?

3. If gear A is turned clockwise, in what direction will gear F turn?

4. If gear A is turned clockwise, in what direction will gear G turn?

ANSWERS AND EXPLANATIONS

In any group of mated gears, the smallest will turn fastest. D has the fewest teeth, so it will turn fastest. The answer to 1 is gear D.

The gear with the most teeth will turn slowest. Gear A has the most teeth. The answer to 2 is gear A.

To answer questions 3 and 4, you need to **look only at the gears the question asks about and the gears in between them.**

Every other gear here will turn in the same direction. So gears A, C, and E turn in the same direction. Because gear A turns clockwise, the answer to question 3 is gear F turns counterclockwise.

We know that with an odd number of gears, the first and last gears turn in the same direction. There are five gears leading from gear A to gear G. They are gears A, B, C, H, and G. So because A is turning clockwise, the answer to question 4 is gear G turns clockwise also.

Internal Gears

Sometimes the teeth of a gear are on the inside edge of a circle rather than on the outside. Here is an example of a large internal gear with a smaller external gear inside it.

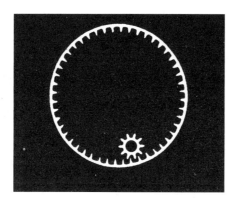

If the small gear turns as shown, which way will the large gear turn?

A. In the direction of arrow A
B. In the direction of arrow B

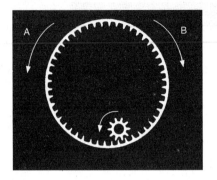

ANSWER AND EXPLANATION

The correct answer is A. If the small gear is turning in the direction of the arrow, the large, internal gear will turn in the same direction.

Gears With Missing Teeth

Each time gear 1 is turned once in the direction of the arrow, its 4 teeth push the teeth of gear 2. Since gear 2 has 16 teeth, gear 2 will make ¼ turn for every turn of gear 1.

It is very different if gear 2 is the driver. Then gear 1 will not make a complete turn. This is because soon gear 1 will be turned so it has no teeth facing gear 2. Then gear 2 will turn without pushing gear 1.

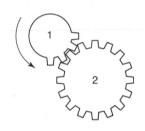

Square Gears

It is hard to believe, but some mated gears are not round! Here is an example of a pair of mated gears that are square. Even though they are not round, they turn, and their teeth mesh, like round gears. What we learned about the speed and direction of round gears also applies to these gears. It is unusual to have questions about square gears on a test.

Worm Gears

Worm gears are like big screws. Here a worm gear is next to a spur gear. If the worm gear turns clockwise, the spur gear will turn counterclockwise.

WHAT CAN I LEARN TO HELP MYSELF DO BETTER?

There are thousands of different gears and gear combinations. You might go to the library and get a few children's books on gears. Each book might contain different types of gears. For example, there are crown gears (the teeth stick up from the rim), worm gears (where one of the gears looks like a screw), helical gears (where the teeth are curved rather than straight), and other, more complex gears. Most of the questions you are asked will be about spur gears, the types of gears described in this chapter.

WHAT ELSE CAN I DO TO PREPARE?

Go to a hardware store and ask to see some gears. Some people who have never seen a gear find it helpful to actually see and touch gears. Many gears are inexpensive (plastic ones may cost less than a dollar), so buy a few and see how they can fit together.

TIPS FOR GEAR QUESTIONS

These tips have been explained already. If you are not sure you understand a tip, go back and reread this chapter.

1. When small and large gears are mated, the gear with fewer teeth will turn faster. The smaller gear will always have fewer teeth.
2. When there are two or more gears in a row, any gears with the same number of teeth will turn at the same speed.
3. Mated spur gears turn in opposite directions.
4. When you have an odd number of gears in a row, the last gear will turn in the same direction as the first gear.
5. When you have an even number of gears in a row, the last gear will turn in the opposite direction from the first gear.
6. If you think the answer is "Can't tell," double-check the other choices.

TIME LIMIT

The time limits for these tests often allow at least some people to finish the test. You should try to finish tests that have this type of question.

HOW TO USE THE PRACTICE QUESTIONS

There are practice questions on the following pages.

- Do the practice questions in this chapter without any time limit.
- Time yourself when you do the practice questions at the end of the book, using the time limit shown there.

Practice Questions

In addition to the questions here, there are more practice questions of this type at the end of this book.

1. If gear B turns as shown, how will gear A turn?

   (A) Same direction
   (B) Opposite direction
   (C) Can't tell

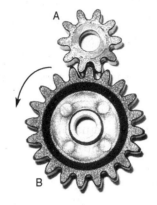

2. If gear A is moved, which gear will turn the most slowly?

   A. Gear A
   B. Gear B
   C. Gear C
   D. Gear D
   E. Gear E

3. If gear D is turned in the direction shown, in what direction will gear A turn?

   A. Same direction
   B. Opposite direction
   C. Can't tell

4. If gear A turns at the rate of 100 rotations per second, gear B will turn _____ rotations per second.

   (A) 150
   (B) 200
   (C) 300
   (D) 400
   (E) 500

5. If gear 1 turns as shown, gear 2 will turn

   (A) Clockwise.
   (B) Counterclockwise.
   (C) Can't tell

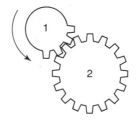

6. If gear A has 40 teeth and turns 5 times a second, gear C will turn _____ times a second.

   (A) 1
   (B) 2
   (C) 4
   (D) 5
   (E) 10

7. How many of these can turn clockwise?

   A. 0
   B. 1
   C. 2
   D. 3

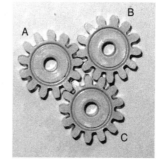

8. If gear A makes 30 turns, how many turns will gear B make?

(A) 10
(B) 15
(C) 30
(D) 35
(E) 40

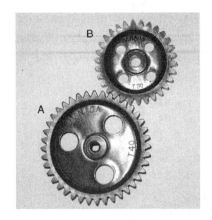

9. If gear A is turning at a rate of 700 turns per second, then gear G will turn at a rate of _____ turns per second?

(A) 100
(B) 300
(C) 700
(D) 1,000
(E) None of the above

10. When turning, how many gears will turn in a clockwise direction?

(A) 0
(B) 1
(C) 2
(D) 3
(E) 4

The answers to these questions are on page 65.

ANSWERS TO PRACTICE QUESTIONS: GEARS

1. **(B)** Two mated spur gears turn in opposite directions.

2. **(C)** The gear with the most teeth turns the slowest.

3. **(B)** D turns counterclockwise, C turns clockwise, B turns counterclockwise, A turns clockwise.

4. **(D)** Gear A has 40 teeth and gear B has 10 teeth, which means gear B has to turn four times for every turn of gear A. So if gear A turns 100 times, then gear B must turn 400 times.

5. **(A)** Gear 1 is turning counterclockwise and mated gears turn in opposite directions.

6. **(E)** Counting the teeth shows gear C has 20 teeth, so it will turn twice as fast as gear A. Two times 5 is 10. (The size of gear B is not important.)

7. **(A)** None of the gears can move. If A moved clockwise, then B would have to move counterclockwise and C would have to move clockwise. But C cannot move clockwise because it is next to A, which is turning clockwise. So none of the gears can turn. They are locked where they are.

8. **(E)** Gear A has 40 teeth and gear B has 30 teeth. Every time gear A turns, gear B must turn 1⅓ times, so every time gear A turns three times, gear B must turn four times. So every time gear A turns 30 times, gear B must turn 40 times.

9. **(C)** Gears A and G are the same size, so they turn at the same rate. Speed of turning does not depend on the number or size of gears in between.

10. **(D)** Every other gear turns in the same direction. Because there are six gears, three will turn clockwise and three counterclockwise.

You will find more questions on gears at the end of this book.

Pulleys

IMPORTANT WORDS IN THIS CHAPTER	
Block	Pulley
Double Pulley	Stable

Some tests ask only about pulleys and ropes, and other tests include a few of these questions together with other types of questions, such as ones about gears. Most of the questions are easy if you know some basic things about pulleys. This chapter will help you learn what you need to know to answer most pulley and rope questions.

WHAT DO THESE QUESTIONS ASK ABOUT?

You will be shown a drawing of two or more pulleys. You will be asked if the pulleys will move or about how hard it will be to move a weight using the pulley.

WHAT DO THESE TESTS LOOK LIKE?

There are many different ways to attach and use pulleys. Usually the pulley questions will ask about relatively simple groups of pulleys.

> **HINT**
>
> You will be asked if the pulley will move or how hard it will be to move a weight using the pulley.

Sample Question

To lift the 100-pound weight, you need to pull with a force of about _____ pounds.

(A) 25
(B) 50
(C) 75
(D) 100
(E) 125

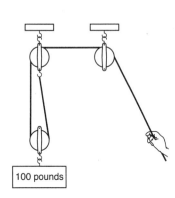

100 pounds

The answer to this sample question is B. A full explanation of this sample question is given on page 73.

Here and on the following pages, we'll learn about different types of pulleys.

Pictures and Diagrams

Some tests use pictures or realistic drawings of pulleys and others use line diagrams. Here is an example of the sample question using a line diagram. We'll use both realistic and line drawings in this chapter so you can get used to both.

Sample Question Using a Line Drawing

To lift the 100-pound weight you need to pull with a force of about _____ pounds.

(A) 25
(B) 50
(C) 75
(D) 100
(E) 125

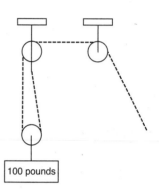

100 pounds

A full explanation of this sample question is given later in the chapter. The answer to this sample question is B.

WHAT ARE THE PARTS OF A SIMPLE PULLEY?

> **VOCABULARY**
>
> Simple pulleys are made of a *wheel* and a *block*, which holds the wheel.

The simple pulleys in this type of question are made of a **wheel** and something called a **block,** which holds the wheel. The wheel usually has a groove in it so that a rope can go around the edge without falling off. The pulley makes it easier for the rope to move.

WHY DO WE USE PULLEYS?

Pulleys are special tools that let us lift heavy objects with little effort and without using electricity or motors. Pulleys can also change the direction of movement. Pulleys are important in many industries. The drawings below show ways a pulley can be used to change the direction of movement. In most of this chapter we will look at ways pulleys are used to make it easier to lift loads.

Three ways to lift a weight

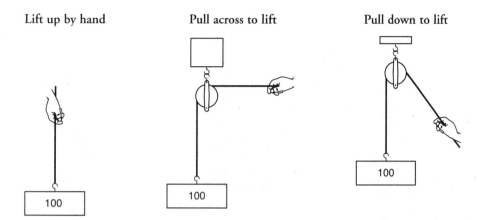

Lift up by hand   Pull across to lift   Pull down to lift

A Few Practical Examples

A few practical examples will help us understand pulleys. These three drawings show how pulleys are sometimes used in everyday living to change direction of movement. For example, when we raise the flag on a flagpole, we do not need to be at the top of the pole pulling the flag up. A pulley lets us raise the flag while standing on the ground and pulling down.

A Close Look at a Pulley

If you have never seen a pulley, they can be mysterious. On the next page are photos of several different simple pulleys. Notice that each pulley has two parts:

- a wheel

- a block or case that holds the wheel

Examples of Pulleys

Thin Wheel, hook on both ends

Plastic, openings at both ends

Thick Wheel

TIP

Hooks or eyes at one or both ends of the blocks are used to hang the pulleys or as a place to tie a rope.

The blocks have hooks or eyes at one or both ends. These are used to hang the pulleys or as a place to tie a rope. (The reason the case is called a block is that many years ago the cases were made from blocks of wood.)

Notice that the wheels have a groove around the outside edge. The rope fits in this groove.

Understanding Why Pulleys Make It Easier to Lift Heavy Weights

Using a pulley is like having another person do part of the lifting. These drawings show the weight supported by each rope.

Here each person holds 50 pounds.

Here the rope tied to the hook holds 50 pounds and the person holds the other 50 pounds.

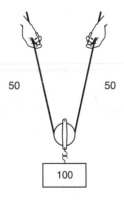

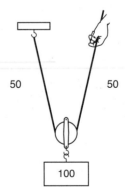

The drawings above show how you can lift 100 pounds using only 50 pounds of effort. In both cases the pulley moves up when the weight is lifted. That is because the pulleys are attached to the weight.

Do the Rope and Pulley Have Weight and Does the Pulley Have Friction?

You should ignore the weight and friction of the rope and the pulleys when you answer questions on this kind of test.

We will look at different ways to use single pulleys.

Using One Pulley

A pulley can be attached in one of two ways:

- to the weight to be lifted

- to an overhead support

If the pulley is attached to the weight, it will move when the weight is moved and the force you need to lift the weight will be half the weight. If the pulley is attached to an overhead support (like the ceiling), it will not move when the weight moves. When you have only one pulley attached to the ceiling, the force you need to lift the weight is the same as lifting without a pulley.

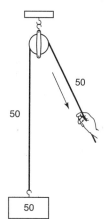

Pulley attached to weight   Pulley attached to ceiling

When is the Force to Lift Less Than the Weight?

We have seen that sometimes one pulley lets you lift a weight using a force equal to the weight and other times one pulley lets you lift the weight using half that force. The key to telling how much force you will need to lift the weight is to count the number of sections of rope supporting the weight. In the drawing on the left there are two sections of rope leading to the weight and each is marked 25, showing that they each hold up 25 pounds. In the drawing on the right, there is only one section of rope supporting the weight. The rope is marked 50, showing it is holding up 50 pounds.

The general rule is

- **divide the weight by the number of sections of rope supporting it to get the force needed to lift the weight.**

Using Two Pulleys

Here are two basic ways to use two pulleys:

- One pulley attached to the weight to be lifted

- Neither pulley attached to the weight to be lifted

The amount of force needed to lift the weight depends on the number of sections of rope supporting the weight.

Two sections of rope supporting the weight

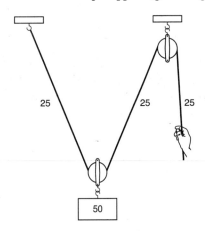

One section of rope supporting the weight

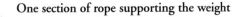
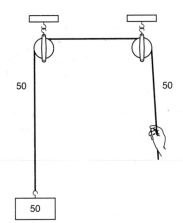

One pulley attached to the weight cuts the force needed to lift the weight in half. This is because there are two sections of rope holding up the weight. The general rule is true here also: **Divide the weight by the number of sections of rope supporting it to get the force needed to lift the weight.** In the drawing on the right, there is one section of rope attached to the weight, so you need a force of 50 pounds to lift it.

Using Three Pulleys

In this drawing there are three sections of rope supporting the weight, so you can lift the 300-pound weight with a force of only 100 pounds.

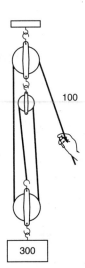

Now we know enough to start answering questions. We will start with the sample question from the first page of the chapter and then go over several more questions.

Sample Question

To lift the 100-pound weight you need to pull with a force of about _____ pounds.

(A) 25
(B) 50
(C) 75
(D) 100
(E) 125

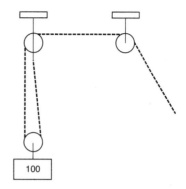

ANSWER AND EXPLANATION

The weight is labeled 100. Because there are two sections of rope supporting the weight, each supports 50 pounds. So we need a force of 50 pounds to lift the weight. The correct answer is B.

Sample Question

To lift the 120-pound weight you need to pull with a force of about _____ pounds.

(A) 10
(B) 12
(C) 20
(D) 24
(E) 30

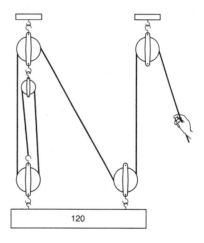

ANSWER AND EXPLANATION

There are five sections of rope holding up the weight. (Three sections of rope go to the lower pulley on the left and two sections of rope go to the lower pulley on the right.) Following the general rule we divide 120 by 5 to get 24. The correct answer is D.

Questions Using the Word *Stable*

Sometimes a question will use the word *stable*. **Stable means the pulleys will not move.** *Unstable* means the pulleys will move. On page 74 is an example of a question that uses the word *stable*.

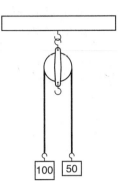

Is this pulley stable?

    (A) It is stable.
    (B) It is unstable.
    (C) Can't tell

ANSWER AND EXPLANATION

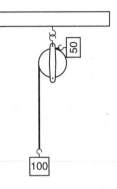

These weights are different, so the heavy weight will move down and the light weight will move up until they cannot move any more. Since the weights will move, they are unstable. The answer is B.

    The pulleys in the question above this one will come to rest in a position like this.

Questions About Whether Weights Will Move

Another type of question asks if the weights shown are balanced or stable, or if they will move. We will look at a few of this type of question now.

Sample Question

Are these weights stable?

    (A) Yes
    (B) No

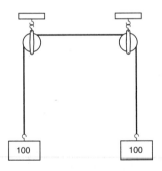

WATCH FOR

A question asking if the weights shown are **balanced** or **stable** is asking "Will these weights stay where they are?"

ANSWER AND EXPLANATION

The question uses the word *stable*. The question means "Will these weights stay where they are?" Because the weights are equal and each weight is held up by one rope, they will not move. The correct answer is A.

Sample Question

Will these weights move?

(A) Yes
(B) No

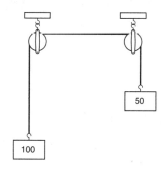

ANSWER AND EXPLANATION

These weights are not balanced. One is twice as heavy as the other, and each is held up with one rope. The heavier weight will move down until it cannot move any more. This will make the lighter weight move up. The correct answer is A.

Sample Question

Will these weights move?

(A) Yes
(B) No

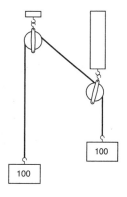

ANSWER AND EXPLANATION

Because the weights are equal and each weight is held up by one rope, they will not move. It doesn't make a difference that one pulley is lower than the other. The correct answer is B.

Sample Question

These pulleys are

(A) stable.
(B) unstable.

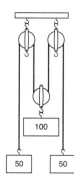

ANSWER AND EXPLANATION

The two 50-pound weights exactly balance the 100-pound weight, so this is stable. The weights will not move. The answer is A.

Questions About Whether Pulleys and Weights Will Move

This type of question also asks if the pulleys shown will move or if they are stable. The key to answering this type of question is to see what is holding each pulley in place. If nothing is holding the pulley in place, it can move.

Sample Question

Will these weights move?

(A) Yes
(B) No

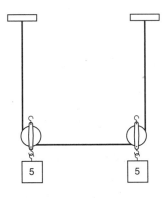

ANSWER AND EXPLANATION

The weights are equal, but there is nothing holding the pulleys in place. So the pulleys are free to move. Because weights always pull down, the weights will move. The weights and pulleys will continue pulling down until they cannot go any farther. The pulleys and weights will come to rest when the weights cannot move down more. This is shown in the diagram at right. The correct answer to this question is A.

The pulleys in the question above will come to rest in a position like this.

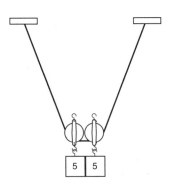

REMEMBER

Pulleys riding on a bar are free to move side to side.

Pulleys Riding on a Bar

These pulleys are not tied in place. Rather, the top pulleys ride on a bar and are free to move side to side. Each top pulley has another pulley attached to it at the bottom. Only the bottom pulleys have rope going around them.

Sample Question

Will these weights move?

(A) Yes
(B) No

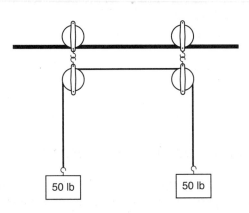

ANSWER AND EXPLANATION

There is nothing stopping the pulleys from sliding together, and the weight on the rope will push the pulleys together. The correct answer is A.

The pulleys in the question on page 76 will come to rest in a position like this.

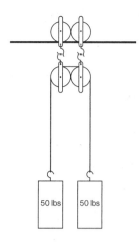

What Do More Complicated Pulleys Look Like?

Sometimes two or more pulley wheels are mounted in the same holder. Even when they are mounted in the same block or case, the pulley wheels do not touch each other, so they turn independently. Here are examples of pulleys with two or three wheels.

Examples of Pulleys with More than One Wheel

Plastic with two wheels   Plastic with three wheels   Metal with two wheels

> **TIP**
>
> A double pulley is just two single pulleys held in the same case.

In each pulley, one wheel can turn without making any other wheel turn. On the next page we will see a double pulley in action.

A Double Pulley in Action

A double pulley is just two single pulleys held in the same case. The wheels in this double pulley are not connected to each other. Each pulley wheel can turn without the other turning.

Lifting with a double pulley   Doing the same with single pulleys

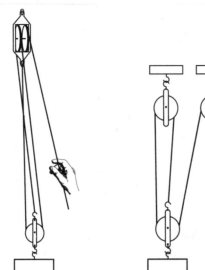
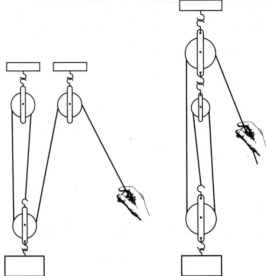

TIP

Even when set in the same block, each pulley wheel turns by itself and the wheels do not touch each other.

WHAT CAN I LEARN TO HELP MYSELF DO BETTER?

There are many different ways to combine pulleys to lift a weight. You might go to the library and get a few children's books on pulleys. Each book will have pictures of pulleys of different sizes and shapes and examples of pulleys being used. You may also want to look at the chapter on General Mechanical Understanding, which teaches about belt pulleys.

WHAT ELSE CAN I DO TO PREPARE?

Go to a hardware store and ask to see some pulleys. Some people who have never seen a pulley find it helpful to actually see and touch one. Many pulleys are inexpensive (small ones may cost about $3), so buy two or three and try to set them up to lift things.

TIPS FOR PULLEY QUESTIONS

1. Divide the weight by the number of sections of rope holding it up to get the force needed to lift the weight.
2. Read the question carefully. Not all questions ask the same thing.
3. The force needed to lift with a pulley will not be more than the weight to be lifted.
4. Ignore the weight of the rope and the pulleys and ignore friction when you answer these questions.

TIP

Look at Chapter 3 on General Mechanical Understanding, which teaches about belt pulleys.

TIME LIMIT

The time limits for these tests often allow at least some people to finish the test. You should try to finish tests that have this type of question.

HOW TO USE THE PRACTICE QUESTIONS

There are practice questions on this and the next pages and more at the end of this book.

- Do the practice questions in this chapter without any time limit.

- Time yourself when you do the practice questions at the end of the book, using the time limit shown there.

Practice Questions

1. To lift the 100-pound weight, you need to pull with a force of about _____ pounds.

   (A) 10
   (B) 25
   (C) 50
   (D) 75
   (E) 100

2. Which would take more force to lift?

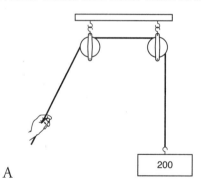

A

B

   (A) Drawing A
   (B) Drawing B
   (C) No difference

3. Which would take more force to lift?

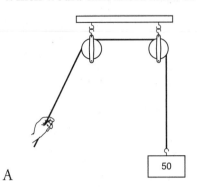

A   B

(A) Drawing A
(B) Drawing B
(C) No difference

4. To lift the weight, you need to pull with a force of about _____ pounds.

(A) 10
(B) 25
(C) 50
(D) 75
(E) 100

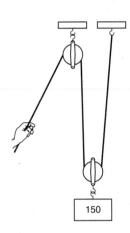

5. Which would take more force to lift?

A   B

A. Drawing A
B. Drawing B
C. No difference

6. Is this stable?

   A. Yes
   B. No
   C. Can't tell

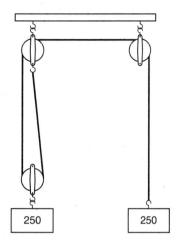

7. Will the weights move?

   A. Yes
   B. No
   C. Can't tell

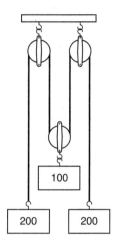

8. To lift the weight, you need to pull up with a force of about _____ pounds.

   (A) 10
   (B) 25
   (C) 50
   (D) 75
   (E) 100

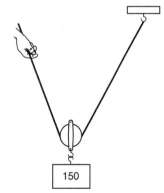

9. To lift the 300-pound weight, you need to pull with a force of about _____ pounds.

(A) 30
(B) 60
(C) 100
(D) 150
(E) 300

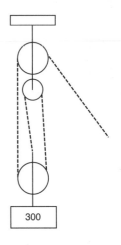

10. To lift the weight, you need to pull with a force of about _____ pounds.

(A) 30
(B) 50
(C) 100
(D) 150
(E) 300

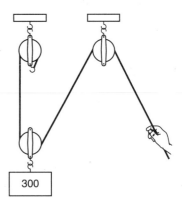

The answers to these questions are below.

ANSWERS TO PRACTICE QUESTIONS: PULLEYS

1. (**E**) There is one supporting section of rope, so the force needed to lift the weight is not less than the weight.

2. (**C**) Both A and B have one supporting section of rope and so require equal force.

3. (**C**) The weight in A is held up by one supporting section of rope, so it takes a force of 50 to lift the weight. The weight in B is held up by two supporting sections of rope, so divide 100 by 2 to get the force needed to lift the weight. A force of 50 is needed to lift either weight.

4. (**D**) There are two supporting sections of rope, so divide 150 by 2.

5. (**C**) Both A and B have one supporting section of rope, and so require equal force. The size of the pulley does not matter.

6. (**B**) The left-hand weight has two supporting sections of rope and the right hand weight has one. So the weights are not stable. The weight on the right will go down and the weight on the left will go up.

7. (**A**) The 100-pound weight will be lifted up by the other two weights.

8. (**D**) There are two supporting sections of rope, so divide 150 by 2.

9. (**C**) There are three supporting sections of rope, so divide 300 by 3.

10. (**D**) There are two supporting sections of rope, so divide 300 by 2. The left hand pulley at the top is really just serving as a place to attach the rope to the ceiling.

You will find more questions on pulleys at the end of this book.

Tools

CHAPTER 6

IMPORTANT WORDS IN THIS CHAPTER

Adjustable Wrench	Needle-nose Pliers
Allen Wrench	Nut
Ball-peen Hammer	Open-ended Wrench
Bolt	Phillips Screwdriver
Box Wrench	Pipe Wrench
C-clamp	Pliers
Channel-lock® Pliers	Retractable Rule
Circular Saw	Rubber Mallet
Claw Hammer	Saber Saw
Combination Wrench	Sledge Hammer
Crescent® Wrench	Slip-joint Pliers
Electric Drill	Slotted Screwdriver
Glue Gun	Socket Wrench
Hacksaw	Square
Hammer Face	Tongue-and-Groove Pliers
Hammer Head	Vise-grip® Pliers
Level	Wing Nut
Locking Pliers	Wood Saw
Machine Screw	Wood Screw

TIP

These questions ask about the names or uses of hand tools, small power tools, and fasteners.

Mechanical aptitude tests may include some questions about tools, fasteners, and other things you might find in an auto or carpentry shop. This chapter will go over the most common types of tools, because these are most likely to be on mechanical aptitude tests.

WHAT DO THESE QUESTIONS ASK ABOUT?

The questions as about the names or the use of hand tools, small power tools, and fasteners, especially those used in carpentry and auto shops, but sometimes also hobbyists' tools.

WHAT DO THESE TESTS LOOK LIKE?

The questions show a picture or name of a tool. You have to choose the name of the tool or tell how it is used by choosing the best answer. There will be several questions on each page.

Sample Question

What kind of wrench is this?

(A) Allen
(B) Pipe
(C) Box
(D) Crescent
(E) Open-ended

ANSWER AND EXPLANATION

The correct answer is D. The other choices list other types of wrenches, all very different from the crescent wrench.

Tests that include questions on tools tend to have longer time limits. The questions do not take long to answer, so usually you will have enough time to answer all of the questions.

Usually there are only a few questions of this type on a test, or there is only a short test as part of a group of tests.

This chapter will go over the types of tools found on these tests.

WHAT KIND OF TOOLS WILL BE ON THE TEST?

Mechanical aptitude tests ask about the most common hand tools and small power tools. Tests that ask about less common tools are usually job knowledge tests, not tests of mechanical aptitude. This chapter will cover some common hand tools, power tools, and fasteners.

WHAT IS COVERED IN THIS CHAPTER?

This chapter will cover tools and fasteners. We will learn the names of many tools and a little about when and how they are used. We will also learn about fasteners such as screws, bolts, and nuts. The major types of tools and fasteners we will learn about in this chapter are:

- hammers
- measures
- pliers
- saws
- screwdrivers

- screws, bolts, nuts, washers
- wrenches
- small electrical power tools
- some other tools

For each of these we will describe

- what it is
- when/why/how it is used
- what it looks like

There are many types of tools and fasteners. We will cover the most common ones, because that is what is likely to be on a test.

We'll start with hammers and then cover the other tools in the order they are listed.

Hammers

Hammers are used to hit or strike something. Some hammers are also made to help take out nails. There are many types of hammers. We will cover four:

- claw hammer
- ball-peen hammer
- rubber mallet
- sledgehammer

CLAW HAMMER

A claw hammer is made of a **handle** and a **head**. At one end of the head is the flat **face** and at the other end is the **claw**. The face of a claw hammer usually is used to hit nails and sometimes to hit other tools. The claw is often used to pull nails out of wood. A claw hammer is almost always used with one hand.

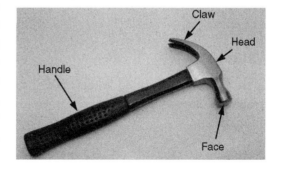

BALL-PEEN HAMMER

A ball-peen hammer is used when working with metal. It is made of a **handle** and a **head**. At one end of the head is the flat **face** and at the other end is a round ball-like **peen**. The peen is smaller than the face and can strike places the face cannot reach. A ball-peen hammer is almost always used with one hand.

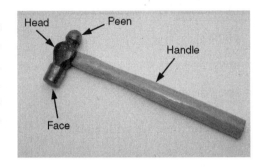

RUBBER MALLET

A rubber mallet is made of a **handle** and a **head**. The head is made of hard rubber. It is used when hitting something that would be damaged by a metal hammer. A rubber mallet is almost always used with one hand.

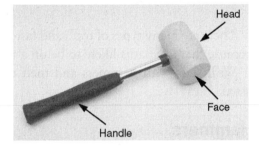

SLEDGEHAMMER

A sledgehammer is made of a **handle** and a metal **head** much larger than a claw or ball-peen hammer. The handle can be several feet long. A sledgehammer is used in construction to drive spikes and for other heavy-duty work. A sledgehammer is almost always used with two hands.

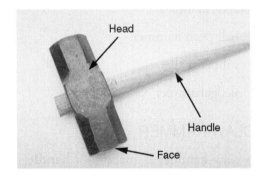

Measures

Measuring tools are used when making or inspecting a finished or partly finished product. There are many different measuring tools. We will talk about a few of the most common:

- retractable rule
- level
- square

RETRACTABLE RULE

This widely used type of metal tape rule is convenient to carry because it rolls up into a small holder. (Although children in school are taught the word *ruler*, a measuring tool like this is called a *rule*.)

LEVEL

A level can be used to see if a part is truly horizontal or vertical. It is a simple tool with two parts: a small, slightly curved tube filled with liquid and a bubble of air, and a holder for the tube. The level to the right has three tubes. That way the level can be used in more than one position. Levels come in various lengths. The one shown here is about 3 feet long and the holder is made of aluminum.

SQUARE

A square is a measuring tool used to check if a part has a 90 degree angle or to mark lines on materials. It is a simple tool with no moving parts. It is metal that is made into an L shape. Squares come in different sizes and styles. The one shown here is about 10 inches long.

Pliers

Pliers are like very strong fingers. They help you hold pieces firmly. Some pliers let you hold small pieces or pieces that are in places that fingers cannot reach. Some pliers are used to cut or bend wire or other metal. Pliers are usually talked about in the plural, so when you talk about a **pair of pliers** you are talking about one tool. Pliers come in various sizes, but they usually are a size to be used with one hand.

At one end of the pliers are the **jaws** that pick up and hold objects, and at the other end are the **handles,** which you hold in your hand and use to open and close and hold the pliers. In the middle is a **joint** where the two pieces of the pliers are joined. These are labeled in the first picture on page 90.

We will cover four types of pliers:

- slip-joint
- needle-nose
- vise-grip®
- channel-lock.

SLIP-JOINT PLIERS

This widely used type of pliers can be adjusted to open more than usual to hold larger objects. The slip joint allows these pliers to open wider.

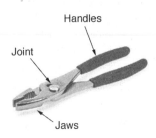

Handles

Joint

Jaws

NEEDLE-NOSE PLIERS

These pliers have a pointed end that can reach into tight places. They are often used in electrical work and sometimes have a cutting edge near the joint for cutting wire. Another name for this is long-nose pliers.

LOCKING PLIERS

Also known as Vice Grip® pliers, these widely used pliers are unusual because they lock onto the part held. They lock strongly to a part, so in some situations after they have been locked in place they can be used without anyone holding them.

TONGUE-AND-GROOVE PLIERS

Also known as Channel-Lock® pliers, and sometimes as pump pliers, these are adjustable to several different open positions. They have long handles which give them a powerful grip. It is easy to damage nuts and bolts with this type of pliers. They should be used only when a wrench that fits is not available. They are often used on larger and odd-shape pieces.

Saws

Saws are used to cut. Different saws are usually used to cut metal or wood. Saws powered by electricity are described in the section on Small Electrical Power Tools on page 95. We will look at two types of saws, one used for metal and one for wood.

HACKSAW

A hacksaw is made to cut metal. It has two parts: a **frame** and a **blade**. The blade has teeth at the bottom that do the cutting. This hacksaw is adjustable, meaning that the frame can be adjusted to use longer or shorter blades. It is best used with two hands, one hand on the handle and the other hand at the front. The hacksaw here is about a foot long.

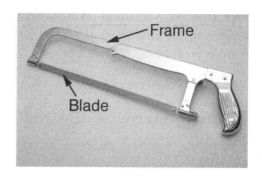

WOOD SAW

This wood cutting handsaw has two parts: a **handle** and a **blade**. The handle is meant to be used with one hand. The blade has teeth at the bottom that do the cutting. The saw to the right is about 3 feet long.

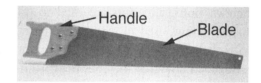

Screwdrivers

Screwdrivers are made to turn screws. Screwdrivers have two parts: a **handle** and a **shank**. The handle is made to be turned with one hand. At the end of the shank is the **tip**, which fits the head of a screw. The tip of the shank usually has one of two shapes, flat or Phillips, to fit one of the two most commonly used screws, which are called slotted and Phillips. You need to turn a screwdriver clockwise to tighten a screw, or counterclockwise to loosen a screw. We will look at two types of screwdrivers now, and then look at some different types of screws.

SLOTTED SCREWDRIVER

Slotted screwdrivers are used to turn screws with a slotted head. They are also called **flat-head screwdrivers**, because the tip is flat. The screwdrivers shown to the right range in length from 2½ inches to a foot.

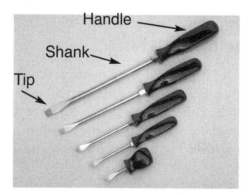

PHILLIPS SCREWDRIVER

This type of screwdriver is also called Phillips tip or Phillips head screwdriver. A closeup of the tip is shown below.

TIP OF A PHILLIPS SCREWDRIVER

The tip of a Phillips screwdriver looks like a cross when looked at from the end.

Screws, Bolts, Nuts, and Washers

Screws, bolts, and nuts are used to hold parts together. Usually they are made of metal. Screws used in wood are tapered, meaning they are thinner at one end than the other. Screws used with nuts are not tapered. A nut is a small block of metal with a threaded hole that matches the thread on a screw. Large untapered screws are called bolts. Two common types of screw heads are slotted and Phillips. The first two drawings below show examples of these types of heads. We will now look at

- wood screws
- machine screws
- nuts

- bolts
- washers

WOOD SCREW

This is a **Phillips head** wood screw. A wood screw is used to attach parts to wood. It is sharp at one end to help it make its own hole as it is screwed into the wood.

MACHINE SCREW

This is a **slotted-head** machine screw. This machine screw has threads along its length. A machine screw cannot make its own hole; rather, a hole has to be made before it can be used. A machine screw can be used with a nut to fasten two pieces together. The threads on a screw and a nut have to be the same size.

NUT

A nut is a small four- or six-sided block of metal with threads inside. It is made to be used with machine screws.

WING NUT

A wing nut is designed to be tightened by hand.

BOLT

A bolt is a large screw. Large bolts can be many inches long. Usually a bolt does not have a slot in the top the way other screws do. The head of a bolt usually has six sides. It is meant to be turned with a wrench, not a screwdriver.

Washers

A washer is shaped like disk with a hole in the middle. Washers are used with machine screws and bolts. The exact shape of the washer depends on the use. Flat washers are smooth. Lock washers come in two general types: split and star washers. When you tighten a screw that has a lock washer, the cut edges of the washer dig in and stop the screw from coming loose on its own.

Flat Washer

Split Washer

Star Washer

Wrenches

A wrench is a tool used to turn nuts and bolts and other objects to make them tighter or looser. We will look at four types of wrenches:

- combination
- adjustable
- socket
- pipe

COMBINATION WRENCH

A combination wrench is a solid, non-adjustable wrench. It combines two types of wrenches in one. One end is an **open-end wrench**. The other end is a **box wrench**. The box wrench is circular. It is called a box wrench because it surrounds the nut. Nonadjustable wrenches often come in sets of different sizes.

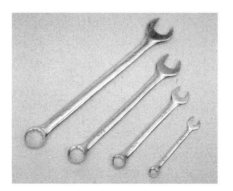

ADJUSTABLE WRENCH

One side of the wrench does not move and the other side is adjusted using a thumbscrew. Because it is adjustable, it can be used with nuts of different sizes, which is convenient. But the correct size box wrench works better than an adjustable wrench. This type of wrench is often called a crescent wrench because it was first made by the Crescent company.

SOCKET WRENCH

A socket wrench has a handle and at least one socket that can be attached to the handle. A socket wrench set has sockets that can be used with nuts of different sizes. Each socket has a square opening at one end that fits on the handle and an opening at the other end that fits nuts of one size or another.

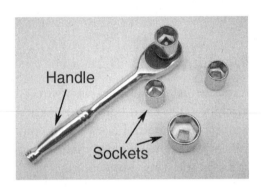

PIPE WRENCH

A pipe wrench is used to turn or hold round objects like pipe. This type of wrench is also called a Stilson wrench.

ALLEN WRENCH

A six sided, L-shaped bar used to loosen or tighten screws or bolts that have a six-sided opening in their head. Allen wrenches come in various sizes, just like screws and screwdrivers. This type of wrench is also called an Allen key, hex key, or hex wrench.

Allen Wrench

Allen Bolt

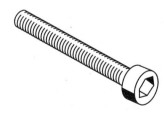

Small Electrical Power Tools

We will learn about a few electrical power tools that can be moved from place to place. Some power tools need to be plugged into an electrical wall socket. Others have rechargeable batteries and do not need to be plugged in while they are being used. The handles of these tools are made to be used with one hand. The electrical power tools we will learn about are

- drill

- saber saw

- circular saw

ELECTRIC DRILL

The electric drill is designed to be used with drill bits of various sizes to drill holes in such things as wood and metal. The drill bit is held in place by a metal clamp on the drill called a chuck. The electric drill can also be used with attachments to sand, polish, and mix paint.

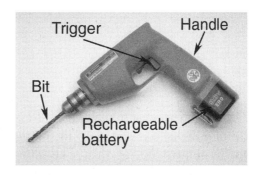

ELECTRIC SABER SAW

The electric saber saw is designed to be used with saw blades of various sizes to cut such things as wood. This type of saw lets you cut smooth curves in wood and light metal. It is also called a **jigsaw.**

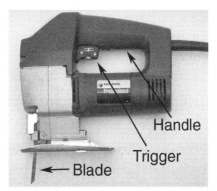

CIRCULAR SAW

The blade of this saw is circular. It is a popular woodworking tool. It is also one of the most dangerous power tools when it is not properly used.

TIP

A **circular saw** is one of the most dangerous power tools when it is not properly used.

Some Other Tools

Here are two other common tools:

- C-clamp

- glue gun

C-CLAMP

A C-clamp is made of a metal frame shaped like the letter C and a screw that can be turned to press into the top of the C. It is used to hold parts in place temporarily, for example, while gluing parts in place.

GLUE GUN

A glue gun uses heat to melt glue. After the glue melts, it is placed on the parts you want to glue together. The glue from a glue gun often works better than other types of glue because it is faster, sticks to almost anything, and is strong.

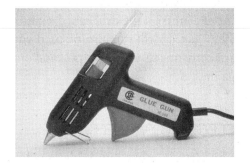

Outlines and Sketches of Tools

Sometimes questions will use rough drawings of tools rather than pictures. It can be more difficult to recognize the tools when all you have is an outline. But if you know the tool, you should be able to recognize it. Here are some drawings of tools to give you some practice recognizing outlines.

COMBINATION WRENCH

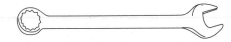

CLAW HAMMER

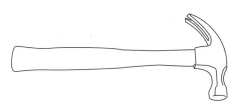

HACKSAW

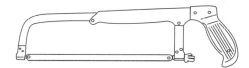

WHAT ELSE CAN I DO TO PREPARE?

Using tools is a good way to learn about them. You can learn how to use tools from a friend or by taking a course. Courses in home repair, car repair, or wood shop are often offered for adults in continuing education courses. Many schools have shop courses for high school or junior high school students. You might also go to the hardware store or the hardware department of a large department store and look at the tools there.

Reading about tools is also a good way to prepare. Search the Internet for tool videos, pictures, and instructions, for example:

- http://home.howstuffworks.com/plumbing-tools.htm

- http://home.howstuffworks.com/hand-tools.htm—has pictures and descriptions of common hand tools and their uses.

- http://landlord.com/diyext_diy.htm—click on hardware and tools for info on fasteners, hand tools, power tools, and more.

- Try using websites for stores like Home Depot (homedepot.com), Sears (sears.com) and Lowe's (lowes.com) to find more pictures of hand tools and power tools.

- You can also go to http://about.com and search the site for "hammer wrench pliers" (search on all three words at once).

> **TIP**
>
> **Memorize** names of tools;, the test may not show pictures.

TIME LIMIT

The time limit for this type of test usually is generous, so you probably will have enough time to answer the questions.

HOW TO USE THE PRACTICE QUESTIONS

There are practice questions on the following pages, and more at the end of this book.

Practice Questions

1. What type of screwdriver should you use with this type of screw?

    (A) Slotted
    (B) Furniture
    (C) Phillips
    (D) Automotive

2. Which part is used to pull out nails?

    (A) A
    (B) B
    (C) Both

    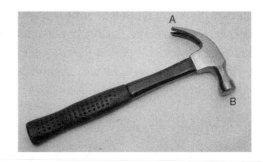

3. What is the name of this tool?

    (A) Open-ended wrench
    (B) Box wrench
    (C) Crescent wrench
    (D) Combination wrench

4. Which of these is best used to tighten a bolt?

    (A) Slip-joint pliers
    (B) Channel-lock pliers
    (C) Combination wrench
    (D) Adjustable wrench

5. Which of these is meant to be tightened by hand?

    (A) Machine screw
    (B) Wood screw
    (C) Wing nut
    (D) Bolt

6. This is made to:

    (A) drive nails.
    (B) work with metal.
    (C) work with soft materials.
    (D) take out nails.

7. Which of these pliers can lock onto a part?

    (A) Slip-joint
    (B) Vise-grip®
    (C) Channel-lock
    (D) Needle-nose

8. This is made to:

    (A) loosen screws and nuts.
    (B) turn pipe.
    (C) remove nails.
    (D) hold objects together.

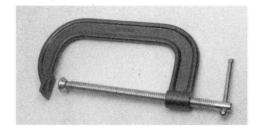

9. A glue gun

    (A) melts glue.
    (B) can shoot glue several inches.
    (C) is used to fix guns.
    (D) None of the above

10. To be sure something is straight up and down you should use a:

    (A) rule.
    (B) level.
    (C) square.

The answers to these questions are below.

ANSWERS TO PRACTICE QUESTIONS: TOOLS

1. (**C**)

2. (**A**)

3. (**D**)

4. (**C**)

5. (**C**)

6. (**B**)

7. (**B**)

8. (**D**)

9. (**A**)

10. (**B**)

You will find more questions about tools at the end of this book.

Map Reading

CHAPTER 7

IMPORTANT WORDS IN THIS CHAPTER

Legend	Northeast/Northwest
North/South/East/West	Southeast/Southwest

In this test, you will answer questions about maps by reading instructions and following compass directions.

WHAT DO THESE QUESTIONS ASK ABOUT?

You will be shown a map or a part of a map. You will be asked to follow directions and answer questions about your location on the map or about how to get from one place to another using the shortest route. There may be written instructions about changes to the map, such as roads that are closed because of construction.

WHAT DO THESE TESTS LOOK LIKE?

All of the questions are based on a map that you will find in the test booklet. The whole map will be on one page. The questions may not all be on the same page as the map. Usually north will be toward the top of the page, but you need to check the compass on each map to be sure. Usually there are one-way streets. You must obey traffic laws in choosing your answers.

> **TIP**
>
> Always check the compass to find north.

> **TIP**
>
> North is *usually* pointing toward the top of the page.

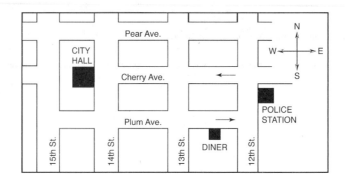

Which of these is the shortest route from city hall to the diner?

(A) North on 14th St., east on Pear Ave., south on 13th St., east on Plum Ave.

(B) East on Cherry Ave., south on 13th St., east on Plum Ave.

(C) South on 14th St., east on Plum Ave.

ANSWER AND EXPLANATION

The correct answer is C.

- Answer A is wrong because you do not have to go north to get to the diner. So this route is not the shortest.

- Answer B is wrong because Cherry Ave. is a one-way street and you may not drive east on Cherry Ave.

In this chapter you will learn the few rules for taking this test, go over some sample questions and answers, review compass directions (north, south, east, and west and more), learn tips for taking this type of test, and get some practice with this type of question.

THE FOUR BASIC COMPASS DIRECTIONS

The maps on this type of test usually use an arrow to show which way is north. Often they show the four directions of a compass: north, south, east, and west. If you know any direction on a map, you can figure out the other directions. Before we look at more test questions, let's review the directions of a compass.

Let's start with a map we have seen often, a map of the United States. If we stand in the middle of the country, we can describe the four directions like this:

- North: Canada

- South: Mexico

- East: Washington, D.C.

- West: California

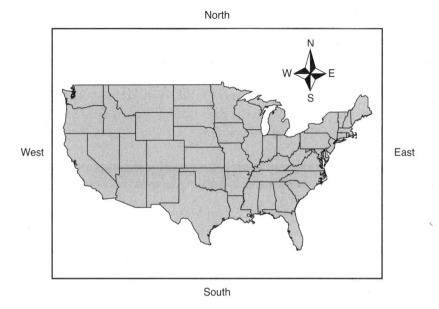

The fancy arrow on the map with the letter N at the top is one of the usual ways of showing which way is north. The letters W, E, and S stand for the directions west, east, and south.

On this page are some other ways of showing the four basic compass directions. You may find any of these on this type of test. Some of these spell out all four directions; others use only the first letter of each direction. Some of these give all four directions; others give only north.

If the map shows only north, it is up to you to know where east, south, and west are.

If north is up, then south is down, and west and east are to the left and right, respectively.

Let's look at a few sample questions. Later we will learn some more about compass directions.

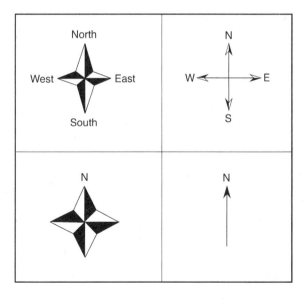

WHAT TYPE OF QUESTIONS WILL I BE ASKED?

Now we will look at some different types of questions. Some of the questions use the same map, but we will show you the map, with each question.

RULE FOR MAP QUESTIONS

There is only one rule in taking this type of test:

- Follow the traffic laws.

Pay close attention to one-way streets. On one-way streets you can walk in either direction but you may drive only in the direction of the arrows. Assume you are driving unless the question says you are walking.

Sample Question Using Compass Directions

You start at the corner of 13th St. and Plum Ave. You go one block east, then one block north, then two blocks west, and finally, two blocks south. Where do you end up?

A. 12th and Walnut
B. 14th and Walnut
C. 12th and Cherry
D. 14th and Cherry

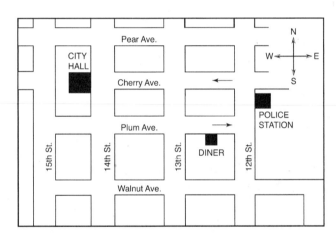

ANSWER AND EXPLANATION

The correct answer is B. This map has some places marked with letters to help you understand how to get the answer.

- First find the place where you start. That place is marked with the letter A.

- After you go one block east, you are at place B.

- After you go one block north, you are at place C.

- After you go two blocks west, you are at place D.

- After you go two blocks south, you are at place E.

HINT

Keep a finger pointing to your destination on the map.

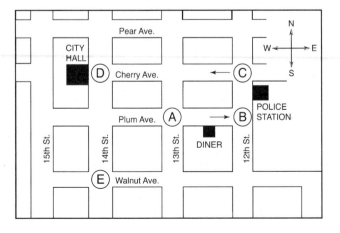

You will find it helpful to use your pencil or finger to point to the location on the map as you answer this type of question. If you are allowed to write in the test booklet, you might make a light check mark to help you remember where you are. This is important because you will be looking back and forth between the map and the question several times as you answer the question.

Sample Question Using Left and Right Turns

You start at the corner of 12th St. and Cherry Ave. You go one block toward city hall, then turn left and go one block, turn left for one block, then turn right for one block. Where do you end up?

A. 12th and Walnut
B. 14th and Walnut
C. 12th and Cherry
D. 14th and Cherry

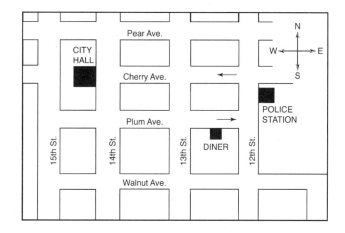

ANSWER AND EXPLANATION

The correct answer is A. This map has some places marked with letters to help you understand how to get the answer.

- First find the place where you start. That place is marked with the letter A.

- After you go one block toward city hall, you are at place B.

- After you turn left and go one block, you are at place C.

- After you turn left and go one block, you are at place D.

- After you turn right and go one block, you are at place E.

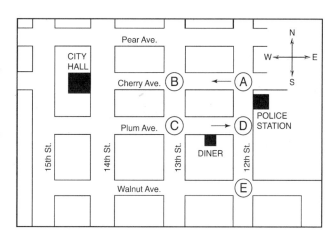

HINT/TIP

Watch out for answer choices that have you driving the wrong way down a one-way street.

For this type of question, some people find it helps to turn the page with the map as they follow the path. It helps to keep the direction you are coming from at the bottom of the page. Otherwise it is easy to make a wrong turn, for example turning left when you should be turning right. Try the questions both ways and see what works best for you.

Sometimes the answer choices do not make sense or are not allowed. For example, an answer choice may have you driving the wrong way down a one-way street. Next we will look at a question like this.

Sample Question with Illegal or Impossible Answers

You are at the diner and want to drive to City Hall. Which of the following is the shortest route?

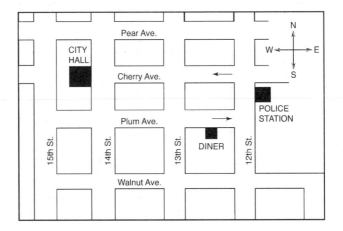

- (A) Take Plum Ave. to 14th St. and turn right.
- (B) Take Plum Ave. to 12th St. Take a left and go to Cherry Ave. Take a left and go to City Hall.
- (C) Take Plum Ave. to 12th St. and turn right. Go to Cherry Ave. and take a left. Go straight on Cherry Ave.
- (D) Take Plum St. to 12th Ave. Take a left and go to Cherry Ave. Take a left and go to City Hall.

ANSWER AND EXPLANATION

The correct answer is B.

- Answer A is wrong because Plum Ave. is one way going east.

- Answer C is wrong because after you take a right turn on 12th St. you will be going away from city hall and you will not get to Cherry Ave.

- Answer D is wrong because there are no streets called 12th Ave. or Plum St.

WHAT IS A LEGEND?

Some maps use symbols and give little explanations of the symbols at the bottom of the map. The place on the map with these explanations sometimes has the title of **Legend.** The legend will usually be different on each map, so you need to look at the legend every time you read a map. The questions on a map reading test may ask about someplace that is mentioned only in the legend. Here are some sample legends. You should look at the different types of symbols and what they sometimes stand for.

This legend has three symbols. The double arrow shows a street where traffic is allowed both ways. A single arrow shows a street that cars can only drive on one way. The circle with a P inside is used to show a parking area.

```
Legend

⟷   Two way street
⟵   One way street
Ⓟ   Parking
```

This legend has three symbols. It does not say Legend at the top, but it shows symbols and what they stand for. In this legend the circle with a P inside is used to show a playground. On the previous legend this symbol was used for a parking area. Be sure you read the legend for each map, because the meaning of some symbols can vary. It is not clear from the legend what the Metro is, but the legend says it is a station, so it must be a bus or train station.

```
Ⓜ   Metro Station
CH   City Hall
Ⓟ   Playground
```

This legend has three symbols.

```
Legend

PS   Police Station
FS   Fire Station
Ⓟ♿  Handicapped
     Parking
```

This legend has five symbols. One is a symbol of a man and woman and it is clear. Police headquarters is shown by the letters PH and a police station by PS. You need to read the letters carefully so you do not confuse a police station with police headquarters.

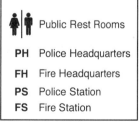

```
🚺🚹  Public Rest Rooms
PH   Police Headquarters
FH   Fire Headquarters
PS   Police Station
FS   Fire Station
```

Now we will look at a sample question that uses a legend.

Sample Question Using a Legend

Using the shortest route, an ambulance can drive from the school to the hospital in _____ blocks.

(A) 3
(B) 4
(C) 5
(D) 6
(E) 7

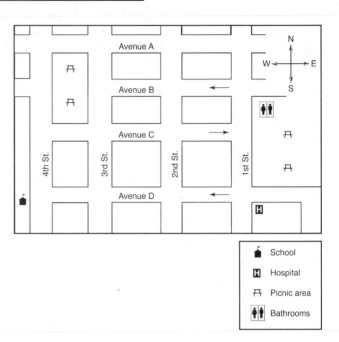

ANSWER AND EXPLANATION

The correct answer is C.

• Answer A would be correct if all the streets were two way. But Avenue D is one way.

• Answer B is wrong because there is no way to get to the hospital by driving exactly four blocks.

• Answer D is wrong because there is no way to get to the hospital by driving exactly six blocks.

• Answer E is wrong because it is not the shortest route.

Eight Basic Compass Directions

Sometimes maps on this type of test show eight directions. These are north, south, east, and west, and the directions between them:

VOCABULARY

Make sure you know these eight directions: N, S, E, W, NE, NW, SE, and SW.

• Northeast (NE) is between north and east.

• Southeast (SE) is between south and east.

• Southwest (SW) is between south and west.

• Northwest (NW) is between north and west.

The symbol on the map might look like this.

Eight Basic Compass Directions

Now we will look at a question that uses some of these eight directions.

Sample Question with Eight Compass Directions

You start at the traffic circle and go 1 block northwest. Then you go 2 blocks east. Then you go 1 block southwest. Where are you now?

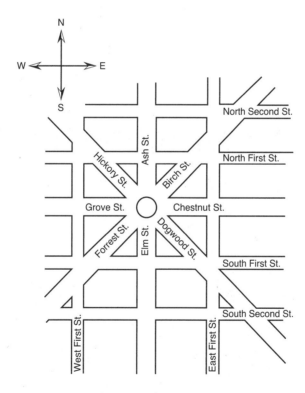

(A) Ash St. and North First St.
(B) East First St. and South First St.
(C) West First St. and South First St.
(D) At the traffic circle

ANSWER AND EXPLANATION

The correct answer is D. This map has some places marked with letters to help you understand how to get the answer.

- You start at the traffic circle in the middle of the map.

- After you go 1 block northwest, you are at place B.

- After you go 2 blocks east, you are at place C.

- After you go 1 southwest, you are back at the traffic circle in the middle of the map.

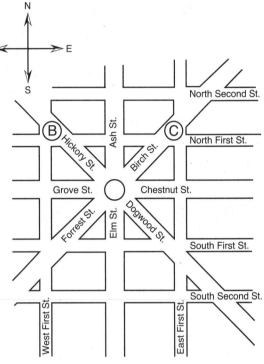

Sample Question with a Temporary Street Closing

The intersection of Cherry and 13th is closed today. What is the shortest way to drive from the police station to city hall?

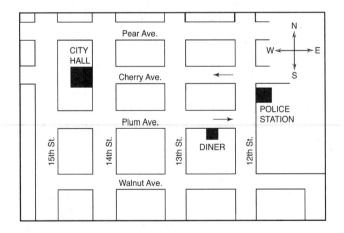

(A) North on 12th and west on Cherry

(B) South on 12th, west on Plum, and north on 14th

(C) North on 12th, west on Pear, and south on 14th

(D) South on 12th, west on Walnut, and north on 14th

ANSWER AND EXPLANATION

The correct answer is C.

- Answer A would be correct if all the streets were open. But the intersection of Cherry Ave. and 13th St. is closed. So this route is not possible.

- Answer B is wrong because Plum is a one-way street going east.

- Answer D will get you to city hall, but it is a longer route than Answer C.

What If North Is Not Facing Up?

Every now and then you will be given a map that does not have north pointing up. You may find it helpful to turn the page so that north is up before answering the questions. Here is a sample of a question that does not have north pointing up.

TIP

Sometimes north does not face up.

Sample Question with North Not Facing Up

You start at the traffic circle and go north one block. Which of the intersections are you closest to?

(A) Quincy and Ohio
(B) Quincy and York
(C) Main and Quincy
(D) Main and Washington

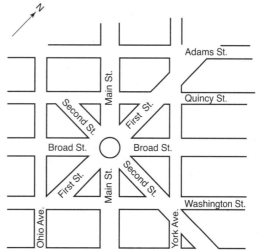

ANSWER AND EXPLANATION

The correct answer is B. To go north one block from the traffic circle you must go on First Street, because First Street goes north-south.

- Answer A is wrong because to get to Quincy and Ohio you would need to go west on Second Street and the question says to go north.

- Answer C is wrong because to get to Main and Quincy you would need to go northwest on Main Street and the question says to go north. Many people choose this wrong answer because Main St. runs in an up-and-down direction, and often North is at the top of a printed map. But on this map north is not at the top. On this map it is First St. that runs north-south.

- Answer D is wrong because to get to Main and Washington you would need to go southeast on Main Street and the question says to go north.

TIPS FOR MAP QUESTIONS

1. Look at the map. Is there a legend with unusual symbols? Try to find north.
2. Read the question carefully. It might tell you about changes to the map.
3. Mark any changes, such as streets closed to traffic, if you are allowed to write in the test booklet.
4. Make sure you know north, south, east, west, northeast, northwest, southeast, and southwest.
5. If you cannot remember which way is west or east, think of a map of America. When north is up, west is to the left and east is to the right.
6. Be careful if streets and places have similar names. Be very careful if a road and an avenue have the same name.
7. Find your starting point on the map before answering the question.
8. Look for arrows showing one-way streets. The arrows may be near the side of the page.
9. Streets that are not marked are two-way streets unless the instructions or the question tells you otherwise.
10. Follow the path with your pencil but write lightly so you do not clutter up the map. If you are not allowed to write in the test booklet, follow your path with your finger.
11. When you are asked to turn left or right, be very careful if you are not coming from the bottom of the page.
12. Read the choices carefully, because there may not be much difference between the right and wrong answers.
13. If the destination is on a one-way street, make sure you arrive from the right direction.
14. Try out all the answers before choosing one. (On many tests you will have enough time to do this.)

WHAT CAN I LEARN TO HELP MYSELF DO BETTER?

Map questions are also reading questions since the questions can have long sentences. Learning to read better may help you answer these questions.

WHAT ELSE CAN I DO TO PREPARE?

Find a map of your neighborhood and make sure you can understand it. Your public library or city hall will have maps of your city or town. This chapter gives the general map information you need for this type of test, but it can't hurt to get some printed maps of cities and rural areas and look at the legends and the symbols used, since there are many different ways to draw maps. The more familiar you are with maps, the less likely you will be confused by map questions.

TIME LIMIT

These tests have relatively long time limits, and most people have time to answer all the questions. So work carefully on this type of test.

HOW TO USE THE PRACTICE QUESTIONS

There are practice questions on the next pages and more at the end of this book.

- Do the practice questions in this chapter without any time limit.

- Time yourself when you do the practice questions at the end of the book, using the time limit shown there.

> **TIP**
>
> Look out for *streets* and *avenues* with the same name.

Practice Questions for Maps

Read the Instructions on page 115 before you begin to answer questions in this section.

Map for Practice Questions

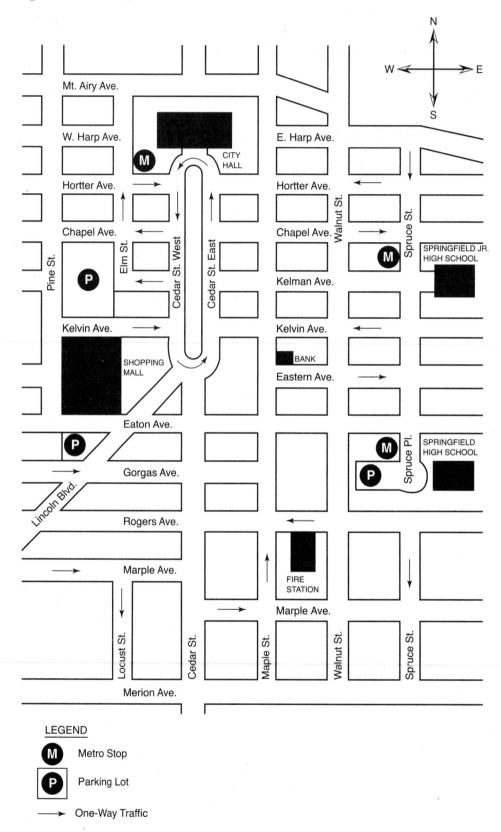

Practice Questions

Instructions: Use the map on the opposite page to help answer the practice questions. Traffic is allowed in both directions unless an arrow shows that only one direction is allowed. Whenever you count blocks, count one whenever you get to a street, whether the street is on the left or the right or both, and regardless of the size or shape of the block.

1. You are at the fire station and are dispatched to a fire at Springfield High School. The most direct route to the school from the fire station is to

    (A) travel west on Rogers Ave., north on Maple St., east on Chapel Ave., south on Spruce St., and east on Kelman Ave. to the school.
    (B) travel west on Rogers Ave., north on Maple St., east on Chapel Ave., and south on Spruce St. to Spruce Pl. to the school.
    (C) travel east on Rogers Ave., north on Walnut St., east on Eaton Ave., and south on Spruce Pl. to the school.
    (D) travel west on Rogers Ave., north on Maple St., and east on Kelman Ave. to the school.
    (E) travel west on Rogers Ave., north on Maple St., east on Eaton Ave., and south on Spruce Pl. to the school.

2. You are at the intersection of Eaton Ave. and Lincoln Blvd. You go two blocks east, turn north and go three blocks, turn east and go one block, turn south and go five blocks, and finally turn east and go one block before stopping. When you stop, you are at the intersection of

    (A) Marple Ave. and Spruce St.
    (B) Kelvin Ave. and Maple St.
    (C) Rogers Ave. and Cedar St.
    (D) Marple Ave. and Walnut St.
    (E) Rogers Ave. and Spruce St.

3. You are at the bank. You exit onto Eastern Ave. You turn left and walk to the corner. You then turn left and walk one block, turn right and walk one block, and finally, turn left and walk one block. You are at the corner of

    (A) Eastern Ave. and Walnut St.
    (B) Kelman Ave. and Spruce St.
    (C) Lincoln Blvd. and Cedar St.
    (D) Gorgas Ave. and Cedar St.
    (E) Eastern Ave. and Spruce St.

The answers to these questions are at the end of this chapter.

Map for Practice Questions

(The map is reprinted here so you will not have to turn pages when you answer the questions.)

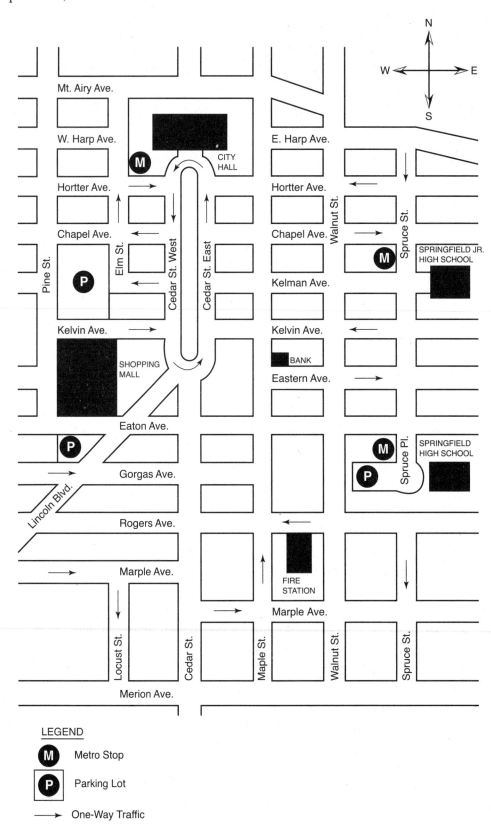

4. You are in the parking lot on the north side of the shopping mall. You are to pick someone up at the Metro stop across the street from Springfield Jr. High School. You exit the parking lot on the south side. The most direct route is to

   (A) travel east on Kelvin Ave., south on Cedar St. West and around the circle onto Cedar St. East, travel north, and turn east on Kelman Ave. to the Metro stop.
   (B) travel east on Kelvin Ave., south on Cedar St. West, south on Cedar St., and east on Eaton Ave. to the Metro stop.
   (C) travel south on Pine, east on Kelvin Ave., south on Cedar St. West and around the circle onto Cedar St. East, travel north, and turn east on Kelman Ave. to the Metro stop.
   (D) travel east on Kelvin Ave., south on Cedar St. West and around the circle onto Cedar St. East, east on Kelvin Ave., and north on Spruce St. to the Metro stop.
   (E) travel east on Chapel Ave., south on Cedar St. West and around the circle onto Cedar St. East, and east on Kelman Ave. to the Metro stop.

5. You are at the fire station and you are sent to city hall. You have been told that you will find parking on Mt. Airy Ave. directly behind city hall. The most direct route to the designated parking area is to

   (A) travel west on Rogers Ave., and north on Cedar St. to city hall.
   (B) travel west on Rogers Ave., north on Maple St., and east on Mt. Airy Ave. to the parking area.
   (C) travel west on Rogers Ave., north on Maple St., and west on Mt. Airy Ave. to the parking area.
   (D) travel north on Maple St., and west on Mt. Airy Ave. to the parking area.
   (E) travel east on Rogers Ave., north on Walnut St., and west on Mt. Airy Ave. to the parking area.

6. You are parked in the lot south of the shopping mall. You must pick up your child up at Springfield High School for a dentist appointment. If the intersection of Cedar St. and Gorgas Ave. is closed for road repairs, then the best way to drive to the school is to

   (A) exit on the north side of the parking lot. Travel east on Eaton Ave., south on Lincoln Blvd., east on Gorgas Ave., north on Maple St., east on Eaton Ave., and south on Spruce Pl. to the school.
   (B) exit on the south side of the parking lot. Travel east on Gorgas Ave., north on Maple St., east on Eaton Ave., and south on Spruce St. to the school.
   (C) exit on the north side of the parking lot. Travel east on Eaton Ave., and south on Spruce Pl. to the school.
   (D) exit on the east side of the parking lot. Travel north on Lincoln Blvd. and around the circle onto Cedar St. East, and east on Kelman Ave. to the school.
   (E) exit on the south side of the parking lot. Travel east on Kelvin Ave., south on Cedar St. West, and continue south on Cedar St. Travel east on Eaton Ave. and south on Spruce Pl. to the school.

The answers to these questions are at the end of this chapter.

Map for Practice Questions

(The map is reprinted here so you will not have to turn pages when you answer the questions.)

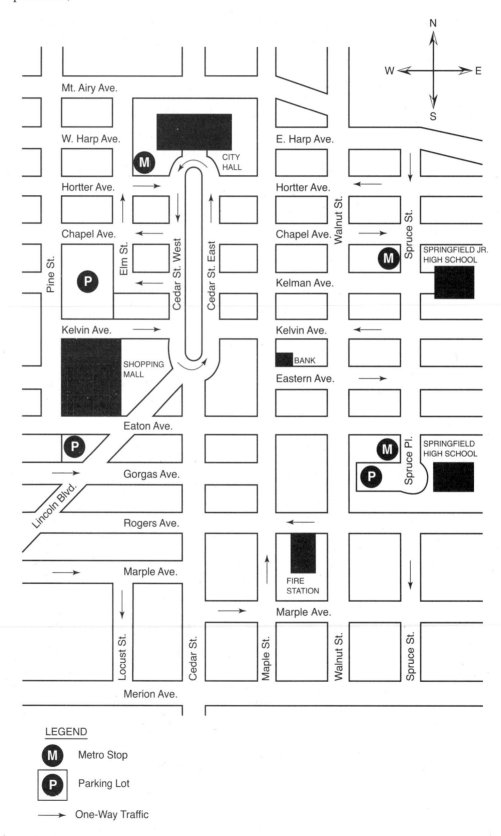

LEGEND

M Metro Stop

P Parking Lot

——→ One-Way Traffic

7. You are at the fire station when you are dispatched to a fire on E. Harp Ave., just west of Walnut St. The most direct route to the fire is to

    (A) travel west on Rogers Ave., north on Maple St., east on E. Harp Ave., and cross Walnut St. to the fire.
    (B) travel west on Rogers Ave., north on Lincoln Blvd., west on Eaton Ave., north on Pine St., and east on W. Harp St. to the fire.
    (C) travel west on Rogers Ave., north on Maple St., west on Mt. Airy Ave., south on Pine St., and east on W. Harp Ave. to the fire.
    (D) travel east on Rogers Ave., north on Walnut St., and west on E. Harp St. to the fire.
    (E) travel west on Rogers Ave., north on Maple St., and east on E. Harp St. to the fire.

8. You live on Locust St. and want to drive to the bank. The most direct route is to

    (A) travel to the corner of Merion Ave. and turn right. Turn left on Maple St. to the bank.
    (B) travel to the corner of Marple St. and turn right. Turn left on Cedar St., right on Gorgas Ave., and left on Maple St. to the bank.
    (C) travel to the corner of Marple St. and turn right. Turn left on Cedar St., right on Eaton Ave., and left on Maple St. to the bank.
    (D) travel to the corner of Merion Ave. and turn left. Turn left on Maple St. to the bank.
    (E) travel to the corner of Merion Ave. and turn right. Turn left on Cedar St., right on Gorgas Ave., and left on Maple St. to the bank.

9. You live in an apartment building at the corner of Eaton Ave. and Walnut St. To get to the closest Metro stop you should walk the following route:

    (A) Walk one block east.
    (B) Walk one block east and one block south.
    (C) Walk one block east and two blocks north.
    (D) Walk two blocks east and one block south.
    (E) Walk three blocks north and one block east.

10. You have jury duty at city hall and decide to eat lunch in the Food Court at the shopping mall. Your car is parked on E. Harp Ave. between Walnut St. and Spruce St. Which of these is the most direct route to drive to the parking lot just north of the mall?

    (A) Travel west on E. Harp Ave. Turn left on Maple St. and right on Eaton Ave. to the parking lot.
    (B) Travel east on E. Harp Ave. Turn right on Walnut St. and right on Eaton Ave. to the parking lot.
    (C) Travel east on E. Harp Ave. Turn left on Walnut St. and left on Eaton Ave. to the parking lot.
    (D) Travel east on E. Harp Ave. Turn right on Spruce St. and right on Eaton Ave. to the parking lot.
    (E) Travel east on E. Harp Ave. Turn right on Spruce St., right on Hortter Ave., right on Cedar St. East and around the circle onto Cedar St. West, and right on Chapel Ave. to the parking lot.

The answers to these questions are on the next page.

ANSWERS TO PRACTICE QUESTIONS: MAPS

1. **(E)**
2. **(A)**
3. **(B)**
4. **(A)**
5. **(C)**
6. **(C)**

7. **(E)**
8. **(D)**
9. **(A)**
10. **(E)**

You will find more map-reading questions at the end of this book.

Line Following

CHAPTER 8

IMPORTANT WORD IN THIS CHAPTER
Jumper

In this test you follow lines from one place to another on the page. This is similar to following wires, pipes, or tubes in some types of industrial diagrams. Like many of the tests of spatial ability, the questions would be easy to answer if you had enough time. But the time limits are short, so you have to work quickly on this type of test to get a good score.

WHAT DO THESE QUESTIONS ASK ABOUT?

You will be asked to look at a page with many lines and you will have to follow the lines from where they start to where they end.

WHAT DO THESE TESTS LOOK LIKE?

All the questions are on one page. Each page has lines in the middle. Each line starts with a number and ends with a letter. You need to follow each numbered line to see which letter it goes to. Sometimes the numbers are on the right hand side of the page, and sometimes they are on the left-hand side of the page.

IMPORTANT

The time limit for this type of test is usually only about 5 minutes, so work fast and make every second count!

VOCABULARY

Curved **jumpers** show where one line jumps over another.

Sample Question

What letters do lines 1, 2, and 3 lead to?

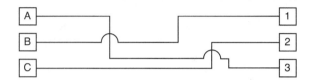

This test may have 20 or more lines to follow. (The sample above is very simple.) Time limits are short, about five minutes. There will be more questions than anyone can answer in the time limit.

ANSWER AND EXPLANATION

Line 1 leads to the letter B, line 2 leads to letter C, and line 3 leads to letter A. So the answers for the sample questions are:

1.   B
2.   C
3.   A

In this chapter we'll learn the few rules for taking this test, learn some hints, and get some practice with this type of question.

Crossing Lines

To make it clear which way the lines go when they cross, one of each pair of lines that cross are drawn with a curved "jumper." These jumpers are like little bridges. They show where one line jumps over another.

In the drawing below you can see that line 1 crosses line 3, and the jumper is going side to side where those two lines cross. Also, line 3 crosses line 2, and the jumper goes up and down where the two lines cross.

Two **jumpers** are shown here in **bold**.

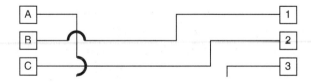

Follow With Your Eyes, Not Your Hands

It is natural to use your finger or pen to trace a line from the beginning to the end. This method works, but most people are faster when they follow a line with their eyes.

WHAT ELSE CAN I DO TO PREPARE?

Doing the practice questions in this chapter and at the end of the book is all that is needed to prepare for this type of test. If you want to do more than this, you might get a book of maze puzzles and do them.

> **TIP**
>
> Don't skip the first questions, since they are usually the easiest.

TIPS FOR LINE-FOLLOWING QUESTIONS

1. Don't skip the first questions, since they are usually easier.
2. Follow the lines with your eyes, not your finger or pen or pencil. (This is really faster!)
3. Always start at the number and trace toward the letter with your eyes.
4. Cross out the choices as you go, so you will know if you are using any of the choices more than once. Try this on the practice questions and see if it helps. (Do this on the real exam only if you are allowed to write in the test booklet.)
5. Be careful when you get to a jumper to be sure you follow the right line.
6. If you are following one of many lines that are parallel, make a mental note about what line you are following (for example, the second line from the top).

> **TIP**
>
> Always start at the number and trace toward the letter.

TIME LIMIT

The time limit for this type of test is usually only about 5 minutes, so work fast and make every second count.

HOW TO USE THE PRACTICE QUESTIONS

There are practice questions on the next page and more at the end of this book.

Practice Questions

Instructions: For each numbered box, follow the line to a lettered box.

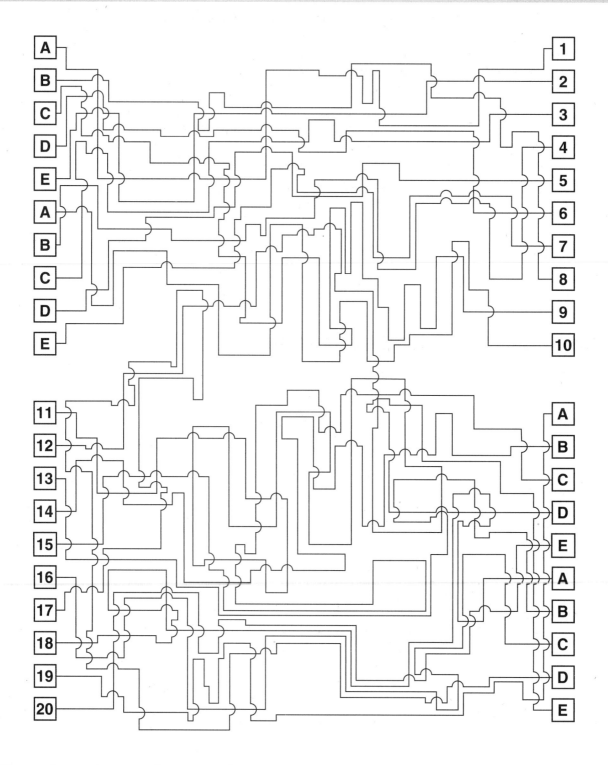

The answers to these questions are on the next page.

ANSWERS TO PRACTICE QUESTIONS: LINE FOLLOWING

1. **(A)**
2. **(E)**
3. **(C)**
4. **(B)**
5. **(D)**
6. **(D)**
7. **(E)**
8. **(B)**
9. **(C)**
10. **(A)**
11. **(E)**
12. **(D)**
13. **(B)**
14. **(B)**
15. **(C)**
16. **(C)**
17. **(D)**
18. **(A)**
19. **(A)**
20. **(E)**

You will find more questions on following lines at the end of this book.

Matching Shapes

This type of test asks you to look at many simple drawings and find pairs that are exactly the same. The questions are mostly easy, but you will have only a few minutes to take the test. You have to work quickly to get a good score.

WHAT DO THESE QUESTIONS ASK ABOUT?

You will be asked to look at two groups of drawings of simple, flat objects and find pairs that are exactly the same size and shape.

WHAT DO THESE TESTS LOOK LIKE?

Each page will have two large boxes, each with 25 or more small drawings of flat objects. The drawings in the first box are labeled with numbers and are in numerical order. The drawings in the second box are labeled with letters and are in random order. Each drawing in the first box is exactly the same as one drawing in the second box. However, the drawings in the second box are in different places and may be rotated. There will be more questions than anyone can answer, and the questions are harder in the second half of the test.

A shortened form of the test might have drawings of flat objects like these:

> **WATCH FOR**
>
> Each drawing in the first box is exactly the same size and shape as a drawing in the second box, and **not** flipped over.

ANSWERS AND EXPLANATIONS

The answer to 1 is B and the answer to 2 is D. For both questions, the answer is in a different place in the box and has been rotated.

Below is a more complete example of this type of question.

Example of Matching Shape Questions with Explanations

The shortened form of the test on this page introduces the answer sheet (page 129) and offers you some practice with the test. For each numbered shape in the top box, find a shape in the bottom box that is exactly the same size and shape.

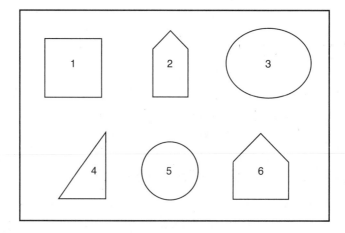

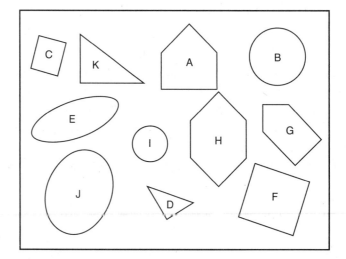

ANSWER SHEET

The answer sheet for this type of question can look a little strange, so we will go over it now. The answer sheet may not have all the choices for each question.

For example, in the question on page 112 there are 11 shapes in the bottom box, lettered A to K. But on the answer sheet there are only 10 choices for each question. So one lettered choice has been left out, but not the same choice for all questions. This can be very confusing, but if you pay attention to what you are doing, you should have no trouble marking your answers. For example, in the answer sheet to the right you can see that choice B is sometimes the first choice in a line, other times it is the second choice, and sometimes it is left out completely.

Mark your answers to the questions here. The correct answers are given below.

Answer Sheet

	A	C	D	E	F		G	H	I	J	K
1	○	○	○	○	○		○	○	○	○	○
	A	C	D	E	F		G	H	I	J	K
2	○	○	○	○	○		○	○	○	○	○
	B	C	D	E	F		G	H	I	J	K
3	○	○	○	○	○		○	○	○	○	○
	A	C	D	E	F		G	H	I	J	K
4	○	○	○	○	○		○	○	○	○	○
	B	C	D	E	F		G	H	I	J	K
5	○	○	○	○	○		○	○	○	○	○
	A	B	C	D	E		F	G	H	I	J
6	○	○	○	○	○		○	○	○	○	○

TIP

The answer sheet can be tricky. One lettered choice may be left out, but not the same letter for all questions (see the sample answer sheet).

Correct Answers

	A	C	D	E	F		G	H	I	J	K
1	○	○	○	○	●		○	○	○	○	○
	A	C	D	E	F		G	H	I	J	K
2	○	○	○	○	○		●	○	○	○	○
	B	C	D	E	F		G	H	I	J	K
3	○	○	○	○	○		○	○	●	○	○
	A	C	D	E	F		G	H	I	J	K
4	○	○	○	○	○		○	○	○	●	●
	B	C	D	E	F		G	H	I	J	K
5	●	○	○	○	○		○	○	○	○	○
	A	B	C	D	E		F	G	H	I	J
6	●	○	○	○	○		○	○	○	○	○

Explanation

1. Moved and slightly rotated

2. Moved and slightly rotated

3. Moved and rotated 1/4 turn

4. Moved and rotated 1/4 turn

5. Moved

6. Moved

Check your answers carefully, because this answer sheet can be tricky.

RULES FOR ANSWERING THE QUESTIONS

1. The answer must be the same size and shape as the numbered question.
2. The answer may be anyplace in the box.
3. The answer may be rotated (turned).

WHAT CAN I LEARN TO HELP MYSELF DO BETTER?

Other than the material in this chapter, there is nothing you need to learn to do well on this type of test.

WHAT ELSE CAN I DO TO PREPARE?

Practice will help you do your best on this type of test. Since this type of test asks you to think about shapes and identify them, you might borrow or buy toys that are made of flat pieces of different sizes and shapes. Spill the pieces on a table and see how quickly you can match pieces of the same size and shape.

REMEMBER

Check for *size* as well as shape, since there may be several objects with the same shape but different sizes.

TIPS FOR ANSWERING MATCHING-SHAPES QUESTIONS

1. Start with the first question and answer the questions in order. Otherwise you may get confused and bubble in the wrong answers. Also, the easier questions are usually at the beginning of the test.
2. To find the right answer, first do a quick scan of the answer choices. If the correct answer does not jump off the page at you, then look in rows, either left to right or top to bottom until you find the object.
3. If you think you see the right answer, check to see if another choice is very similar to it. There may be several shapes that look the same but are different in size.
4. If you have trouble with one shape, skip it and go to the next question. But make sure that you skip that question number on the answer sheet.
5. Use each lettered answer shape only once because each lettered answer is correct only once. When you use an answer, cross it out so that you don't have to look at it for another question. (Do not do this if the instructions tell you not to write on the test.)
6. If you don't see the answer to a question, put a mark in the margin of the answer sheet. After you have done more questions and crossed out more choices, you can go back to the question you missed. (Do not do this if the instructions tell you not to write on the test.)
7. Make sure that you check for size as well as shape of an object. There are often two or three drawings with the same shape but different sizes. If you reach a point where most of the answers are crossed out and the only answer that looks similar to the question is too big or too small, go back to the other questions that asked about this shape. It may be that you chose the wrong size object for one of the earlier questions and you can switch your answers to make them correct.
8. Be careful when using the answer sheet, because not all the letter choices are there. For example, choice C might not be the third bubble.
9. Sometimes it helps to count the number of sides or corners, especially if there are six-, seven-, and eight-sided objects that are similar in size.
10. Work quickly. It is better to make a few mistakes and answer many questions than to go very slowly and make no mistakes.

TIME LIMIT

The time limit for this type of test is often about 5 minutes, which is not much time for 50 or more questions. Most of the questions are easy. You need to work quickly to do well on this type of test.

HOW TO USE THE PRACTICE QUESTIONS

There are practice questions on page 132, and more at the end of this book.

- Do the practice questions in this chapter without any time limit.

- Time yourself when you do the practice questions at the end of the book. There is a suggested time limit for each test at the back of the book.

IMPORTANT

You need to work quickly to do well on this type of test.

Practice Questions

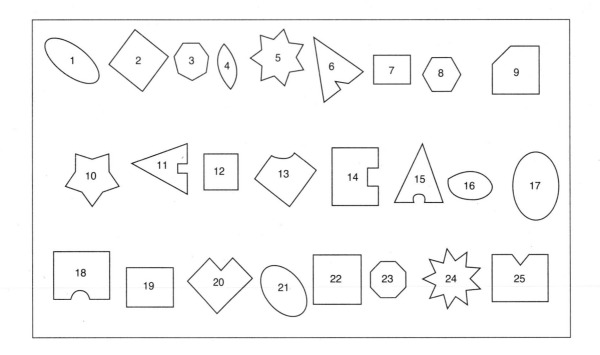

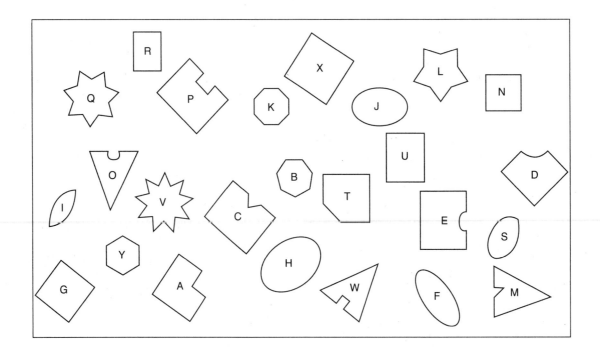

Answer Sheet

PRACTICE QUESTIONS: MATCHING SHAPES

	B	F	H	I	J	K	L	Q	S	V			B	F	H	I	J	K	L	Q	S	Y
1	○	○	○	○	○	○	○	○	○	○		16	○	○	○	○	○	○	○	○	○	○

	C	D	E	G	N	P	R	T	U	X			B	F	H	I	J	K	L	Q	S	V
2	○	○	○	○	○	○	○	○	○	○		17	○	○	○	○	○	○	○	○	○	○

	B	F	H	I	J	K	L	Q	S	Y			A	C	D	E	M	O	P	T	W	X
3	○	○	○	○	○	○	○	○	○	○		18	○	○	○	○	○	○	○	○	○	○

	B	F	H	I	J	K	L	Q	S	V			C	D	E	G	N	P	R	T	U	X
4	○	○	○	○	○	○	○	○	○	○		19	○	○	○	○	○	○	○	○	○	○

	B	F	H	I	J	K	L	Q	S	V			A	C	D	E	M	O	P	T	W	X
5	○	○	○	○	○	○	○	○	○	○		20	○	○	○	○	○	○	○	○	○	○

	A	C	D	E	M	O	P	T	W	X			B	F	H	I	J	K	L	Q	S	Y
6	○	○	○	○	○	○	○	○	○	○		21	○	○	○	○	○	○	○	○	○	○

	C	D	E	G	N	P	R	T	U	X			C	D	E	G	N	P	R	T	U	X
7	○	○	○	○	○	○	○	○	○	○		22	○	○	○	○	○	○	○	○	○	○

	B	F	H	I	J	K	L	Q	S	Y			B	F	H	I	J	K	L	Q	S	Y
8	○	○	○	○	○	○	○	○	○	○		23	○	○	○	○	○	○	○	○	○	○

	A	C	D	E	M	O	P	T	W	X			B	F	H	I	J	K	L	Q	S	V
9	○	○	○	○	○	○	○	○	○	○		24	○	○	○	○	○	○	○	○	○	○

	B	F	H	I	J	K	L	Q	S	V			A	C	D	E	M	O	P	T	W	X
10	○	○	○	○	○	○	○	○	○	○		25	○	○	○	○	○	○	○	○	○	○

	A	C	D	E	M	O	P	T	W	X
11	○	○	○	○	○	○	○	○	○	○

	C	D	E	G	N	P	R	T	U	X
12	○	○	○	○	○	○	○	○	○	○

	A	C	D	E	M	O	P	T	W	X
13	○	○	○	○	○	○	○	○	○	○

	A	C	D	E	M	O	P	T	W	X
14	○	○	○	○	○	○	○	○	○	○

	A	C	D	E	M	O	P	T	W	X
15	○	○	○	○	○	○	○	○	○	○

The correct answers are on the next page.

Answers

PRACTICE QUESTIONS: MATCHING SHAPES

	B F H I J	K L Q S V		B F H I J	K L Q S Y
1	○ ● ○ ○ ○	○ ○ ○ ○ ○	16	○ ○ ○ ○ ○	○ ○ ○ ● ○
	C D E G N	P R T U X		B F H I J	K L Q S V
2	○ ○ ○ ● ○	○ ○ ○ ○ ○	17	○ ○ ● ○ ○	○ ○ ○ ○ ○
	B F H I J	K L Q S Y		A C D E M	O P T W X
3	● ○ ○ ○ ○	○ ○ ○ ○ ○	18	○ ○ ● ○ ○	○ ○ ○ ○ ○
	B F H I J	K L Q S V		C D E G N	P R T U X
4	○ ○ ● ○ ○	○ ○ ○ ○ ○	19	○ ○ ○ ○ ○	○ ○ ○ ● ○
	B F H I J	K L Q S V		A C D E M	O P T W X
5	○ ○ ○ ○ ○	○ ○ ● ○ ○	20	● ○ ○ ○ ○	○ ○ ○ ○ ○
	A C D E M	O P T W X		B F H I J	K L Q S Y
6	○ ○ ○ ○ ●	○ ○ ○ ○ ○	21	○ ○ ○ ● ○	○ ○ ○ ○ ○
	C D E G N	P R T U X		C D E G N	P R T U X
7	○ ○ ○ ○ ○	○ ● ○ ○ ○	22	○ ○ ○ ○ ○	○ ○ ○ ○ ●
	B F H I J	K L Q S Y		B F H I J	K L Q S Y
8	○ ○ ○ ○ ○	○ ○ ○ ○ ●	23	○ ○ ○ ○ ○	● ○ ○ ○ ○
	A C D E M	O P T W X		B F H I J	K L Q S V
9	○ ○ ○ ○ ○	○ ○ ● ○ ○	24	○ ○ ○ ○ ○	○ ○ ○ ● ○
	B F H I J	K L Q S V		A C D E M	O P T W X
10	○ ○ ○ ○ ○	○ ● ○ ○ ○	25	○ ● ○ ○ ○	○ ○ ○ ○ ○
	A C D E M	O P T W X			
11	○ ○ ○ ○ ○	○ ○ ○ ● ○			
	C D E G N	P R T U X			
12	○ ○ ○ ○ ●	○ ○ ○ ○ ○			
	A C D E M	O P T W X			
13	○ ○ ● ○ ○	○ ○ ○ ○ ○			
	A C D E M	O P T W X			
14	○ ○ ○ ○ ○	○ ● ○ ○ ○			
	A C D E M	O P T W X			
15	○ ○ ○ ○ ○	● ○ ○ ○ ○			

You will find more questions about matching shapes at the end of this book.

Visual Comparison

In this type of test, you have to decide which of different similar objects are identical.

WHAT DO THESE QUESTIONS ASK ABOUT?

In each question, you will be presented with five similar objects, only two of which are identical. The objects might be different from each other in any of several ways, such as different sizes. We'll discuss other types of differences in this chapter.

WHAT DO THESE TESTS LOOK LIKE?

These tests have 30 to 40 questions. Each question is made up of five lettered shapes. All five shapes are similar, but only two of them are exactly the same.

Sample Question

Which two squares are exactly the same size?

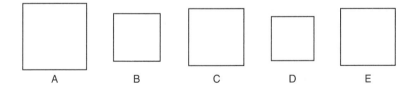

ANSWER AND EXPLANATION

The correct answer is C and E. These are the only two squares that are exactly the same size.

Sometimes the differences between objects will be hard to see. It may seem like there is more than one correct answer. However, there will always be only two objects that are exactly the same. Your job is to find them.

This type of test usually has a time limit of 10 minutes for 30 to 40 questions, so you have to work quickly to do well.

TIPS FOR ANSWERING VISUAL-COMPARISON QUESTIONS

1. Don't spend more than a minute on one question. There is not much time to complete the test.
2. The questions get harder as the test goes on, so try not to skip too many questions in the beginning of the test.
3. Rule out clearly wrong answers. Then it will be easier to decide which of the objects left are the same.
4. Spot what part of the objects is different. Compare just that part of the objects.
5. If more than one part of the objects are different, look at one part at a time to rule out wrong answers.

Different Lengths

In the first sample question, the size of the objects was different. Here's an example where their length is different.

Sample Question

Which two are exactly the same size?

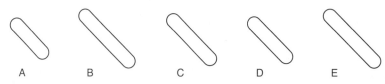

A   B   C   D   E

ANSWER AND EXPLANATION

The correct answer is B and E. These are the only two that are exactly the same size. In the first two sample questions, the size of the objects was different. There are other ways the objects can be different. We'll look at one next.

Different Arrangements

Here's an example where the objects are each made of five pieces, but only two objects are put together in the same way.

Sample Question

Which two are exactly the same?

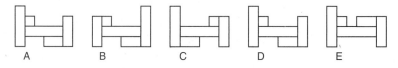

A   B   C   D   E

ANSWER AND EXPLANATION

The correct answer is A and D. These are the only two objects with the five pieces in exactly the same places.

SUGGESTED APPROACH TO ANSWERING QUESTIONS

Sometimes the answer will be clear, but most of the time the different choices will be very similar and you will have to figure out the correct answer. Try to find the correct pair by eliminating the wrong answers. Here is a suggested step-by-step way to answer these questions.

TIP

If you have ruled out even one object but you don't know the right answer, guess.

SUGGESTED APPROACH

1. See if you can just see two objects that are the same. If you can, check the other objects. It may be that you have chosen two objects that are very close, but not exactly the same.
2. If you can't see the correct answer, rule out objects that aren't similar to any other.
3. When you are left with a few very similar objects, look at them more closely to see how they are different. Then try to find two that are exactly the same.
4. If you have ruled out a few objects but are not sure of the answer, guess.
5. If the question is too hard, go on to the next question.

HOW TO FILL IN THE ANSWER SHEET

To answer a question just fill the circles for the **two** objects that are the same. If the two objects that are the same are B and D you would fill in

IMPORTANT

To answer a question, fill the circles on the answer sheet for the *two objects* that are the same.

WHAT CAN I LEARN TO HELP MYSELF DO BETTER?

Other than the material in this chapter, there is nothing you need to learn in order to do well on this type of test.

WHAT ELSE CAN I DO TO PREPARE?

Practice will help you maximize your visual judgment abilities so you will do your best on this type of test. Doing jigsaw puzzles will help you develop your ability in this area.

TIME LIMIT

You are not given much time for this type of test—less than half a minute per question—so work quickly.

HOW TO USE THE PRACTICE QUESTIONS

There are practice questions on this and the next page and more at the end of this book.

- Do the practice questions in this chapter without any time limit.

- Time yourself when you do the practice questions at the end of the book.

Practice Questions

Instructions: For each question, choose the two objects that are exactly the same.

TIP

Try using your finger or your pencil as a measuring tool if you're not sure which objects are the same size or length.

1.

2.

3.

4.

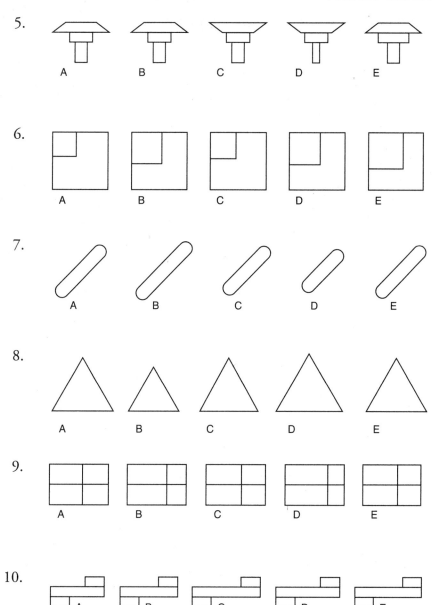

The answers to these questions are on the next page.

ANSWERS TO PRACTICE QUESTIONS: VISUAL COMPARISON

  1. (B), (C)

  2. (A), (C)

  3. (D), (E)

  4. (A), (D)

  5. (A), (B)

  6. (B), (D)

  7. (A), (E)

  8. (A), (E)

  9. (C), (E)

10. (C), (E)

You will find more visual-comparison questions at the end of this book.

Finding Rotated Shapes

CHAPTER 11

IMPORTANT WORDS IN THIS CHAPTER
Rotate
Turned Over

Each question on this type of test shows you a different flat shape. You have to find which of five other flat shapes is exactly the same as the first.

WHAT DO THESE QUESTIONS ASK ABOUT?

These questions ask about flat shapes that have been moved in one of two ways: rotated or turned over. You have to choose the shape that has been rotated and not turned over.

WHAT DO THESE TESTS LOOK LIKE?

Each question shows a shape on the left and five similar shapes on the right with a letter near each one.

- All the shapes are the same size.

- All the lettered shapes are rotated.

- Four lettered shapes are turned over.

- One lettered shape is not turned over.

Your job is to find the lettered shape that is the same as the shape to the left of the line: **it can be rotated but not turned over**.

Sample Question

Choose the letter of the shape that is the same as the shape to the left of the line.

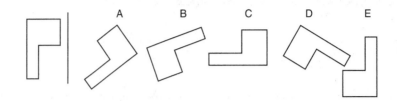

Other than being rotated or turned over, all the shapes in a question are exactly the same.

This test may have 50 or more questions. Time limits are short—about seven minutes. There will be more questions than anyone can answer in the time limit, so work quickly.

ANSWER AND EXPLANATION

Only shape E is not turned over. This chapter will explain how to tell if a shape has been turned over or rotated.

Examples of Turning Over and Rotating

It is easy to tell when a coin is turned over. Let's look at turning over and rotating coins and letters now. Then we will look at shapes.

Examples of Turning Over and Rotating			Examples of Just Rotating	
Start with This	Turned Over	Turned Over and Rotated	Start with This	Rotated
F	Ⅎ	ⅎ	F	ⅎ
P	ꟼ	d	P	d
Q	Ọ	Ơ	Q	Ơ
R	Я	ⱨ	R	ⱨ

The coin example shows what we mean by turning a coin over. Now let's look at letters that are turned over.

The backward F is turned over. There is no way to make a regular F face backward by just rotating it. Now look at each of the letters.

VOCABULARY

To **flip** or turn over a shape, you need to *lift* it off the page and turn it over in the air.

- Look at the difference between letters in the first two columns (letters turned over).

- Look at the difference between letters turned over and letters both turned over and rotated (in the second and third columns).

- Most important, look at the difference between letters that are both turned over and rotated and letters just rotated (in the third and last columns).

Here is a good way to think about the difference.

- You can **turn over** a coin or letter **by picking it up off the paper and flipping it over.**

- You can **rotate** a coin or letter **by sliding it to a new position on the paper.**

Next we will look at turning over and rotating other flat shapes.

Rotating and Turning Over Flat Shapes

To understand rotating and turning over flat shapes, think of the shapes as things you can move. In turning over a shape you need to lift it off the page and flip it over. In rotating a shape you slide it along the page in any direction. Here are two examples.

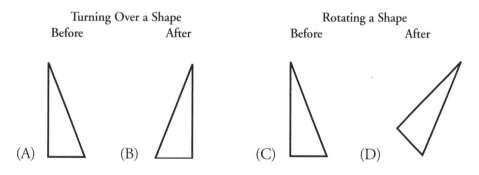

Turning Over a Shape
Before   After

Rotating a Shape
Before   After

(A)   (B)   (C)   (D)

REMINDER

On this test, if you have to turn the object over to match the original shape, then that answer is wrong.

There is no way to make shape A look like shape B without picking it off the paper and flipping it over. You can make shape C look like shape D by sliding it on the paper. If you are not clear about this, go back and read about turning over and rotating letters on the previous page.

Sample Questions with Explanations

We'll start with a simple example and then go on to explain a few harder ones.

Sample Question

Choose the letter of the shape that is the same as the shape to the left of the line.

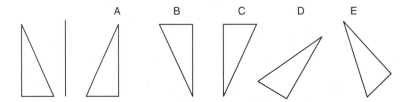

ANSWER AND EXPLANATION

To get choice A we would have to turn over the shape on the left of the line, so choice A is wrong. Choices D and E are the same as choice A, just rotated a little, so they are wrong. You can rotate choice C to make it look exactly like choice A, so choice C is wrong. You can rotate choice B to get the shape on the left of the line, so choice B is correct.

Sample Question

Choose the letter of the shape that is the same as the shape to the left of the line.

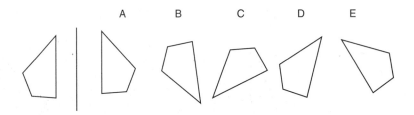

ANSWER AND EXPLANATION

To get choice A we would have to turn over the shape on the left of the line, so choice A is wrong. Choices B, C, and E can be rotated to be exactly like choice A, so they are wrong. You can rotate choice D a little to make it look exactly like the shape on the left of the line, so choice D is correct.

Sample Question

Choose the letter of the shape that is the same as the shape to the left of the line.

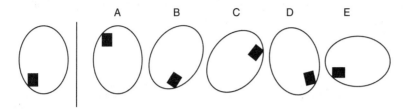

ANSWER AND EXPLANATION

There is no way to rotate the shape on the left of the line to get choice A, because the black box moves with the oval. Choices B, D, and E can be rotated to be identical to choice A, so they are wrong. Choice C can be rotated to look exactly like the shape to the left of the line, so C is the correct answer.

Sample Question

Choose the letter of the shape that is the same as the shape to the left of the line.

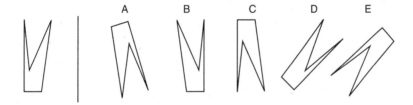

ANSWER AND EXPLANATION

If you turned over the shape on the left of the line, you would get choice B, so B is wrong. Choice C, D, and E can be rotated to get choice B, so they are wrong. Choice A can be rotated to look exactly like the shape to the left of the line, so A is the correct answer.

SUGGESTED APPROACH TO ANSWERING THESE QUESTIONS

Sometimes you can just see the answer. If not, try to find the right answer by eliminating the wrong answers. The box on the next page is a summary of this approach.

SUGGESTED APPROACH

1. First look for the right answer. If you see it, do not spend time looking at the wrong answers. If you don't see it, look at each choice until you find the one that is correct.
2. Remember, if two answers have the same shape but are rotated differently, they are both wrong (because there is only one correct answer).
3. If the question is too hard, go on to the next question.

WHAT CAN I LEARN TO HELP MYSELF DO BETTER?

Other than the material in this chapter, there is nothing you need to learn in order to do well on this type of test. Practice will help you do your best.

WHAT ELSE CAN I DO TO PREPARE?

Because this type of test asks you to tell the difference between flat shapes that are rotated and turned over, you might make, borrow, or buy flat shapes and use them to make practice questions. Flat shapes may be made out of paper or cardboard.

TIP

There is only one right answer, so if two answers are the same, they are both wrong.

TIPS FOR ROTATED-SHAPES QUESTIONS

1. If an answer looks correct, quickly look at the other answers to see if any others look exactly like it.
2. If two choices are the same, then they must both be wrong. The choices include the right answer and four answers that are turned over.
3. When you are comparing shapes, pay attention to one part of the shape at a time, such as a corner or another easily identified feature.
4. For a shape that seems to be rotated a little, turn your head a bit to see the shape straight up and down. Or you can turn the page to do this. Turn the booklet upside-down if you need to.
5. If you think a shape with objects inside it was rotated 180 degrees, check by rotating it slowly in your mind so you can tell where the objects inside belong.
6. Skip hard questions. Do not spend too long on any one problem. There is not much time for this test.

TIME LIMIT

You need to work quickly to do well on this type of test.

• These tests have short time limits, some as short as 7 minutes.

HOW TO USE THE PRACTICE QUESTIONS

There are practice questions on the next pages and more at the end of this book.

• Do the practice questions in this chapter without any time limit.

• Time yourself when you do the practice questions at the end of the book.

Practice Questions

For each question, choose the letter of the shape that is the same as the shape to the left of the line.

1.
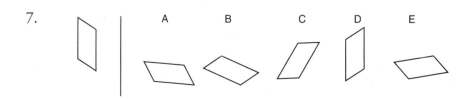

2.
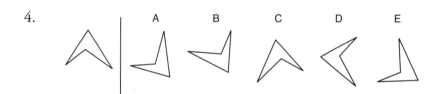

3.
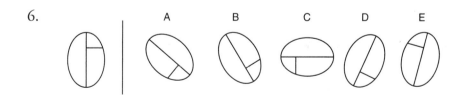

4.
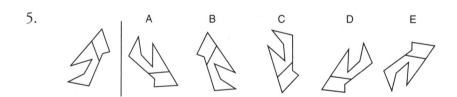

5.
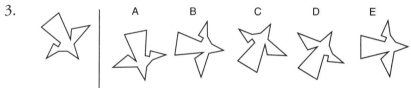

6.

7.
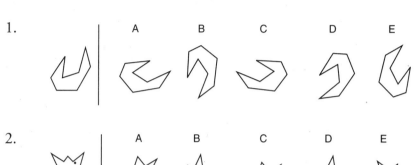

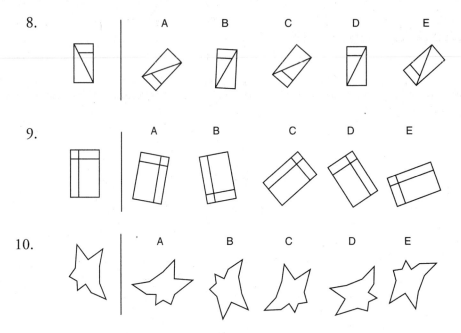

8.   A   B   C   D   E

9.   A   B   C   D   E

10.   A   B   C   D   E

The answers to these questions are below.

ANSWERS TO PRACTICE QUESTIONS: FINDING ROTATED SHAPES

1. **(A)**
2. **(E)**
3. **(D)**
4. **(B)**
5. **(A)**
6. **(A)**
7. **(B)**
8. **(E)**
9. **(C)**
10. **(D)**

You will find more questions on finding rotated shapes at the end of this book.

Cut-Ups

This type of test shows you flat shapes that have been cut into pieces. You have to match the pieces with the shape they came from. The shapes and pieces are usually simple, but the questions are sometimes hard.

WHAT DO THESE QUESTIONS ASK ABOUT?

This type of test shows you four flat shapes, which are used for all the questions. In each question, one of the shapes has been cut up into two to five flat pieces. The test question shows you the pieces. For each question your job is to look at the pieces and figure out which flat shape was cut up.

This is a speeded test, with more questions than anyone can answer in the time limit, especially because many questions are hard. You need to work quickly to get a good score.

WHAT DO THESE TESTS LOOK LIKE?

Usually 25 to 50 questions are on this type of test. The same answer choices are used for all questions. They are given on the same page as the questions or on a separate page. Each question is made up of two to five pieces. You have to tell which shape you can make from the pieces. A sample question is on page 150.

> **REMEMBER**
>
> Each question shows two to five pieces that you must fit together to find what shape the pieces make up.

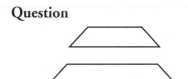

Question

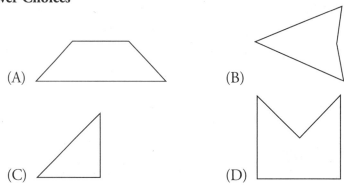

Answer Choices

(A)   (B)

(C)   (D)

ANSWER AND EXPLANATION

The correct answer is A. It is the only shape that can be made from the two pieces.

Read the Directions

Each test has its own set of directions. Read them carefully on the day of the test. Here are the usual rules for answering this type of question.

> **TIP**
>
> You may want to review rotating and flipping shapes over in the chapter we just finished.

RULES FOR ANSWERING THE QUESTIONS

1. The answer must contain all the pieces.
2. The answer may not contain any extra pieces.
3. The pieces may be moved in one or more of these three ways:
   - moved to another place on the page
   - flipped over
   - rotated (turned)
4. The pieces must stay the same size and shape.
5. You cannot cut up or fold the pieces.

Example: Moving Pieces Just a Little

For the sample question on this page, you should try to make one of the following four answer choices from the two flat pieces at the bottom of this page.

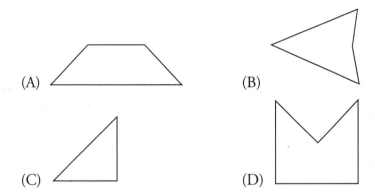

(A)

(B)

(C)

(D)

Sample Question

Which one of the four answer choices above can you make from these two pieces?

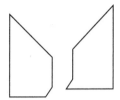

ANSWER AND EXPLANATION

You can think about sliding these two pieces together to make shape D. There is no way to fit these two pieces together to make one of the other three shapes. The correct answer is D. The drawing on the next page shows how these pieces fit together to make shape D.

SOLUTION DIAGRAM

The correct answer is D.
The line inside this target shape shows how the pieces fit together to make this shape.

SUGGESTED APPROACH TO ANSWERING THESE QUESTIONS

Sometimes with this type of question the answer is immediately clear. If you are sure of the answer, just go on to the next question. If you are not really sure, try using this simple approach.

SUGGESTED APPROACH

1. Look quickly at the pieces and the answer choices.
2. If one choice looks right, think about whether the pieces are really the right size for that choice. (Sometimes a wrong choice seems to work, but the final shape is the wrong size.)
3. If no choice looks right, try to find the right answer by eliminating the wrong choices based on the size or shape of the pieces.
4. If no choice looks right, think creatively about different possible ways to put the pieces together.
5. If the question is too hard, go on to the next question.

HINT

If no choice looks right, try eliminating clearly wrong choices based on the size or shape of the pieces.

EXAMPLE: LOOK AT THE GENERAL SHAPE

ANSWER CHOICES

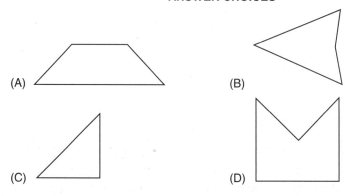

SAMPLE QUESTION

Which one of the four answer choices above can you make from these two pieces?

ANSWER AND EXPLANATION

Look at the shape of the pieces.

- The large piece looks a lot like target shape B, since it has a bent side that none of the other shapes have. The small piece on the left can fit into the indent on the right side of the larger piece to complete the shape.

- These pieces cannot make any of the other three answer choices.

- The correct answer is B.

(Example continued from preceding page)

SOLUTION DIAGRAM

The drawing below shows how the pieces come together to make shape B.

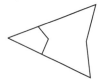

The correct answer is B.

EXAMPLE: RULE OUT WRONG ANSWERS

ANSWER CHOICES

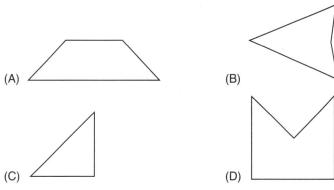

(A)

(B)

(C)

(D)

SAMPLE QUESTION

Which one of the four answer choices above can you make from these pieces?

ANSWER AND EXPLANATION

If you can just see the answer, that's great. If not, you will have to think about it. Because this question has only two pieces, it is relatively easy to rule out some answer choices.

- You cannot make A, B, or C from the two pieces because neither of the two pieces looks close to these answer choices.

- To be sure D is the correct answer you need to be able to move the pieces to make shape D. If the triangle was moved to sit on top of the larger piece, it would look like D. The correct answer is D. The drawing on the next page shows how these pieces come together to make shape D.

SOLUTION DIAGRAM

The correct answer is D.

EXAMPLE: THINK CREATIVELY

ANSWER CHOICES

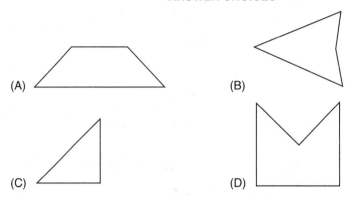

(A)   (B)

(C)   (D)

SAMPLE QUESTION

Which one of the four answer choices above can you make from these pieces?

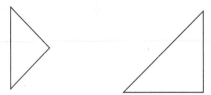

ANSWER AND EXPLANATION

If you cannot see the answer immediately, you will need to do some serious thinking.

- You might think you can rule out answer choices B and D because both have an indentation, and these two pieces do not.

- Also, it seems impossible to make target shape A from these two pieces so you can rule out A.

- The only choice left is C, but there is no way to fit the two pieces together to make shape C.

Some of your reasoning must be wrong, so you need to rethink and to think creatively. One of the answer choices that was ruled out as impossible must be possible. Think about this question for a while before looking at the solution below. Hint: The two sides that meet are different lengths.

SOLUTION DIAGRAM

The correct answer is D.

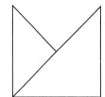

EXAMPLE: QUESTIONS WITH THREE PIECES

ANSWER CHOICES

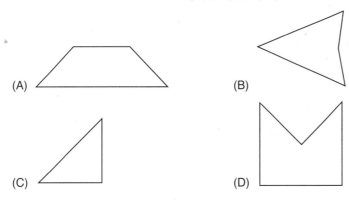

(A)

(B)

(C)

(D)

SAMPLE QUESTION

Which one of the four answer choices above can you make from these pieces?

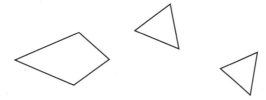

ANSWER AND EXPLANATION

Three pieces makes this a more complicated question. You might immediately see the correct answer. If not, it is possible to rule out some answer choices.

- The three pieces cannot make choice A because there is no way to make the straight bottom and top of choice A.

- Choice C is wrong because there is no way to make the right angle in the lower right-hand corner of choice C.

- Choice D is wrong because it is too big to be made from the three pieces, and it has three long, straight sides.

To get the right answer you have to use your imagination. You can move the two triangles so that they are next to the same-size sides of the larger object. See the diagram below.

SOLUTION DIAGRAM

The correct answer is B.

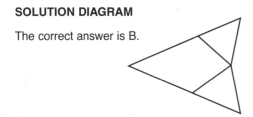

LEARNING THIS WILL HELP YOU TO DO WELL

Other than the material in this chapter, there is nothing you need to learn in order to do well on this type of test. Practice should help you do better.

WHAT ELSE CAN I DO TO PREPARE?

Games that involve making shapes from pieces are available for free on the Web and also sold in stores. One of the games available for free on the Web is called Tangrams (see, for example, http://rexgames.com/game.html). A similar game, available in stores, is called Tangoes (manufactured by Rex Games; see http://rexgames.com). Practice making shapes will help you with this type of test. The more you practice, the better.

HOW HARD ARE THE QUESTIONS?

REMEMBER

If the question is too hard, go on to the next question.

Some of the questions are easy. Most of the questions can be answered if you think about them long enough. A few of the questions are much harder than the others. Do not waste time on very hard questions. Answer the questions you can as quickly as you can.

REMEMBER

Each test has its own set of directions, so make sure you read them carefully on the day of the test.

TIPS FOR ANSWERING CUT-UPS QUESTIONS

1. Before answering any questions, look at the answer choices to see in what ways they are different.
2. Look to see if any of the pieces match part of one of the choices, such as a corner.
3. Sometimes some shapes are larger than others. If the pieces are not big enough to make a large shape, then the correct answer is one of the other shapes.
4. Because the same answer choices are used for many questions, some people find that it helps to make up names for the four answer choices.
5. If you are having too much trouble with one question, go on to the next question.

TIME LIMIT

The time limit for this type of test is often about 10 minutes, which is not much time for 40 or more questions. You have to work quickly to get a good score on this type of test. Often the easier questions are near the beginning of the test. Don't worry if you are not able to finish all the questions.

HOW TO USE THE PRACTICE QUESTIONS

There are practice questions on the next pages and more at the end of this book.

- Do the practice questions in this chapter without any time limit.

- Time yourself when you do the practice questions at the end of the book. There is a suggested time limit for each test at the back of the book.

Practice Questions

Instructions: Use these answer choices to answer the questions on these pages.

ANSWER CHOICES

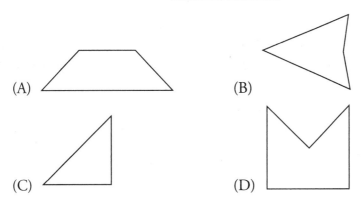

1. Which one of the four answer choices above can you make from these pieces?

2. Which one of the four answer choices above can you make from these pieces?

3. Which one of the four answer choices above can you make from these pieces?

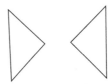

4. Which one of the four answer choices above can you make from these pieces?

5. Which one of the four answer choices on page 157 can you make from these pieces?

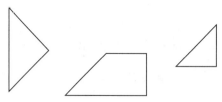

6. Which one of the four answer choices on page 157 can you make from these pieces?

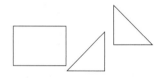

7. Which one of the four answer choices on page 157 can you make from these pieces?

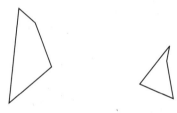

8. Which one of the four answer choices on page 157 can you make from these pieces?

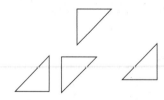

9. Which one of the four answer choices on page 157 can you make from these pieces?

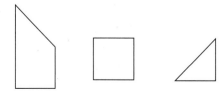

10. Which one of the four answer choices on page 157 can you make from these pieces?

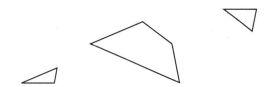

ANSWERS TO PRACTICE QUESTIONS: CUT-UPS

1. **(C)**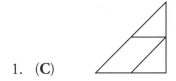

2. **(A)**

3. **(C)**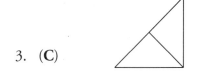

4. **(A)**

5. **(D)**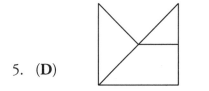

6. **(A)**

7. **(B)**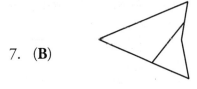

8. **(C)**

9. **(D)**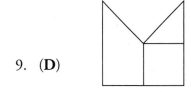

10. **(B)**

You will find more questions about cut-ups at the back of this book.

Jigsaw Puzzles

> ### IMPORTANT WORDS IN THIS CHAPTER
>
> | | |
> |---|---|
> | Flip | Rotate |
> | Move | Turn |

Taking this type of test is like doing little jigsaw puzzles in your mind.

The good news about this type of test question is that the jigsaw pieces are usually simple, with only a few straight sides or only a few simple curved sides, and the time limit is longer than for many spatial ability tests. The bad news is that often the questions are hard and the tests have many questions, so no one finishes these tests. You have to work quickly to get a good score.

WHAT DO THESE QUESTIONS ASK ABOUT?

Each question shows you two to five separate, flat jigsaw pieces and five larger flat shapes. Your job is to choose the larger flat shape that you can make using all the jigsaw pieces.

WHAT DO THESE TESTS LOOK LIKE?

Each page will have several questions, each inside its own box. Each question has:

- jigsaw pieces in the upper left hand corner

- five complete shapes, lettered A, B, C, D, or E, which are the five answer choices.

Your job is to think about how you could fit the jigsaw pieces together to look like one of the answer choices.

Another way to think about this type of question is to ask yourself which of the choices is divided into pieces that are exactly the same as the jigsaw pieces in the upper left hand corner of the question.

Usually there are about 50 questions on this type of test. The first few questions in the test are easier than the questions later in the test.

> **USEFUL INFO**
>
> This type of test is like doing little jigsaw puzzles in your mind.

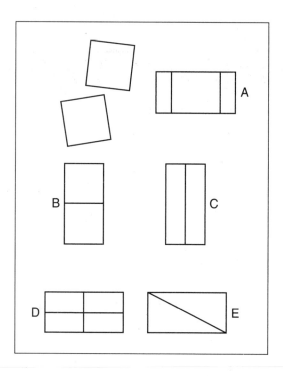

The box to the right shows a sample question. We'll explain the question and the answer on the next page.

THE JIGSAW PIECES

Below are the jigsaw puzzle pieces from the sample question. You can see there are two squares, both the same size.

Jigsaw Pieces

THE ANSWER CHOICES

Each answer choice in this type of question shows you the outline of the same flat shape. In the sample on this page, it is a rectangle.

What makes the choices different is the lines drawn inside. These lines divide each choice into two or more pieces. Sometimes the choices differ in size.

On the next page are the choices for the sample question.

- Choice A is divided into three pieces.

- Choice B is divided into two pieces.

- Choice C is divided into two pieces.

- Choice D is divided into four pieces.

- Choice E is divided into two pieces.

ANSWER AND EXPLANATION

The correct answer is choice B. This is the only choice that is made up of two square jigsaw pieces.

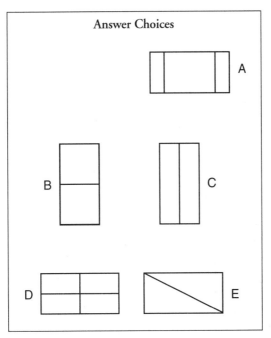

READ THE DIRECTIONS

Each test has its own set of directions. Read them carefully on the day of the test. Following are the usual rules for answering this type of question.

RULES FOR ANSWERING THE QUESTIONS

1. The answer must contain all the jigsaw pieces.
2. The answer may not contain any extra pieces.
3. The jigsaw pieces may be moved in any of these ways:
   - **moved** to another place on the page
   - **flipped** over
   - **rotated** (turned)
4. The jigsaw pieces must stay the same size and shape.
5. You cannot cut up or fold the jigsaw pieces.

REMEMBER

The jigsaw pieces must stay the same shape and size, and you cannot cut them up or fold them.

In this question, the jigsaw pieces are the two triangles in the upper left-hand corner. Find the answer choice you could make from these pieces.

HINT

Count how many jigsaw pieces there are, and rule out answers that contain a different number of pieces.

ANSWER AND EXPLANATION

We could move the two triangles together so their long sides touch. Then they would make a rectangle. That rectangle would look like choice E. The other choices are wrong.

- Choice A is made of three pieces, but there are only two jigsaw pieces.

- Choice B is made of three pieces, but there are only two jigsaw pieces.

- Choice C has only one piece, but there are two jigsaw pieces.

- Choice D is made of pieces that do not look like the jigsaw pieces. Its two pieces are unequal in size, but the jigsaw pieces are both the same size. One piece in choice D has five sides, but the jigsaw pieces are both triangles.

- The correct answer is E. It uses all the jigsaw pieces and no extra pieces.

There are more suggestions and sample questions and explanations on the next few pages.

SUGGESTED APPROACH TO ANSWERING THESE QUESTIONS

Sometimes with this type of question the answer is immediately clear. If you are sure of the answer, just go on to the next question. If you are not really sure, try using this simple approach.

SUGGESTED APPROACH

1. Look at the jigsaw pieces and the choices.
2. If one choice looks right, compare it with any similar choices.
3. If no choice looks right, try to find the right answer by eliminating the wrong choices.
4. If the question is too hard, go on to the next question.

Sample Question: Size of Pieces

Which of the lettered circles could be made from the two pieces in the upper left-hand corner?

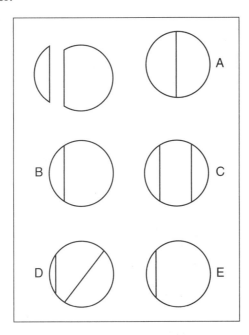

ANSWER AND EXPLANATION

There are two jigsaw pieces in the upper left-hand corner, and they are very different in size.

- Choice A is wrong because it shows the circle cut into equal halves and the jigsaw pieces are not equal in size.

- Choice C is wrong because it shows the circle cut into three pieces, but there are only two jigsaw pieces in the upper left-hand corner of the question.

TIP

If you think you've found the right answer but you're not sure, try moving the pieces around in your mind to make them fit together into the answer choice.

- Choice D is wrong for the same reason and because the pieces are the wrong size and wrong shape.

The correct answer must be either choice B or choice E. Look at the size of the pieces in each choice.

- Choice E is wrong because its small piece is smaller than the small piece shown in the upper left-hand corner. Also the large piece in E is too large.

- The correct answer is choice B. The two pieces that make up choice B are the same size and shape as the two jigsaw pieces in the upper left-hand corner.

Sample Question: Turning Pieces

Which of the figures could be made from the two triangles in the upper left-hand corner?

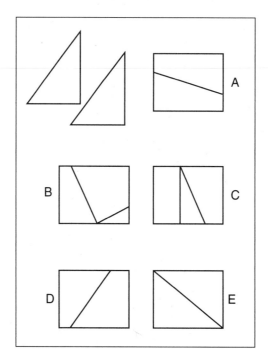

ANSWER AND EXPLANATION

The jigsaw pieces in the upper left-hand corner are two equal triangles. You might just see the right answer. If not, you can find the correct answer by elimination.

- Choices A and D are not made of triangles.

- Choice B is made from three pieces.

- Choice C is made from three pieces.

- In choice E both jigsaw pieces have been moved around. In your mind you can rotate and slide the top triangle so that its longest side lines up with the bottom triangle and forms a rectangle. Then you can turn and move that rectangle so that one of its long sides is on the bottom. It will then look like choice E. The correct answer is choice E.

Sample Question: Turning and Moving Pieces

Which of the figures could be made from the two triangles in the upper left-hand corner?

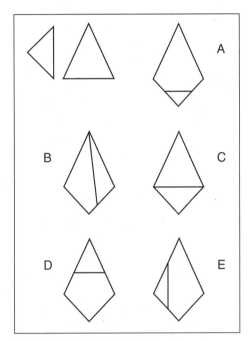

HINT

Look carefully at the shape and size of each piece.

ANSWER AND EXPLANATION

To get the answer to this question you need both to count the number of pieces and look carefully at the size of the pieces. You can see that there are two jigsaw pieces in the upper left-hand corner. Both jigsaw pieces have three sides and the pieces are different in size.

- Choices A, B, D, and E are wrong because none of them are made up of two triangles.

- In choice C the smaller triangle is pointed in a different direction. It has been moved and is at the bottom of the larger triangle. Often you have to move pieces in your mind to answer this type of question. The correct answer is C.

Sample Question: Flipping a Piece Over

Which of the figures could be made from the pieces in the upper left-hand corner?

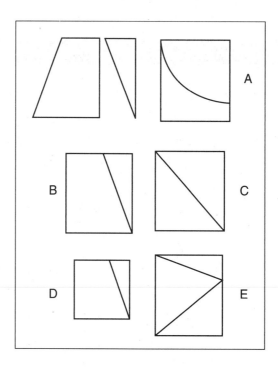

ANSWER AND EXPLANATION

The two jigsaw pieces are unequal in size and only one is a triangle. A quick look at this question shows that four choices are clearly wrong.

- Choice A is wrong because the pieces have curved sides.

- Choice C is wrong because they are equal in size and both are triangles.

- Choice D is wrong because the whole shape is too small.

- Choice E is wrong because it is made from too many pieces.

It seems that choice B must be correct, but to be sure, let's see if we can fit the jigsaw pieces together to look like choice B. We can do that if we flip over the large jigsaw piece. Choice B is correct.

Sample Question: Small Differences in Size

Which of the figures could be made from the three pieces in the upper left-hand corner?

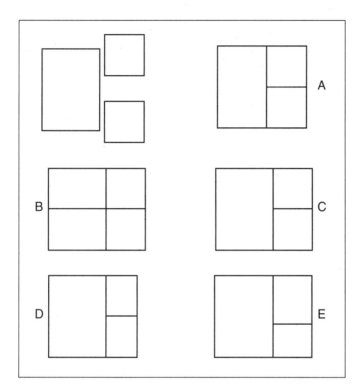

ANSWER AND EXPLANATION

Counting the number of pieces will help here, but you also need to look carefully at the size and shape of the jigsaw pieces in the upper left-hand corner. There are three jigsaw pieces and two of them are squares that are equal in size.

- Choice B cannot be correct because it is made of four pieces.

- Choice E is wrong because it does not have two same-size squares.

- Choice D is wrong because it does not contain two squares.

  The correct answer must be either A or C.

- Choice A is wrong because the large piece is too small.

- The large piece in C is the same size as the large piece in the upper left-hand corner. The correct answer is C.

Sample Question: Very Hard Question

Which of the figures could be made from the pieces in the upper left-hand corner?

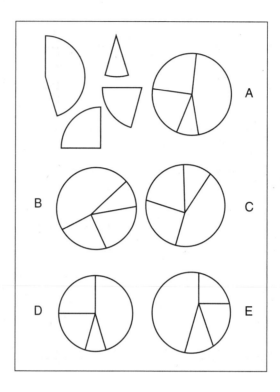

ANSWER AND EXPLANATION

If you do not see the answer immediately, try looking at the center of the circle.

- Choices B and E are wrong because the inside lines meet too far from the center of the circle.

  Now look at the overall size.

- Choice D is too small, overall.

  Now look at each piece.

- Choice C does not have a piece that looks like a quarter of a circle.

- Choice A is the correct answer. We have shown this by ruling out the other choices, but you can also see that the pieces are all the right shape and size.

WHAT CAN I LEARN TO HELP MYSELF DO BETTER?

Other than the material in this chapter, there is nothing you need to learn in order to do well on this type of test.

WHAT ELSE CAN I DO TO PREPARE?

Practice will help you do your best on this type of test. Because this type of test asks you to do little jigsaw puzzles, you might borrow or buy some puzzles that involve shapes.

TIPS FOR ANSWERING JIGSAW QUESTIONS

1. If you think you see the right answer, check to see whether another choice is very similar to it. If so, look to see how they are different. It may be that you have chosen an answer that is close, but wrong.

2. Some questions are much harder than others. If you are having too much trouble with one question, just go on to the next question. If you find yourself skipping too many questions, then stop skipping questions and spend your time trying to answer some of them.

3. If the correct answer is not clear to you, try some of these tips.

   - Identify wrong answers. Then find the correct answer or make a good guess. There are several ways to find the wrong answers.

   - **Count** the number of pieces in the choices. If the number of pieces in the choices is different from the number of pieces in the assembled drawing, that choice is wrong.

   - Look at the **shape** of each jigsaw piece. If a choice has a piece that does not match up with any of the separate jigsaw pieces, then that choice is wrong. You can compare pieces one by one, starting with the largest piece.

   - Look at the **size** of each jigsaw piece. If the choice has a piece that does not match up with any of the separate jigsaw pieces, then that choice is wrong. You can look at and compare pieces one by one, starting with the largest piece. You might be able to use your pencil as a rough measuring device to compare the size of the pieces.

   - **Notice and compare** any unusual features. For example, if two of the jigsaw pieces are equal in size, they should be equal when they are in an answer choice. Or if one of the jigsaw pieces has a curved side, then any choice without a piece with a curved side is wrong.

4. Remember, for this type of question you can move, turn, and flip over the pieces in any way. (But always follow the instructions printed on the test, if they say something else.)

5. Pay attention to how many sides each piece has. If a jigsaw piece has three sides but in one of the choices the only similar piece has four sides, the choice is wrong. Sometimes people do not notice an extra side when it is small and near a corner. Pay special attention to what the pieces in the choices look like at the **corners**.

6. Sometimes a wrong answer looks like the right answer, but is a little bigger or smaller overall. If the choice is not the same **size** as the pieces, it is a wrong answer.

7. If you are still stuck on a question, pick one jigsaw piece and see if every choice has that piece. Think about both size and shape. If that does not work, then look very carefully at the corners of the pieces to see if the jigsaw pieces match the choices. If you still cannot tell which answer is correct and which answers are wrong, skip the question and go on to the next one.

8. **Read the instructions carefully.** Some tests allow you to flip pieces over and others do not, so read the instructions carefully. Do the sample questions on the test, if there are any.

TIME LIMIT

The time limit for this type of test is often about 20 minutes, which is not much time for 50 or more questions. You need to work quickly to do well on this type of test.

HOW TO USE THE PRACTICE QUESTIONS

There are practice questions on the next pages, and more at the end of this book.

- Do the practice questions in this chapter without any time limit.

- Time yourself when you do the practice questions at the end of the book. There is a suggested time limit for each test at the back of the book.

Practice Questions: Jigsaw Puzzles

Instructions: For each question, you should pick the shape that can be made from the pieces in the upper left-hand corner.

1.

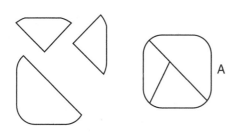

3.

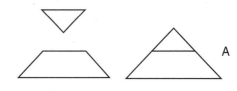

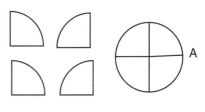

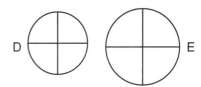

2.

4.

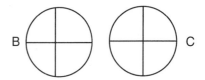

5.

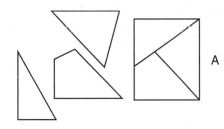

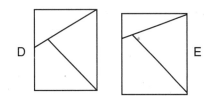

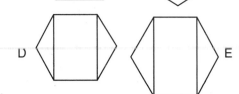

6.

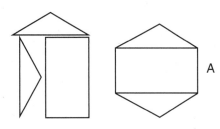

7.

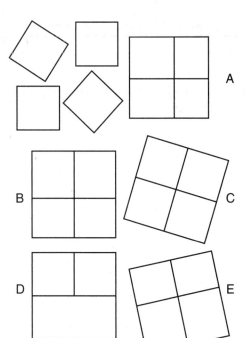

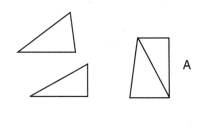

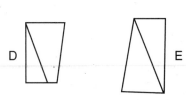

8.

9.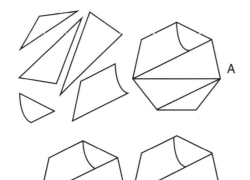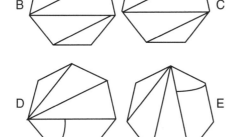

10.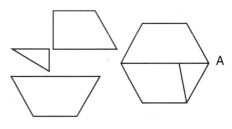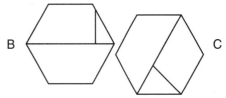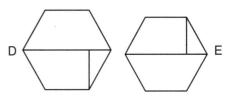

ANSWERS TO PRACTICE QUESTIONS: JIGSAW PUZZLES

1. **(D)** The sizes or shapes of the pieces in the other answers are wrong. This is easiest to see by looking at the smaller pieces. Choice D has been rotated (which is allowed).

2. **(C)** Choice B is too small, overall. The two smaller pieces should be equal in size and shape. In choice D the two smaller pieces are a little different (look at the corners).

3. **(A)** Look at the size of both the top and bottom pieces. Choice E is missing a horizontal line, so it is wrong.

4. **(C)** Look at the shape and size of the pieces. Choice A is wrong because the two right-hand side pieces are unequal in shape (the top right-hand piece is a little less than a quarter circle). Choice B has pieces that are unequal in size. Choice D is too small. Choice E is too large.

5. **(B)** In choice A the upper left-hand side of the lower left-hand piece is too long. In choice C this side is even longer. In choice E this side is too short. Choice D is too narrow.

6. **(E)** The triangles in A are too big. In B and C the rectangle is too big. D is too small overall.

7. **(C)** Only C has four pieces exactly the same size and shape.

8. **(A)** B has a four-sided shape. The lower right-hand corner of C has a larger angle than any of the jigsaw pieces. D has a four-sided piece. The lower left-hand piece of E is too big. Note that the upper right-hand triangle in A has been flipped over.

9. (**A**) B is too small overall. In C the curved line does not exactly meet the top corner. In D the piece in the lower left-hand corner is too big. In E that piece is flipped over so the piece it fits with is shaped wrong. (This is a very hard question.)

10. (**D**) In choices A and C the small triangle is the wrong shape. In choice B the inside line does not meet the upper right-hand corner. Choice E is too small.

You can find more questions about jigsaw puzzles at the back of this book.

Hole Punching

This type of test asks you to imagine folding a piece of paper and then punching a hole in it. To answer the questions correctly you must unfold the piece of paper in your mind and figure out where the holes would be.

WHAT DO THESE QUESTIONS ASK ABOUT?

Each question on this test shows you a piece of paper and shows you how it will be folded. Then it shows where one hole will be punched on the folded piece of paper. It is up to you to imagine how the paper would look after it is unfolded and to tell where in the paper the holes would be.

WHAT DO THESE TESTS LOOK LIKE?

The steps the question uses for folding the piece of paper are shown to you as a series of drawings. The drawings are arranged from left to right. The first drawing shows the first fold. The last drawing shows where the hole is punched. To the right of each question is an answer grid for marking where the holes would be. Your job is to draw circles on the grid to show where the holes would be.

This type of paper-folding test usually has a short time limit and 10 to 20 questions.

> **TRY IT**
>
> Imagine folding a piece of paper once or twice, punching a hole in it, unfolding it, and then seeing where the holes would be.

Sample Question

The first drawing shows the paper was folded in half once. The second drawing shows where a hole was made. Where would the holes be seen when the paper is unfolded?

ANSWER AND EXPLANATION

The correct answer is shown above. Because the paper was folded once and then a hole was made, there will be two holes when the paper is opened up. The next two pages tell how to read this type of question and give a more detailed explanation of this question and answer.

How to Read These Drawings

The drawings are arranged in order from left to right. The solid lines show the outside edges of the paper and where it has been folded. The dashed lines indicate the outline of the whole piece of paper.

Here is what each drawing means.

- The first drawing on the left shows the paper after the first fold.

- The second drawing shows the piece of paper after the second fold, and so on.

- The last drawing does not show a new fold. It shows where a hole has been punched.

- The drawing on the far right is the answer grid where you mark your answer. Each circle on the answer grid shows you a possible hole location on the piece of paper.

The questions have no words, only drawings, so understanding the drawings is very important. Let's look at the sample question more closely.

What Does the Sample Question Mean?

The questions leave out some steps. We are just starting to learn about these questions, so let's look at all the steps for the sample question.

REMEMBER

Solid lines show the outside edges of the paper, while dashed lines show the outline of the unfolded paper.

1. Start with a piece of paper.

2. The piece of paper is folded like this.

3. On the test the folded paper would look like this.

4. Make a hole in the folded paper.

5. On the test it would look like this.

6. Start to open up the folded paper.

7. The unfolded paper would look like this.

8. Mark the answer grid to show where the holes are.

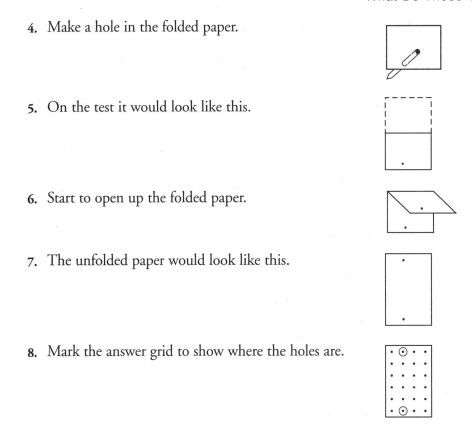

The sample question on the first page of this chapter has only two of these drawings. You have to imagine the other steps in the question.

The paper can be folded and punched only in certain ways. We will learn about this next.

Where Can the Holes Be Made?

Holes can be punched in the paper only in the places the answer grid shows. No holes will be made anywhere else.

Where Can the Paper Be Folded?

The paper will be folded so that the holes line up with the answer grid. The paper may be folded horizontally, vertically, or diagonally. The folds will all be made neatly, like this:

- A horizontal fold will be exactly in the middle between two rows of holes.

- A vertical fold will be exactly in the middle between two columns of holes.

- A diagonal fold will go through a diagonal row of holes.

Exactly Where Will the Folds Be?

The paper will be folded only in certain places. The drawings below show the places where the paper may be folded. The paper will not be folded in any other places. The possible hole locations are shown as dots, just like on an answer grid. The dashed lines show where a fold may be made.

Folds the short way will be made only here.
These folds are made **between the dots.**

Folds the long way will be made only here.
These folds are made **between the dots.**

Diagonal folds will be made only here.
These folds are made **on the dots.**

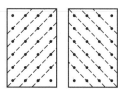

SUGGESTED APPROACH TO ANSWERING THESE QUESTIONS

1. Look at the drawings and see how the paper was folded in each step.
2. Figure out how many layers of paper were punched through. This way you'll know how many holes are in the correct answer.
3. Start with the last drawing. Unfold the paper once in your mind and pay attention to where the hole ends up. Whenever you see a hole in a part of the paper that is fully unfolded, circle that hole on the answer grid. Repeat this for each drawing.
4. Remember, you will find the location of another hole every time you unfold the paper.

Now that we know more about this type of question, let's look at an example and answer it using this suggested approach.

TIP

The number of layers of paper punched equals the number of holes you should mark in your answer.

Sample Question

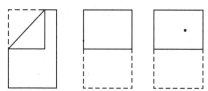

ANSWER AND EXPLANATION

The answer is shown below and on page 182. We'll use the suggested approach with this question.

1. First we'll think about how the paper was folded in each step. In the first step, the upper left-hand corner was folded down. In the second step, the bottom half of the paper was folded up.

2. When the upper left-hand corner was folded down, we got two layers of paper. When the bottom half of the paper was folded up, we added one layer of paper. So there are three layers of paper where the hole was made, meaning there will be holes in three places. We will need to circle three points on the answer grid.

3. We will start with the last drawing and mark the answer grid with that hole. Then we will unfold the paper once and circle that hole on the answer grid. We will repeat this for each drawing. We'll show how we do this with the following drawings.

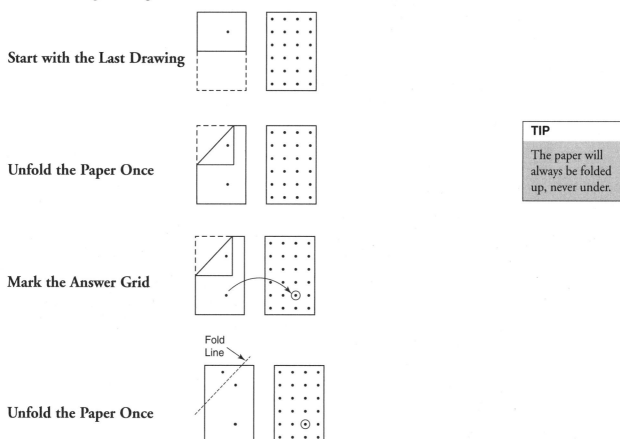

Start with the Last Drawing

Unfold the Paper Once

Mark the Answer Grid

Unfold the Paper Once

Fold Line

TIP

The paper will always be folded up, never under.

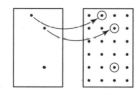

Mark the Answer Grid

The steps we used to find the right answer to this example are the same steps you would use to answer any paper-folding question.

TIPS FOR HOLE-PUNCHING QUESTIONS

1. Imagine the paper lying on a table. Some part of it is always flat on the table.
2. The paper will always be folded up. It will never be folded under. If you can't see the edge of the paper after it has been folded, that means that the edge is on top of another fold or edge.
3. Don't skip the first questions, because they are usually easier.

SAMPLE QUESTIONS

We will look here at some different questions. Try to answer each question before you look at the answer.

Sample Question

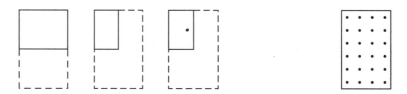

ANSWER AND EXPLANATION

The answer is shown below. In the first drawing the bottom half of the paper was folded up. In the second drawing the right half of the paper was folded over to the left. This means that there are four layers of paper and that there will be four holes.

ANSWER TO SAMPLE QUESTION

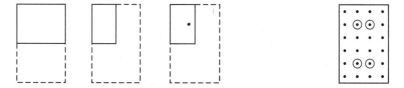

Sample Question

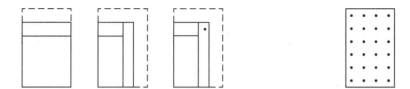

ANSWER AND EXPLANATION

The answer is shown below. In the first drawing the paper was folded between the first and second rows. In the second drawing the paper was folded between the third and fourth columns. This means that there are four layers of paper and that there will be four holes.

ANSWER TO SAMPLE QUESTION

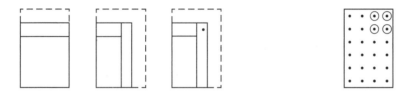

WHAT ELSE CAN I DO TO PREPARE?

The best way to understand these questions is to try them with a piece of paper. There is a large answer grid at the end of this chapter. Cut it out and use it to answer some of the practice questions in this book. Fold the paper and punch it the way the question does. Then unfold the paper and see where the holes are. This will help train your mind for taking this test.

TIME LIMIT

The time limits for these tests are short, so work quickly.

HOW TO USE THE PRACTICE QUESTIONS

There are practice questions on the following pages and more at the end of this book.

• Do the practice questions in this chapter without any time limit.

• Time yourself when you do the practice questions at the end of the book.

Practice Questions

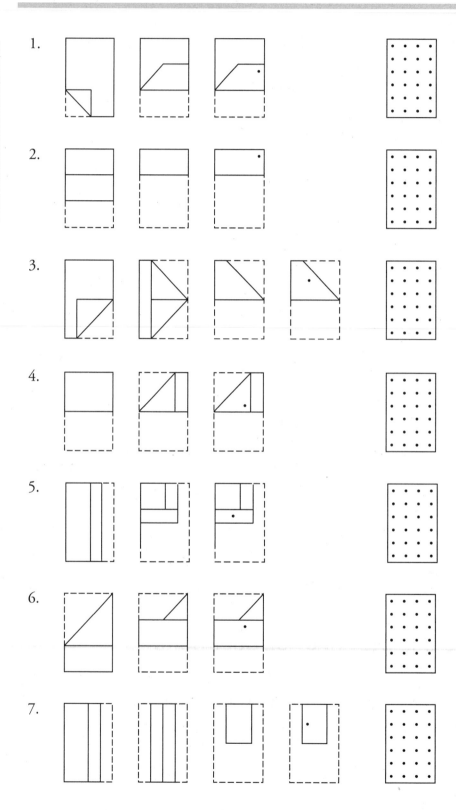

1.

2.

3.

4.

5.

6.

7.

8.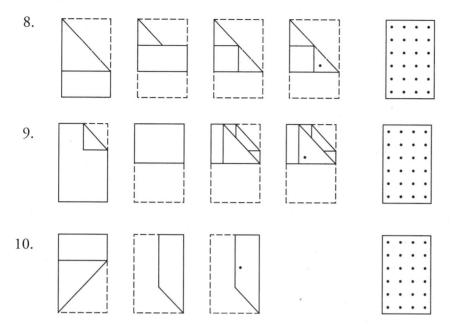

9.

10.

The answers to these questions follow.

ANSWERS TO PRACTICE QUESTIONS: HOLE PUNCHING

1.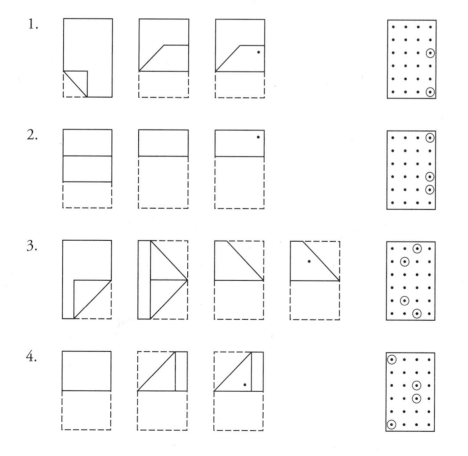

2.

3.

4.

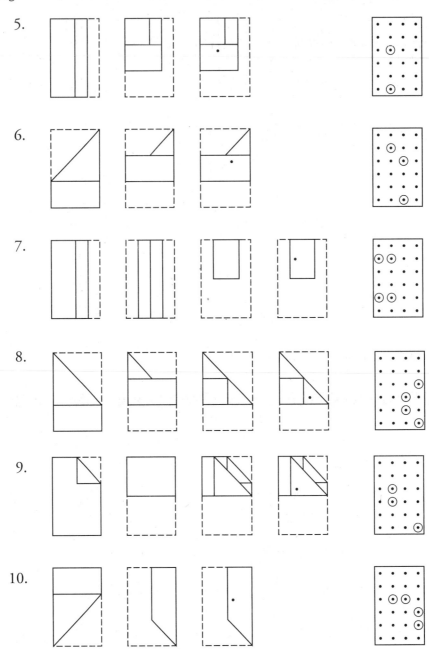

You will find more hole-punching questions at the end of this book.

Large-Size Hole-Punching Answer Grid

Tear out this page and use it to help you understand any questions you found hard.

Hidden Blocks

IMPORTANT WORDS IN THIS CHAPTER
Hidden Block
Partly Hidden Block
Supporting Block

This type of test uses drawings of stacks of blocks to measure spatial ability, which is an important part of mechanical aptitude. The questions are usually easy, but there are more questions than anyone can answer in the time limit. To get a good score, you need to work quickly.

WHAT DO THESE QUESTIONS ASK ABOUT?

You will be shown drawings of stacks of blocks. Some of the blocks will be hidden from view. You will be asked how many blocks are in each stack.

WHAT DO THESE TESTS LOOK LIKE?

Each question shows a stack of blocks. A test may have 25 or more questions. Your job is to count the number of blocks in the stack.

You need to count:

- blocks you can see.

- blocks that are hidden but supporting blocks you can see.

TIP

Count the blocks you can see as well as the blocks that are *hidden* but are *supporting* other blocks.

How many blocks are there?

The blocks in this type of question are **all the same size and are all cube shaped**. Usually the piles have only a few blocks. The questions are drawings, so the test has few or no sentences after you get past the instructions.

These tests have short time limits, some as short as five minutes. No one is expected to answer all the questions. Because the questions tend to be easy, your grade is based mainly on the speed with which you answer the questions.

ANSWER AND EXPLANATION

A full explanation of the answer to this sample question is given later in this chapter. The answer to this sample question is eight blocks.

Next, we'll learn about hidden blocks and go over a good approach to counting blocks.

Counting Hidden Blocks

It is the hidden blocks that make these questions a test of spatial ability rather than the ability to count. In some stacks of blocks you can see only the top blocks, but you know that some other blocks must be there to hold them up. The blocks that must be there but cannot be seen are called **hidden blocks**.

Sample Question: Hidden Block

All the blocks are the same size and shape.
How many blocks are there?

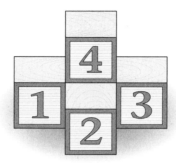

To show how these questions work, we will look at two other views of these blocks.

FRONT DIAGONAL VIEW

In this view we can still see only four blocks.

BACK DIAGONAL VIEW

This view from the back shows that there is a fifth block. It holds up block 4. It cannot be seen from the front, so it is a hidden block.

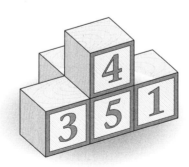

ANSWER AND EXPLANATION

The correct answer is five blocks. It is true that we can see only four blocks in the question, but it is clear that there must be a block holding up block 4. We cannot see that block but we know it is there, and because it is there we must count it.

Sample Question: Hidden Blocks

How many blocks are there?

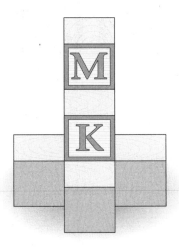

We can see five blocks, but one hidden block is holding up block K and two hidden blocks are holding up block M. The drawing below helps you see these hidden blocks.

ANSWER AND EXPLANATION

Here you can see the two blocks holding up block M and that there must be a hidden block holding up block K. There are eight blocks here.

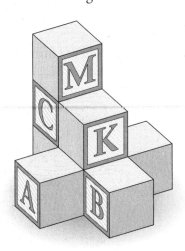

Partly Hidden Blocks

Sometimes you can see the corner of a block. Whenever you see a part of a block, you know the whole block is there because all the blocks are the same size and shape.

Sample Question: Partly Hidden Blocks

How many blocks are there?

> **REMEMBER**
>
> Sometimes you will see the corner of a **partly hidden** block, which means the whole block must be counted in the total.

EXPLANATION

Three blocks are partly hidden. The hardest one to see is the one in the back with only a small corner showing. If you were able to look at the pile from another view you would see these three blocks more clearly.

SIDE VIEW

This shows the partly hidden blocks more clearly. They are labeled 1, 2, and 3.

ANSWER

There are eight blocks in this stack.

SUGGESTED APPROACH TO ANSWERING THESE QUESTIONS

Unlike some types of tests where sometimes you can see the answer, this type of question makes you count to get the answer. Here is a simple approach that should help you.

An Orderly Approach to Counting Blocks

One good way to count blocks in a large stack is to count each row separately. Start with the row closest to you. We'll look at a question and then show how to count by rows.

Sample Question

How many blocks are there?

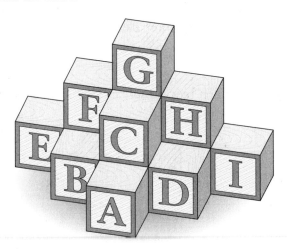

EXPLANATION OF ANSWER

To show how to count each row separately, we'll label all the blocks you can see and show you a drawing for each row.

There is 1 block in the front row, labeled A.

There are 4 blocks in the second row. Three are labeled B, C, and D, and 1 is hidden. We know the hidden block is there because there must be a block holding up block C.

There are 9 blocks in the back row. Five are labeled E, F, G, H, and I, and 4 blocks are hidden. We know there is 1 hidden block holding up block F, and 1 holding up block H, and 2 hidden blocks holding up block G.

Adding the number of blocks in each row we can be sure this stack of blocks has 14 blocks because 1 + 4 + 9 = 14.

WHAT CAN I LEARN TO HELP MYSELF DO BETTER?

Other than the material in this chapter, there is nothing you need to learn to do well on this type of test. Practice may help you do your best.

WHAT ELSE CAN I DO TO PREPARE?

Because this type of test asks you to count blocks, you might borrow or buy block toys and use them to make practice questions.

TIPS FOR COUNTING-BLOCKS QUESTIONS

1. Only count blocks you can see or that must be there. There are no unnecessary blocks that are completely hidden. A space you cannot see will have a block only if it is holding up another block.

2. If the test instructions allow, use your pencil to mark each block (or each row) when you count it. (Do not do this if the instructions say "Do not write on the test.")

3. Use a system to count the blocks. Count row by row, starting with the front row. In each row, count the blocks you can see and the hidden blocks.

4. If two stacks of blocks are equal in height and you can see how many blocks are in one of the stacks, the other stack has the same number of blocks.

5. Read the instructions carefully, because they are not repeated for each question.

6. Remember, all the blocks are the same size and shape.

> **TIP**
>
> These tests have short time limits. Practice these questions until you can do them quickly.

TIME LIMIT

You need to work quickly to do well on this type of test. These tests have short time limits, some as short as five minutes.

HOW TO USE THE PRACTICE QUESTIONS

There are practice questions on the following pages and more at the end of this book.

• Do the practice questions in this chapter without any time limit.

• Time yourself when you do the practice questions at the end of the book.

Practice Questions

In addition to the questions here, there are more practice questions of this type at the end of this book.

1. All the blocks are the same size and shape. How many blocks are there?

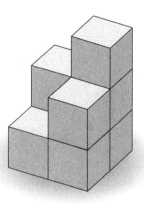

2. All the blocks are the same size and shape. How many blocks are there?

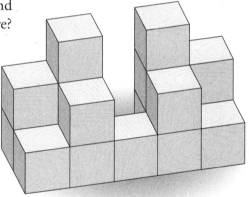

3. All the blocks are the same size and shape. How many blocks are there?

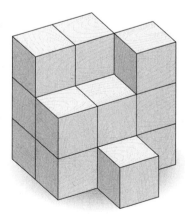

4. All the blocks are the same size and shape. How many blocks are there?

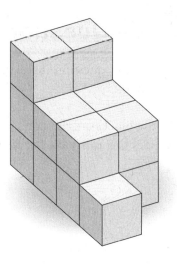

5. All the blocks are the same size and shape. How many blocks are there?

6. All the blocks are the same size and shape. How many blocks are there?

7. All the blocks are the same size and shape. How many blocks are there?

8. All the blocks are the same size and shape. How many blocks are there?

9. All the blocks are the same size and shape. How many blocks are there?

10. All the blocks are the same size and shape. How many blocks are there?

The answers to these questions are below.

ANSWERS TO PRACTICE QUESTIONS: HIDDEN BLOCKS

1. **8** First row: 3
Second row: 5

2. **17** First row: 7
Second row: 10

3. **14** First row: 1
Second row: 7
Third row: 6

Note that there is a place in the last row where there could be a block hidden from view. Because the rules are that hidden blocks are found only where they are supporting a block that can be seen, there can be no block there.

4. **15** First row: 1
Second row: 4
Third row: 4
Fourth row: 6

5. **27** First row: 1
Second row: 4
Third row: 7
Fourth row: 15

6. **23** First row: 6
Second row: 8
Third row: 9

7. **20** First row: 1
Second row: 2
Third row: 7
Fourth row: 10

8. **20**   First row: 1
Second row: 7
Third row: 12

9. **19**   First row: 2
Second row: 7
Third row: 10

10. **17**   First row: 4
Second row: 5
Third row: 8

You will find more questions about hidden blocks at the end of this book.

CHAPTER 16

Counting Touching Blocks

IMPORTANT WORD IN THIS CHAPTER
Touching Block

Counting touching blocks is another test that uses drawings of stacks of blocks to measure spatial ability. The good news about this type of test is that usually all the questions are easy. The bad news is that it has short time limits, and you have to work quickly to get a good score.

WHAT DO THESE QUESTIONS ASK ABOUT?

You will be shown drawings of stacks of blocks, and a few of the blocks will be identified by a letter. You will be asked how many blocks each lettered block is touching.

WHAT DO THESE TESTS LOOK LIKE?

Each page may have five or more stacks of blocks. There are usually five questions about each stack, each asking about a different block in the stack. Often there are 25 to 50 questions in a test. All the questions on a test are similar.

To answer these questions you must

- understand what is counted as touching.

- think about blocks that are partly hidden by other blocks.

USEFUL
These questions are usually very easy, but you must work fast to get a good score.

Sample Question

How many blocks is block A touching?

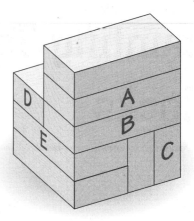

The blocks in this type of question are **all the same size and shape**. The questions are easy, and people generally correctly answer all or most of the questions they try. But there are more questions than anyone can answer in the time limit.

• No one is expected to answer all the questions. Your grade is based mainly on the speed with which you answer them.

Before we answer the sample question, we need to know how to count touching blocks. We'll learn the rule for counting touching blocks on these two pages and then answer this sample question.

What Is Counted as Touching?

Now we will explain the most widely used definition of touching blocks and give some examples.

RULE FOR COUNTING TOUCHING BLOCKS

Two blocks are counted as touching if they are side by side or on top of each other. Blocks are not counted as touching if they meet at only one or two corners.

How to Count Touching Blocks—Example One

How many blocks is block A touching?

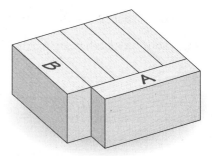

ANSWER

- Block A is touching the four blocks behind it.

- Blocks A and B are **not** counted as touching.

EXPLANATION

We count blocks as touching only if they are touching along a side. Blocks A and B meet at two corners and along the line that connects the two corners. We do not count that as touching. So, following the usual rules for this test, we say that block A is touching four blocks.

How to Count Touching Blocks—Example Two

How many blocks is block A touching?

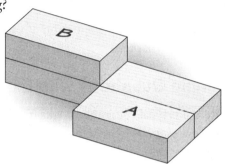

ANSWER AND EXPLANATION

- Block A is touching the block behind it.

- We do not count block A as touching block B or the block under it.
Following the most typical rules for this test we say that block A is touching one block.

How to Count Touching Blocks—Example Three

How many blocks is block A touching?

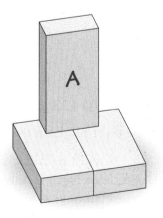

ANSWER AND EXPLANATION

Block A is on top of two blocks, so we say it is touching two blocks.

SUGGESTED APPROACH TO ANSWERING THESE QUESTIONS

Unlike some types of tests where the answer sometimes jumps off the page at you, this one makes you go through the counting process to get the answer. Here is a simple approach that should help you.

SUGGESTED APPROACH

1. First count the touching blocks above, then the touching blocks below, and then the touching blocks to the side. Remember: **above, below, and to the side.**

2. Look at the top and bottom of blocks standing up, and the left and right sides of blocks lying flat to catch all the touching blocks.

3. If the question is too hard, go on to the next question.

Following is a full explanation of the answers to the sample question from the first page of this chapter.

Sample Questions with Explanations

Here is a typical touching-blocks question. It shows one stack of blocks. You can see five blocks labeled with a letter. The question is the same for each of these five blocks: How many blocks is the block touching?

Sample Question

How many blocks is block A touching?

How many blocks is block B touching?

How many blocks is block C touching?

How many blocks is block D touching?

How many blocks is block E touching?

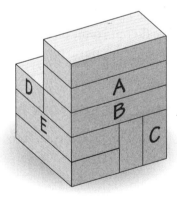

ANSWER AND EXPLANATION

There are eight blocks in this stack.

- Block A is touching 2 blocks: the one above it and the one below it. Note that block A meets block D only at two corners and the line that connects them, and this is **not counted** as touching.

- Block B is touching 5 blocks: block A above it, blocks C and E and the block next to C below it, and block D behind it.

- Block C is touching 3 blocks: blocks B and D above it, and the block next to it.

- Block D is touching 4 blocks: blocks E and C and the block next to block C below it, and block B to the side.

- Block E is touching 4 blocks: blocks B and D above, the block below it, and the block next to block C to the side.

Example: Partly Hidden Blocks

This is a harder touching-blocks question because more blocks are partly hidden by other blocks. Remember, **all the blocks are the same size and shape**.

Sample Question

How many blocks is block A touching?

How many blocks is block B touching?

How many blocks is block C touching?

How many blocks is block D touching?

How many blocks is block E touching?

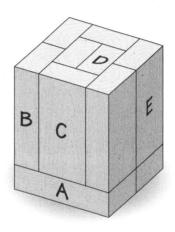

ANSWER AND EXPLANATION

There are 10 blocks in this stack.

- Block A is touching 6 blocks: blocks B, C, and D and two more blocks above it, and one block to the side (the block behind it).

- Block B is touching 4 blocks: block A below it, and block C and two more blocks next to it.

- Block C is touching 5 blocks: block A below it, and blocks B and D and two more blocks next to it.

- Block D is touching 7 blocks: block A and another block below it, and blocks C and E and 3 other blocks next to it.

- Block E is touching 4 blocks: 1 block underneath it, and block D and 2 other blocks next to it.

WHAT CAN I LEARN TO HELP MYSELF DO BETTER?

Other than the material in this chapter, there is nothing you need to learn in order to do well on this type of test. Practice may help you do your best.

WHAT ELSE CAN I DO TO PREPARE?

Because this type of test asks you to think about blocks and how they fit together, you might borrow or buy block toys and see what types of shapes you can make out of them.

TIPS FOR ANSWERING TOUCHING-BLOCKS QUESTIONS

1. Follow a system. First count the touching blocks above, then the touching blocks below, and then those to the side. Remember: **above, below, and to the side.**

2. Look at the **top and bottom of blocks standing up,** and the **left and right sides of blocks lying flat** to catch all the touching blocks.

3. Take it one block at a time. Do not try to count the number of blocks A touches at the same time you count the number for B.

4. Remember, all the **blocks are the same size and shape.**

5. If you are not sure how far back a block goes because part of the block is hidden by another block, you can often tell by looking at a block near it, because all blocks are the same size and shape.

6. Remember to **count unlabeled blocks** (not just those with letters).

7. Don't count just what you can see. Use your imagination to "see" hidden sides of blocks. Make sure you check whether blocks touch other blocks in the middle area where you often cannot see.

8. Blocks that are covered up by other blocks must be touching those other blocks.

9. Go as quickly as you can, since this is a speed test. But don't rush so much that you make careless mistakes.

10. Keep a positive attitude. Remember, you don't have to be a mechanical genius to figure it out; you just have to **think carefully and logically.**

11. Remember that only blocks whose **flat sides touch are counted as touching.** Blocks that come together at one or two corners don't count as touching.

12. You might try pointing at the blocks with the eraser side of your pencil to help you count. But do not make marks, because you have to use the same group of blocks to answer several questions.

13. Read the instructions carefully. The word *touch* may mean different things in different tests. Read the instructions carefully and do the sample questions if there are any.

> **IMPORTANT**
>
> Count unlabeled blocks as well as blocks marked with letters.

TIME LIMIT

You need to work quickly to do well on this type of test. These tests have short time limits, some as short as five minutes.

HOW TO USE THE PRACTICE QUESTIONS

There are practice questions on the following pages and more at the end of this book.

- Do the practice questions in this chapter without any time limit.

- Time yourself when you do the practice questions at the end of the book, using the time limit shown there.

Practice Questions

1. How many blocks is block A touching?

2. How many blocks is block B touching?

3. How many blocks is block C touching?

4. How many blocks is block D touching?

5. How many blocks is block E touching?

6. How many blocks is block A touching?

7. How many blocks is block B touching?

8. How many blocks is block C touching?

9. How many blocks is block D touching?

10. How many blocks is block E touching?

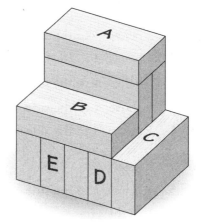

11. How many blocks is block A touching?

12. How many blocks is block B touching?

13. How many blocks is block C touching?

14. How many blocks is block D touching?

15. How many blocks is block E touching?

16. How many blocks is block A touching?

17. How many blocks is block B touching?

18. How many blocks is block C touching?

19. How many blocks is block D touching?

20. How many blocks is block E touching?

The answers to these questions are below.

ANSWERS TO PRACTICE QUESTIONS: TOUCHING BLOCKS

1. **5** 2 below, 3 to the side
2. **5** 2 below, 3 to the side
3. **5** 1 below, 4 to the side
4. **6** 5 above, 1 to the side
5. **5** 1 below, 4 to the side

6. **2** 2 below
7. **5** 4 below, 1 to the side
8. **1** 1 to the side
9. **5** 3 above, 2 to the side
10. **5** 3 above, 2 to the side

11. **5** 1 above, 3 below, 1 to the side
12. **2** 2 below
13. **4** 3 below, 1 to the side
14. **5** 3 above, 1 below, 1 to the side
15. **6** 3 above, 3 to the side

16. **1** 1 below
17. **4** 3 below, 1 to the side
18. **2** 1 above, 1 below
19. **2** 1 above, 1 to the side
20. **3** 2 above, 1 to the side

You will find more questions about touching blocks at the end of this book.

Making Rectangular Boxes

CHAPTER **17**

E ach question on this type of test shows you a flat drawing or pattern that can be folded to make a box. You are shown four similar boxes and asked to find one that can be made from the pattern.

WHAT DO THESE QUESTIONS ASK ABOUT?

The key to these questions is in the painting or shading or designs on the sides. All the boxes are the same size and shape, but the sides look different. You have to tell which box could be made from the pattern based on what the sides look like.

WHAT DO THESE TESTS LOOK LIKE?

Each question shows a flat pattern and four boxes that are the same size but have different sides. Your job is to look for the box that can be made from the pattern.

Sample Question

Which box can be made from this pattern?

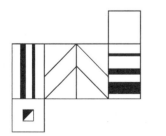
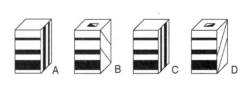

This test may have 50 questions. Time limits are short—about 10 minutes. There will be more questions than anyone can answer in the time limit, so work quickly.

ANSWER AND EXPLANATION

Only box A can be made from this pattern. Box B is wrong for two reasons. First, the top of the box shows the little box with the shaded triangle, but the little box should be on the bottom. Second, the side with the slanted lines should show the line starting near the thick stripe, but B shows them starting near the thin stripe. Box C is wrong because the thicker of the two up-and-down lines should be next to the side with the horizontal stripes. Box D is wrong because the little box with the shaded triangle should be on the bottom. The correct answer is A.

Think About Folding the Pattern to Make a Box

> **REMEMBER**
>
> The key things to look at are *which sides touch each other* and *which corners touch each other.*

Look at the pattern in the sample question on the next page. You can see that one end of the box will be blank and the other end will have a box with a shaded triangle on it. These shaded triangles are important to answering the sample questions on the first pages of this chapter.

If you would like more help learning how to fold the pattern, you should cut out a pattern and actually fold it to make a box. (Of course, you should do this at home, not at the exam.) On the fourth page of this chapter is a large pattern that you can cut out and fold into a box.

Look at the Marks on the Sides

The marks on the sides of the box are the key to answering this type of question. You should look back and forth at the choice and the pattern to see which choices are possible. The key things to look at are

- which sides touch each other and

- which corners touch each other.

Look at Sides That Touch

All the choices have the same side facing front. Look at that side on the pattern and see which sides are next to it. **Sides that meet on the choices must meet on the pattern or the choice is wrong.** This will be the best way for you to decide whether a choice is correct or wrong.

Look at Corners That Touch Each Other

Sometimes it is easier to pay attention to the corners: look to see what patterns come together at a corner of a choice and then look to see if the pattern allows that.

A Box May Be Upside Down

The box may be upside down. This makes the question harder. You might find it useful to turn the booklet upside down when you study the pattern for the questions where the box is upside down.

None of These

This type of question can have a fifth choice: "none of these." If none of the boxes can be made from the pattern, then you should choose E on the answer sheet.

Examples of Questions with Explanations

It is not possible to have simple examples of this type of question, so the examples will be hard. The questions on the test will be no harder than these examples.

Sample Question

Which box can be made from this pattern?

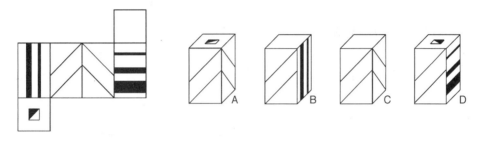

ANSWER AND EXPLANATION

Only box C can be made from this pattern. In box A the lines form an upside down V and the top of the box has the little box with the shaded triangle. But the pattern shows that when the sides with the lines come together to make an upside down V, the top of the box is blank. So box A is wrong. In box B the side with the diagonal lines meets the side with the up-and-down lines on the wrong side. The diagonal line should touch the side with a thin up-and-down line. So box B is wrong. In box D the side with the diagonal line is meeting the side with the side-to-side lines, but the diagonal lines are pointing to the thin side-to-side line. But the pattern shows that the diagonal lines point to the thick side-to-side lines, so D is wrong. In box C the lines form an upside down V and the top of the box is blank. The pattern shows that this is correct. The correct answer is C.

If this explanation is not clear to you, cut out the pattern on the next page and fold it to make the box. Then look at the box and the choices until you see the errors in each choice.

Sample Question

Which box can be made from this pattern?
(If none of the boxes can be made from the pattern, choose E.)

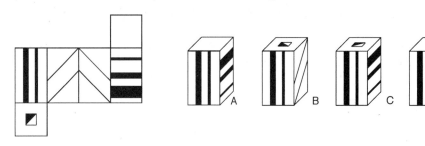

ANSWER AND EXPLANATION

Box A is wrong because when the side with the up-and-down lines is facing front with the thinner line on the right, the side on the right should have two diagonal lines. Box B is wrong because with the two sides shown, the top should be blank. Box C is wrong for the same reason as box A. Box D is wrong because the diagonal lines are going in the wrong direction. Because none of the choices is correct, you should choose E on the answer sheet.

If this explanation is not clear to you, cut out the pattern on the next page and fold it to make the box. Then look at the box and the choices until you see the errors in each choice.

More Help Understanding Patterns

If you would like more help understanding how patterns are turned into boxes, you can use this pattern. This is the pattern used in the sample questions earlier in this chapter.

- Cut out this pattern.

- Fold it into a box and tape it together.

- For each sample question example on the earlier pages of this chapter, compare each choice to the box and see why the wrong answers are wrong.

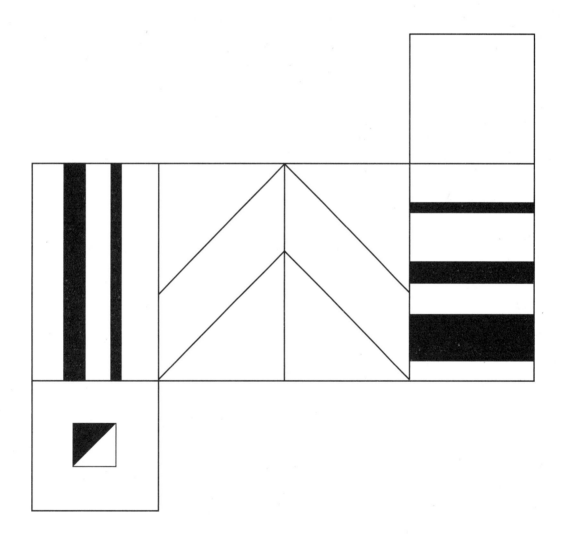

SUGGESTED APPROACH TO ANSWERING THESE QUESTIONS

You need to think about each choice and decide whether it is correct.

SUGGESTED APPROACH

1. Look at the pattern. If you can just "see" the answer, choose it and go on to the next question. Otherwise, try to eliminate wrong answers.
2. Look at the choices and see which side of the box is facing you. Then find that side in the pattern and see which sides are touching it.
3. Check each choice to see if the sides that are showing are sides that touch in the pattern.
4. If a question is hard for you, skip it.

HINT

For each choice, first look at the front of the box and find that side in the flat pattern.

HOW TO ANSWER THESE QUESTIONS MORE QUICKLY

The key to answering this type of question quickly is to look at the front of the boxes. The front of each box is the same. Find this front side in the pattern. Then look to see which end is attached to it and must be the top. Use that to rule out any choice with a different top. Then look at the pattern to see which sides touch the front side. Use this to eliminate any choice that has another side touching the front. Be careful if there are two sides in the pattern that look the same or that would look the same when turned upside down.

In summary:

- Look at the front of the box.

- Find that side in the flat pattern.

- Use the flat pattern to see which end must be the top and eliminate any choice with a different top.

- Use the flat pattern to see what sides touch the front and eliminate any choice with a different side.

- Be careful when two sides look the same or are very similar.

WHAT CAN I LEARN TO HELP MYSELF DO BETTER?

Other than the material in this chapter, there is nothing you need to learn in order to do well on this type of test. Practice will help you do your best.

WHAT ELSE CAN I DO TO PREPARE?

You might make, borrow, or buy flat shapes and use them to make practice questions. Flat shapes may be made out of paper or cardboard.

TIPS FOR QUESTIONS ON MAKING RECTANGULAR BOXES

1. If the correct answer is clear to you, do not spend time checking other answers to see if they are wrong.

2. If the correct answer is not clear, check each choice against the pattern to see if it is correct.

3. If two choices are the same except for one difference, then one must be wrong. It is likely that one of these is correct.

4. A side will look different if the box is shown upside down from the pattern. Sometimes it helps to turn the test booklet upside down when you look at a box.

5. Don't forget that some tests have an option E—"none of the these." Don't use it all the time, but don't forget that it exists.

6. If you think the answer is E, double check all choices before deciding on E.

7. Some questions will be harder for you than others. Skip any that you find very hard.

8. Questions get harder toward the end, so don't skip too many at the beginning.

9. There is one pattern for several questions. Look at each new pattern when you get to it.

HINT

Work fast to get a good score.

TIME LIMIT

You need to work quickly to do well on this type of test. These tests have short time limits, some as short as 10 minutes.

HOW TO USE THE PRACTICE QUESTIONS

There are practice questions on the following pages and more at the end of this book.

- Do the practice questions in this chapter without any time limit.

- Time yourself when you do the practice questions at the end of the book.

Practice Questions

Instructions: For each line of boxes below, answer this question:

Which box can be made from this pattern? If none of the boxes can be made from the pattern, choose E.

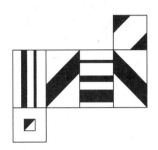

1.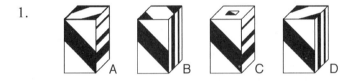

2.

3.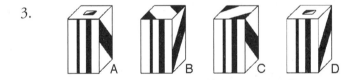

4.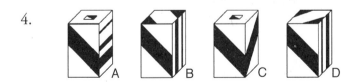

5.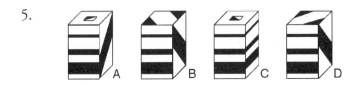

For each line of boxes below, answer this question:

Which box can be made from this pattern? If none of the boxes can be made from the pattern, choose E.

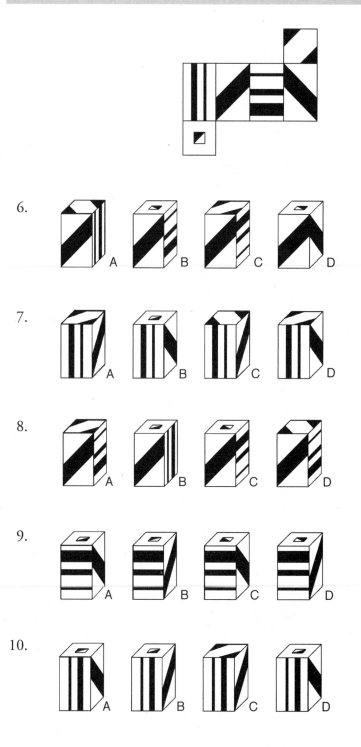

The answers to these questions are on page 221.

ANSWERS TO PRACTICE QUESTIONS: MAKING RECTANGULAR BOXES

1. **D**
2. **C**
3. **A**
4. **E**
5. **B**
6. **E**
7. **C**
8. **A**
9. **B**
10. **D**

You will find more questions about making rectangular boxes at the end of this book.

Paper Folding— Shape Known

CHAPTER 18

IMPORTANT WORD IN THIS CHAPTER

Inside Out

Each question on this type of test shows you a flat drawing or pattern that can be folded to make a solid object. You are shown several solid objects and must choose the one that matches the flat pattern based on the coloring of the sides.

WHAT DO THESE QUESTIONS ASK ABOUT?

Each question shows you a pattern and four or five solid objects. All the objects are the same size and shape, but they look different because some of their sides are shaded or have designs on them. You have to tell which solid could be made from the pattern.

Sample Question

Which solid can be made from this pattern?

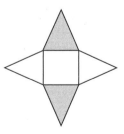

      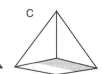

Answer and Explanation

The correct answer is D. The other answers are wrong for these reasons:

- A shows the bottom is half shaded, but the pattern shows it is white.

- B shows two shaded sides next to each other, but the pattern does not.

- C shows the bottom is half shaded, but the pattern shows it is white.

- E shows the bottom is shaded, but the pattern shows it is white.

This type of test may have as many as 50 questions with a time limit of about 25 minutes. In addition, many of the questions are hard, so do not waste time when you take this test.

The Answers Show You the Solids

Making solid shapes out of flat patterns can be difficult, but luckily you don't have to do that; these questions show you the shapes. Each question has its own pattern, and the correct shape for that pattern is shown in the choices. All you have to do is decide which solid shape can be made from the flat pattern.

Look at the Shading and Marks on the Sides

> **USEFUL**
>
> You must choose the solid object that matches the flat pattern based on the coloring of the sides.

The shading and the marks on the sides of the shape are the key to answering this type of question. You should look back and forth at each choice and the pattern to see which choice is possible. The key things to look at are

- which sides touch each other and

- which corners touch each other.

Choose the Best Answer

There is always a correct answer. Some other tests ask you to choose "none of these" if none of the choices is correct, but this type of test does not work that way. So choose the best answer because one of them is correct.

Sample Questions with Explanations

We'll start with a simple example and then explain a few harder ones.

Sample Question

Which shape can you make from this pattern?

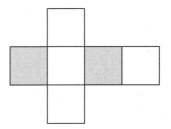

ANSWER AND EXPLANATION

The correct answer is D. The other answers are wrong for these reasons:

- Box A shows 3 shaded sides but the pattern shows only 2.

- Box B shows 2 shaded sides touching, but the pattern shows that the shaded sides do not touch.

- Box C is wrong because the pattern shows that no 3 white sides meet at one corner.

Sample Question

Which shape can you make from this pattern?

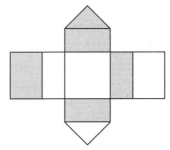

  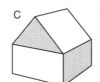

ANSWER AND EXPLANATION

The correct answer is B. The other answers are wrong for these reasons:

- A and C each have one rectangular end white, but in the pattern both rectangular ends are shaded.

- D has a shaded side under the shaded side of the roof, but the pattern shows a white side under the shaded roof.

Sample Question

Which shape can you make from this pattern?

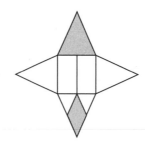

ANSWER AND EXPLANATION

The correct answer is D. The other answers are wrong for these reasons:

- A and B each have the two shaded sides next to each other, but the pattern shows that the shaded sides are separated.

- In C the bottom point of the shaded portion does not touch the line that goes down the middle of the bottom, but the pattern shows that it should.

Sample Question

Which shape can you make from this pattern?

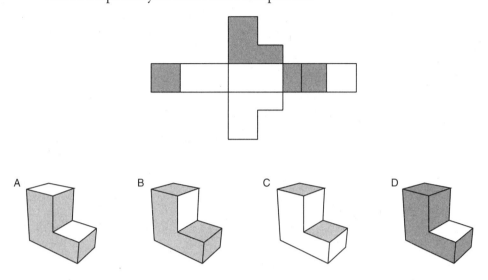

ANSWER AND EXPLANATION

The correct answer is B. The other answers are wrong for these reasons:

- A has a white top, but the pattern shows the top is shaded.

- C has a white front, but the pattern shows that part is shaded.

- D has a white horizontal piece, but the pattern shows that part is shaded.

Inside Out is Wrong: The Correct Way to Fold the Pattern

After the first few questions on the test you will get to some questions that can be very confusing. Some may seem to have no answer, and others may seem to have two answers. This will happen if you make a mistake in thinking about how to fold the patterns. The way to avoid being confused is to learn the correct way to fold a pattern.

You need to pay attention to the inside and outside of the pattern. The pattern shows you the outside side. There are two ways to fold the pattern, but only one way is correct. You will get wrong answers if you fold the pattern so the side you see becomes the inside of the shape. **Think of the pattern as being white on the side that is facedown.**

- **You must fold the pattern so the side of the pattern that faces you becomes the outside of the shape.**

IMPORTANT

Fold the pattern so that the side facing you (the shaded side) becomes the outside of the folded shape, and the side facing down (the white side) is on the inside. (See page 229.)

Which shape can you make from this pattern?

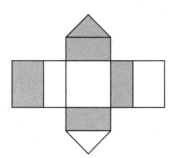

ANSWER AND EXPLANATION

The correct answer is C. The other answers are wrong for these reasons:

- A is wrong because the right side of the house should be white.

- B is wrong because when the roof is white, the whole front should be shaded.

- D is wrong because when the whole front is shaded, the roof should be white.

If you thought B or D was correct, you are probably folding the pattern with the wrong side out. The next page goes over the right and wrong way to fold the pattern for this question.

The Right Way and the Wrong Way to Fold a Pattern

There is a right way and a wrong way to fold a pattern. Think about every pattern as being shaded only on the side you see and white on the other side. You should fold a pattern so that the shaded sides are on the outside. To learn how to fold the pattern, cut out the pattern on this page and actually fold it both ways. This will help you see that the way you fold the pattern makes a difference.

- Cut out this pattern.

- Fold it into the shape of a house and tape it together.

- **The shaded sides must be on the outside of the house. If they are on the inside, you have folded it inside out.**

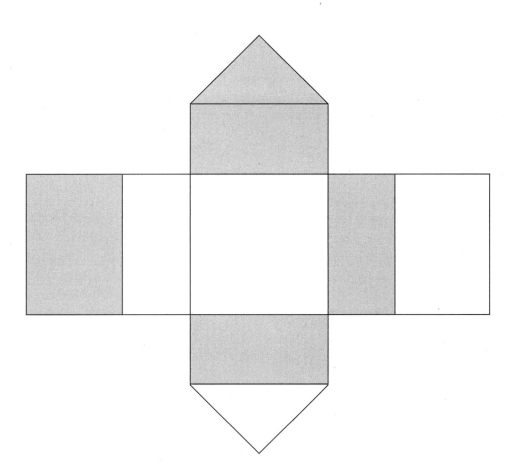

SUGGESTED APPROACH TO ANSWERING THESE QUESTIONS

If the right answer does not leap off the page at you, then think about each choice and decide whether it is correct. Compare the pattern with the solid shapes to see

• which sides are next to each other in the pattern and in the solid shapes, and

• how the sides are drawn. A wrong answer may show a side upside down.

SUGGESTED APPROACH

1. Glance at the pattern and see if it is simple and something you recognize. For simple patterns you recognize, look immediately to see what the shading or markings are on the sides.
2. For more complex patterns, first look at the choices to see what type of solid shape is being made. Then look at the pattern to see the shading or markings on each side.
3. If you can just "see" the answer, mark the answer sheet and go on.
4. If you are not sure of the answer, compare the pattern with each choice.
5. Pay attention to which sides are next to each other in the pattern.
6. Pay attention to orientation of the sides. (Often a wrong answer will show a side upside down.)

WHAT CAN I LEARN HELP MYSELF DO BETTER?

Other than the material in this chapter, there is nothing you need to learn in order to do well on this type of test. Practice will help you do your best.

WHAT ELSE CAN I DO TO PREPARE?

You might make, borrow, or buy flat shapes and use them to make practice questions. You can make flat shapes out of paper or cardboard.

TIPS FOR QUESTIONS ON PAPER FOLDING—SHAPE KNOWN

1. If the correct answer is clear to you, do not spend time checking other answers to see if they are wrong.
2. If two choices are the same except for one difference, then one must be wrong. It is likely that one of these is correct.
3. Often you can eliminate one or two choices because of obvious errors. For example, the choice might have two shaded sides touching but the pattern does not.
4. Some questions will be harder for you than others. Skip any you find very hard.
5. Questions get harder toward the end, so don't skip too many at the beginning.

TIME LIMIT

These tests have relatively long time limits, some as long as 25 minutes. However, there may be 50 or more questions, so you do not have much time for each question. You need to work quickly to do well on this type of test.

> **MORE PRACTICE**
>
> These questions ask you to match flat patterns to folded solid objects, so you may want to also review the chapter *Making Rectangular Boxes* (Chap. 17) for more practice.

HOW TO USE THE PRACTICE QUESTIONS

There are practice questions on this and the following pages and more at the end of this book.

- Do the practice questions in this chapter without any time limit.

- Time yourself when you do the practice questions at the end of the book, using the time limit shown there.

Practice Questions

1.

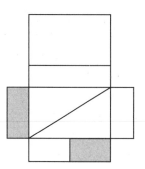

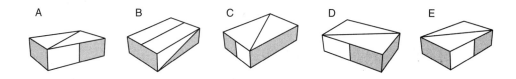

2.

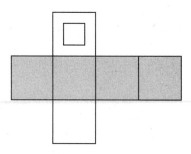

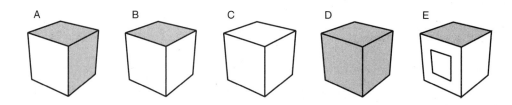

3.

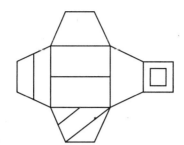

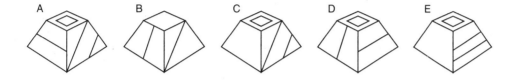

A   B   C   D   E

4.

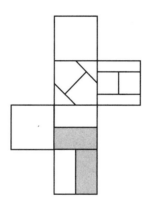

 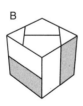

A   B   C   D   E

5.

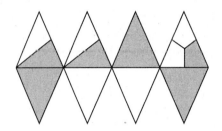

A  B C D E

6.

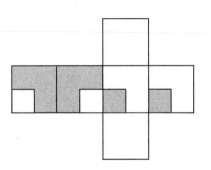

A 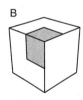 B C D E

7.

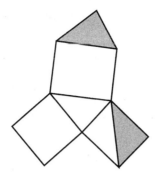

A   B   C   D   E

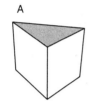 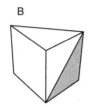 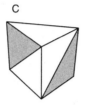 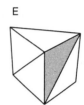

8.

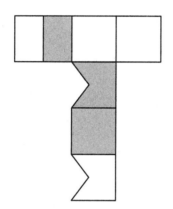

A   B   C   D   E

 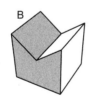

9.

 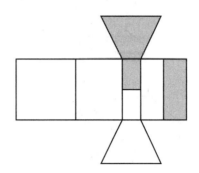

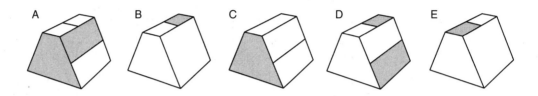

10.

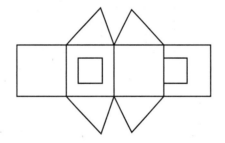

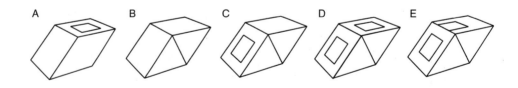

The answers to these questions are on the next page.

ANSWERS TO PRACTICE QUESTIONS: PAPER FOLDING—SHAPE KNOWN

1. **A**

2. **A**

3. **C**

4. **A**

5. **E**

6. **D**

7. **B**

8. **C**

9. **D**

10. **C**

You will find more questions on paper folding—shape known at the end of this book.

Paper Folding— Shape Unknown

Each question on this type of test shows you a flat drawing or pattern that can be folded to make a solid object. You are shown different shapes and have to choose the one that can be made from the pattern. Some of these questions seem very hard, but if you study this chapter, you will find that these questions get easier with practice.

WHAT DO THESE QUESTIONS ASK ABOUT?

Each question shows you a pattern and four or five solid objects. You need to fold the pattern on the dotted lines to make a solid object. All the solid objects are different shapes. The sides are not shaded or colored. You have to tell which solid could be made from the pattern.

Sample Question

Which solid could you make by folding the pattern on the dotted lines?

> **HINT**
>
> Some of these questions seem very hard, but you will find that these questions get easier with practice.

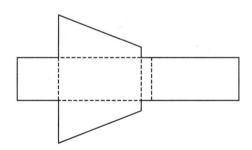

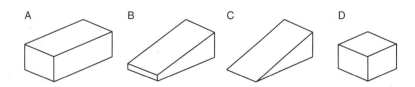

ANSWER AND EXPLANATION

The correct answer is B. When you fold the pattern on the dotted lines, the solid shape will have 6 sides and the top will be on a slant.

- Choices A and D are wrong because the top is not on a slant.

- Choice C is wrong because it has only 5 sides.

These tests are usually speed tests. You will have only about five minutes or so to answer 20 questions. No one finishes all the questions, but the more you get right, the better your score, so you need to work quickly. No training or experience is needed to answer these questions.

Making solid shapes out of flat patterns can be difficult, but one of the answers shown is always correct. This chapter will give you some practice and tips for answering these questions.

CHOOSE THE BEST ANSWER

There is always a correct answer. Some other tests ask you to choose "none of these" if none of the choices is correct, but this type of test does not work that way. So choose the best answer, because one of them is correct.

Sample Questions with Explanations

We'll start with a simple example and then go to a few harder ones. These questions have no words, only drawings. The flat shape is the question, and the solids are the answer choices.

Sample Question

> **WATCH OUT**
>
> Every dotted line on the flat pattern becomes the edge of a side when the shape is folded. In other words, two sides of the pattern will not be put together to make one larger side on the folded shape.

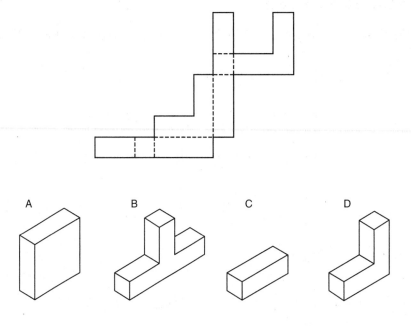

ANSWER AND EXPLANATION

The correct answer is D.

- Choices A and C are wrong because they are much too simple.

- Choice B is wrong because it is a T shape and the pattern is not in that shape.

Sample Question

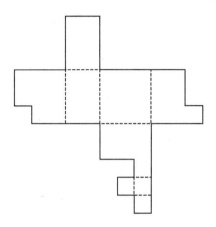

> **HINT/TIP**
>
> When counting the sides of a solid shape, don't forget to count *hidden sides* that are obviously there but you can't see.

A    B 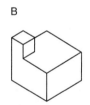   C 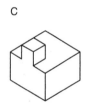   D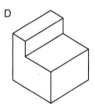

ANSWER AND EXPLANATION

The correct answer is B.

- Choice A is wrong because it does not have a large square shape, but the pattern does.

- Choice C is wrong because the little cube on the top is not at a corner.

- Choice D is wrong because the pattern does not show a long piece on top.

You could also count sides to help answer this question. The pattern has 9 sides. Choice A has 11 sides, choice C has 10 sides, and choice D has 8 sides. Only choice B has 9 sides.

The diagram below shows how to count the number of sides on this pattern.

THIS PATTERN HAS NINE SIDES

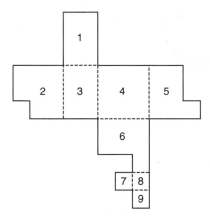

Counting Sides

Sometimes counting the number of sides is a quick and easy way to find the answer or to eliminate wrong answers. Other times it is difficult to count sides on the solid objects. Try counting sides if you are stuck, and see if it helps you. An example of counting sides is given in the previous example.

Don't Worry About Inside Out

Patterns can be folded so the side you see is on the outside or on the inside. In some other tests described in this book this difference is very important. For the questions in this chapter, the difference is not important. This type of test will not show you a wrong choice that is folded inside out. It usually works best if you fold the pattern so the side you see is the outside.

TIPS AND SUGGESTED APPROACH

1. Look at the pattern and the choices. If you can just "see" the answer, choose it and go on to the next question. Otherwise, try to eliminate wrong answers.

2. Notice the size and shape of the sides of the pattern and look for these in the choices. If you do not find them in a choice, the choice is wrong.

3. Count the number of sides in the pattern. The solid must have that number of sides. Eliminate any choices with the wrong number of sides.

4. Often the questions look hard but are easy.

5. Don't spend more than 30 seconds on a question.

6. If a question seems too hard for you, skip it.

Drawings Side By Side

Some tests show the pattern next to the solids. Below is an example like that.

Sample Question

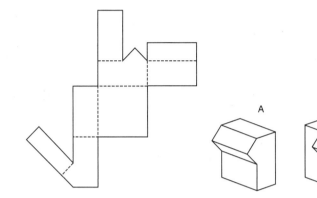

ANSWER AND EXPLANATION

The correct answer is A.

- Choice B is wrong because the pointed part is not long enough.

- Choices C and D are wrong because they each have two pointed parts but the pattern shows only one.

You could also rule out choices B, C, and D because they have too many sides. The pattern has 8 sides. Choice B has 9 sides, choice C has 10 sides, and choice D has 9 sides.

WHAT CAN I LEARN TO HELP MYSELF DO BETTER?

Other than the material in this chapter, there is nothing you need to learn in order to do well on this type of test. However, this type of test is somewhat similar to what you would learn in a drafting course. You might want to take a drafting course to become more familiar with different ways to look at solid parts.

WHAT ELSE CAN I DO TO PREPARE?

At the end of this chapter are large copies of the patterns for the 10 practice questions. It would help if you cut out the shapes in the practice questions and fold them into solids. Do this for any questions you find confusing.

TIME LIMIT

The time limits for these tests are very short, about five minutes. Most people finish only half the questions on this type of test. Try to do as many questions as you can.

HOW TO USE THE PRACTICE QUESTIONS

There are practice questions on this and the following pages and more at the end of this book.

- Do the practice questions in this chapter without any time limit.

- Time yourself when you do the practice questions at the end of the book.

Practice Questions

1.

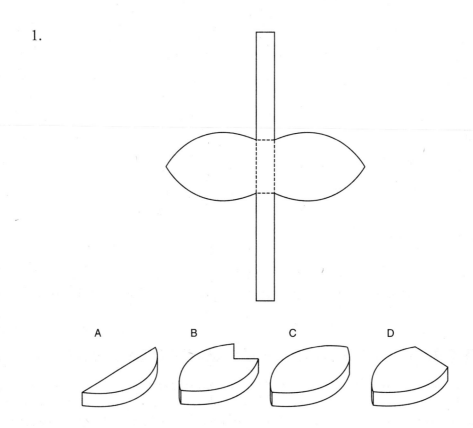

A   B   C   D

2.

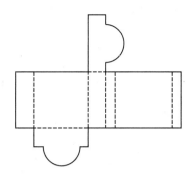

A

B

C

D

3.

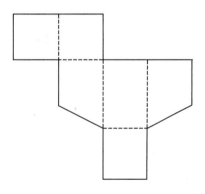

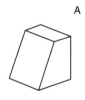
A

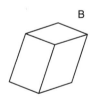
B

C

D

4.

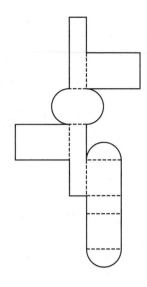

A 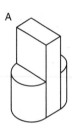 B  C 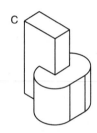 D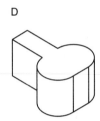

5.

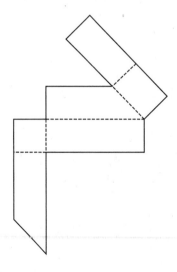

A 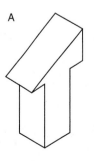 B 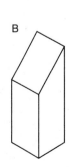 C 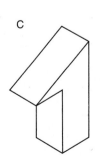 D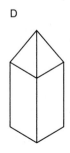

6.

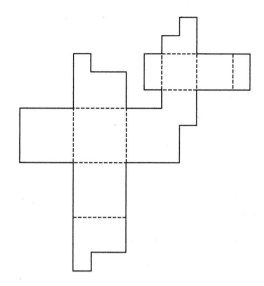

A   B   C   D

 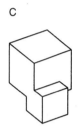 

7.

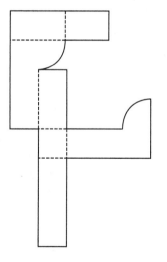

A   B   C   D

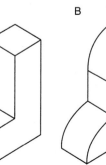 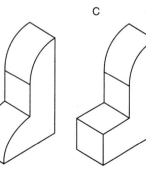 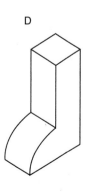

8.

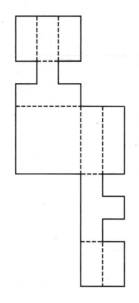

A 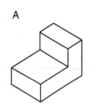 B 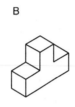 C 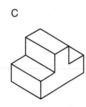 D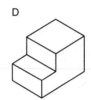

9.

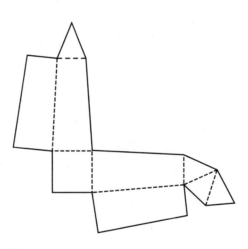

A  B 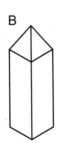 C  D

10.

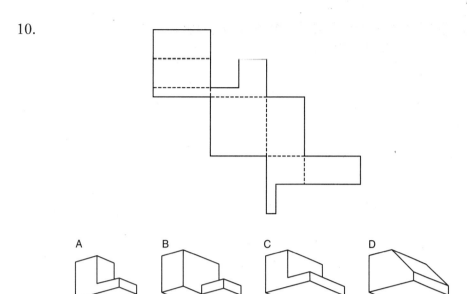

The answers to these questions are on the next page.

You will find more questions about paper folding—shape unknown at the end of this book.

ANSWERS TO PRACTICE QUESTIONS: PAPER FOLDING—SHAPE UNKNOWN

1. **D**
2. **B**
3. **C**
4. **A**
5. **B**
6. **D**

7. **D**
8. **C**
9. **C**
10. **C**

There are more practice questions of this type at the end of this book.

Large Copy of the Pattern for Practice Question 1

To better understand this question, cut out this pattern and fold it into a solid.

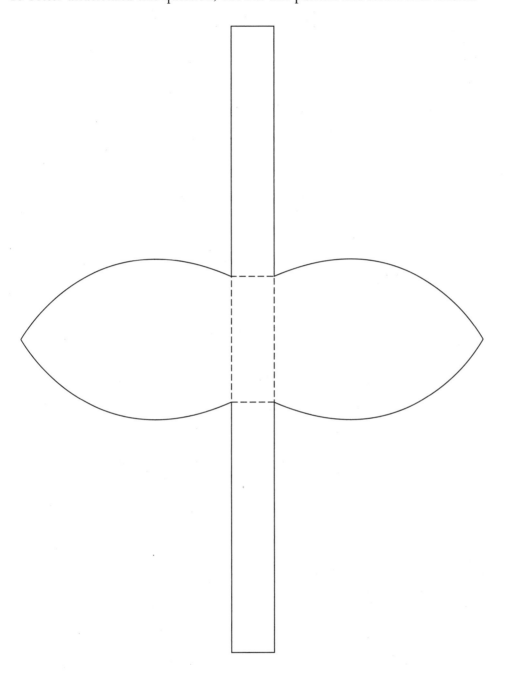

Large Copy of the Pattern for Practice Question 2

To better understand this question, cut out this pattern and fold it into a solid.

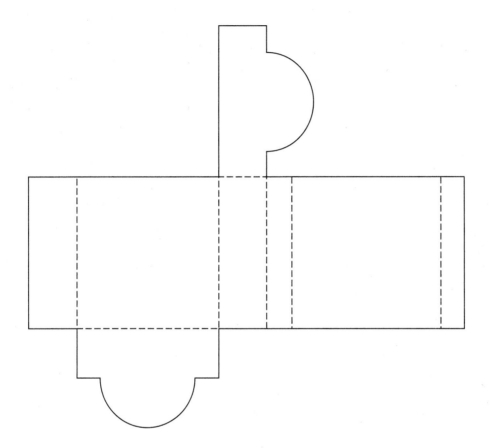

Large Copy of the Pattern for Practice Question 3

To better understand this question, cut out this pattern and fold it into a solid.

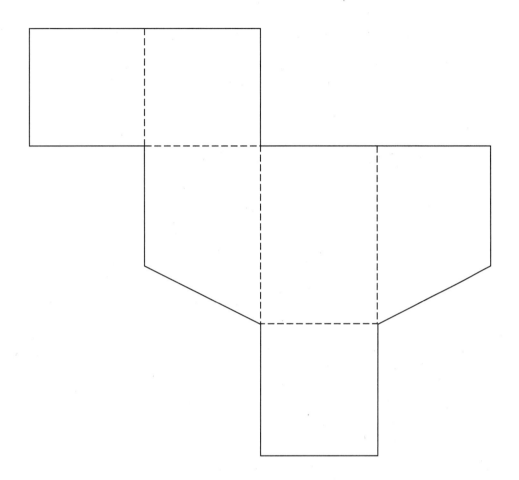

Large Copy of the Pattern for Practice Question 4

To better understand this question, cut out this pattern and fold it into a solid.

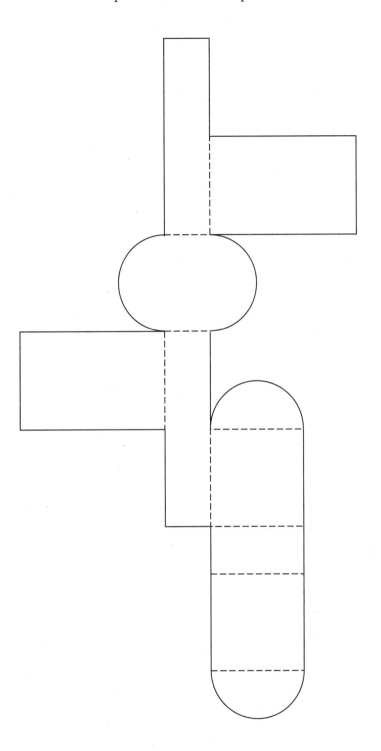

Large Copy of the Pattern for Practice Question 5

To better understand this question, cut out this pattern and fold it into a solid.

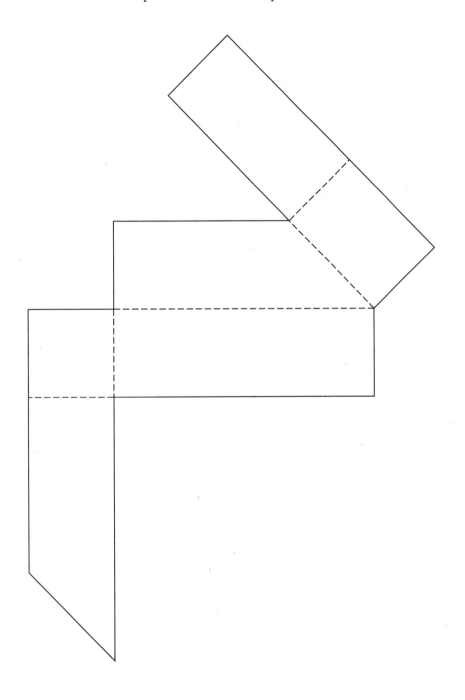

Large Copy of the Pattern for Practice Question 6

To better understand this question, cut out this pattern and fold it into a solid.

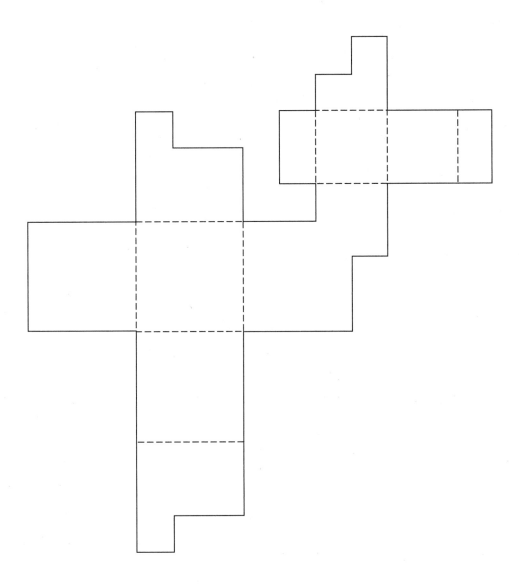

Large Copy of the Pattern for Practice Question 7

To better understand this question, cut out this pattern and fold it into a solid.

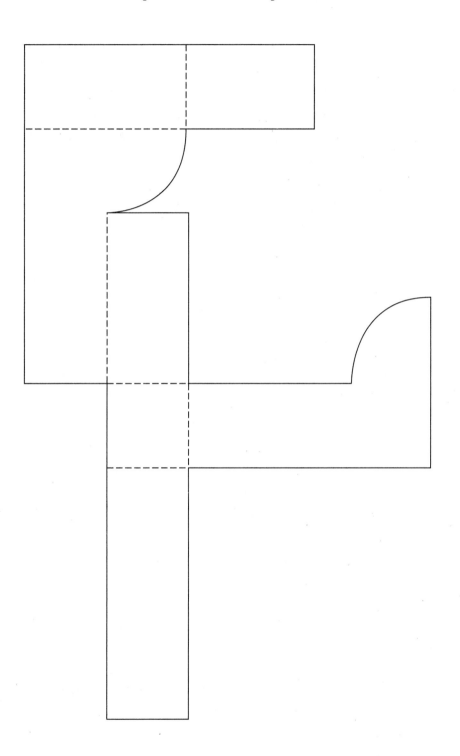

Large Copy of the Pattern for Practice Question 8

To better understand this question, cut out this pattern and fold it into a solid.

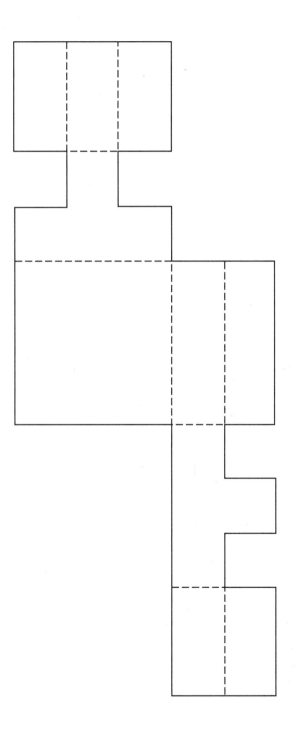

Large Copy of the Pattern for Practice Question 9

To better understand this question, cut out this pattern and fold it into a solid.

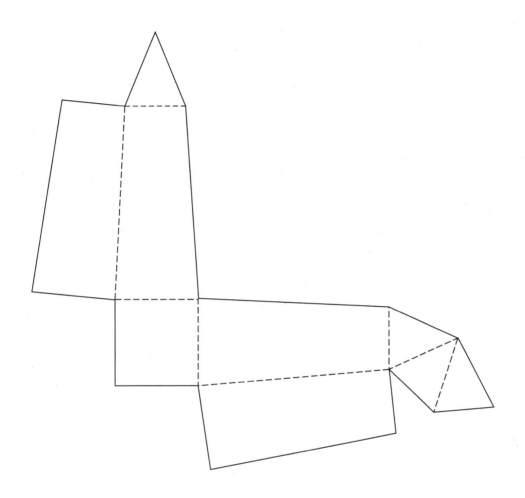

Large Copy of the Pattern for Practice Question 10

To better understand this question, cut out this pattern and fold it into a solid.

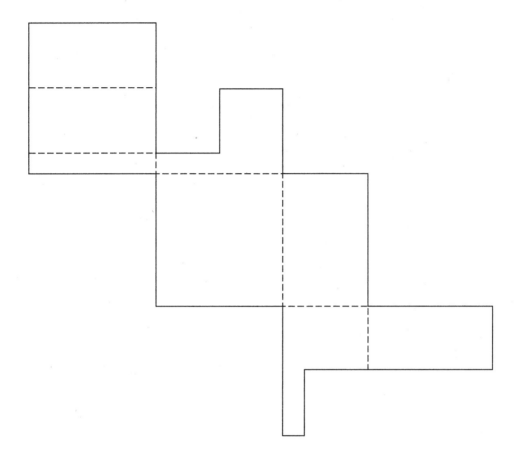

Parts Assembly

These questions ask you to think about moving and turning solid mechanical parts so that they fit together. Some of these questions seem very hard, but if you study this chapter you will find they get easier with practice.

WHAT DO THESE QUESTIONS ASK ABOUT?

These questions ask you to put mechanical parts together in your mind, following instructions in a diagram.

WHAT DO THESE TESTS LOOK LIKE?

Each question has small but clear drawings of from three to six parts. The questions have no words. Letters in the drawings show how the parts are supposed to be put together. The answer choices are drawings of the parts assembled. Your job is to choose the answer that shows the parts as they should be put together.

This is a speed test. You have only five minutes or so to answer 20 questions, so you need to work quickly. No training or experience is needed to answer these questions. Here is a sample question. We will give and explain the correct answer on the next page.

OVERVIEW

Each question shows from three to six drawings of mechanical parts and asks you what they would look like if they were put together correctly.

Sample Question

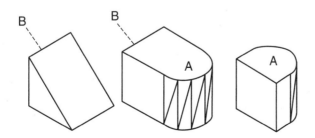

ANSWER

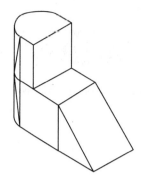

Rules for Putting Parts Together

Here are the three rules for putting parts together.

- **Put together sides with the same letter printed on them.** In the sample question, the letter A is printed on two parts. These parts should be put together so that the sides with the letter A are touching.

- **Put together hidden sides pointed to by the same letter and dashed lines.** Dashed lines are used to point to sides you cannot see. In the sample question two parts have the letter B with a dashed line pointing to the back of the part.

- **You can lift, turn, and move parts when you put them together.**

Answer and Explanation

In the sample question only the correct answer is given. We will explain the correct answer now, first looking at the parts marked A and then looking at the parts marked B.

- Two parts have the letter A printed on them. This means the sides marked with A should be put together so they are touching. In the correct answer you see that the smaller part marked A has been picked up, turned upside down, and put on top of the larger part marked A. You cannot see the letters in the answer because when the parts are on top of each other, they hide the letters.

- Two parts have the letter B with a dashed line pointing to the back of each part. This means the backs should be put together so they are touching. In the correct answer the larger part with the letter B has been turned around and the smaller part with the letter B has been moved so the two marked sides are touching.

Examples

The way these questions work will become clearer as we go through some examples. The questions have no words, only drawings. The question is in the upper left-hand corner, and the choices are labeled A, B, C, D, and E.

Sample Question

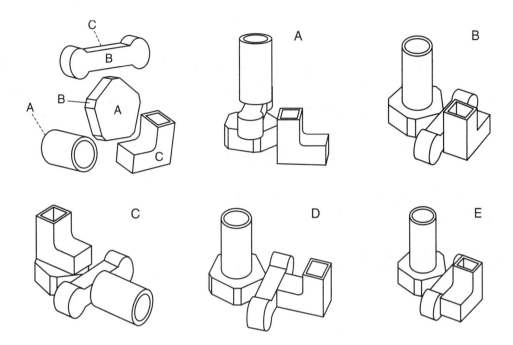

ANSWER AND EXPLANATION

The correct answer is B.

- Choice A is wrong because the cylinder should be standing directly on the large flat part (the one marked with both A and B).

- Choice C is wrong because the cylinder should be standing on the large flat part.

- Choice D is wrong because the part on the right is attached wrong. The L-shaped side of that part should be touching the other parts rather than the square end.

- Choice E is wrong because the part on the right is attached wrong. The other L-shaped side of that part should be touching.

REMEMBER

You are allowed to turn, lift, and move parts when you put them together.

Rules

This test has only a few rules:

- The parts can be moved, rotated, or turned over when you put them together.

- Letters can be on or point to different places on a part, such as a side you can see, a side that is hidden, a hole, or an edge.

- Dotted lines point to places you cannot see, like the back of a part.

- Solid lines point to places you can see, like the front of a part. (Questions use solid lines when the part is too small to mark with a letter.)

SUGGESTED APPROACH TO ANSWERING THESE QUESTIONS

Think about each pair of letters, starting with the As, then the Bs, and so on.

SUGGESTED APPROACH

1. Look at the pattern and the choices. If you can just "see" the answer, choose it and go on to the next question. Otherwise, try to eliminate wrong answers.

2. Put together the marked parts in your mind. Then look at the choices and eliminate any that put these parts together wrong. If the correct answer is clear, choose it.

3. Repeat step 2 for the other letters. You can go in alphabetical order or choose a letter that fits with the parts already assembled.

4. If a question is too hard for you, skip it.

Sample Question

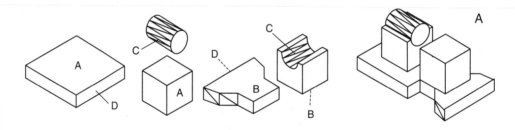

WATCH OUT

Dashed lines are used to point to sides you cannot see.

REMEMBER

Letters can either be on or point to different places on a part, such as a *side you can see*, a *side that is hidden*, a *hole*, or an *edge*.

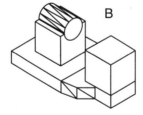

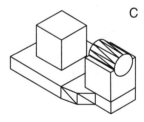

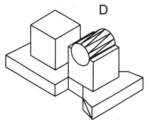

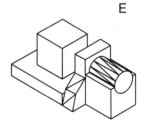

ANSWER AND EXPLANATION

The correct answer is C. There is more than one way to get the correct answer to this question. We will use the suggested approach just described to help us find it.

- Looking at the parts marked A we see the cube should be on top of the flat square. So choices A and B are wrong.

- Since the flat square part is marked D, look at the other part marked D. The long hidden side of that part should be next to the flat, square part, so choices D and E are wrong. Because all the other choices are wrong, choice C must be correct.

SMALLER DRAWINGS

On the real tests, the drawings can be small. Below is an example with smaller drawings.

> **TIP**
>
> Use a system to fit the parts together, starting with the As, then the Bs, and so on.

Sample Question

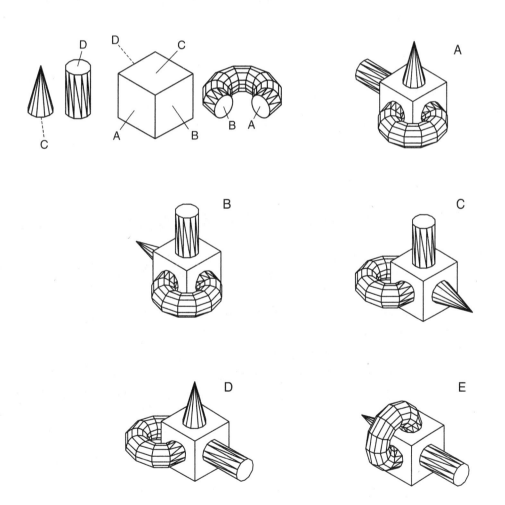

ANSWER AND EXPLANATION

The correct answer is A. There is more than one way to get the correct answer to this question. We will use the suggested approach just described to help us find it.

- Looking at the parts marked A we see the curved tube fits against the cube in two places. All the choices have this.

- Looking at the parts marked C, we see the cone must be on the cube pointing in a different direction than the curved tube. So choices B and C are wrong.

- Looking at the parts marked D we see the straight cylinder must be on the cube on a side next to the cone, so choice E is wrong. Also, the cylinder must be on the left of the curved tube, so choice D is wrong. All the other choices are wrong, so choice A must be correct.

WHAT CAN I LEARN TO HELP MYSELF DO BETTER?

This type of test is somewhat similar to what you would learn in a drafting course. You might want to take a drafting course to become more familiar with different ways to look at solid parts.

WHAT ELSE CAN I DO TO PREPARE?

You could practice doing solid puzzles, the kind that come apart and you have to put together to make a certain shape. Puzzles like these are available in toy stores and on the Web (for example, http://cleverwood.com/puzzles_by_type.htm, which has some puzzles for less than $5). Free puzzles are also available on the Web. You have to cut out and paste together the parts, but the price is right. See, for example, http://subhelp.com/pyramid_index.htm.

TIP

If you've narrowed it down to two similar answers, try to figure out what is different about the two answers to help you pick the one that is correct.

TIPS FOR PARTS-ASSEMBLY QUESTIONS

1. Use the suggested approach on page 274 to answer these questions.
2. Answers that are different from most of the other answers in obvious ways are often wrong.
3. Often the wrong answers have obvious errors.
4. If you have no idea what the answer is, go on to the next question.
5. Don't spend too much time on any one question.
6. If you are allowed to write in the test booklet, draw a line through wrong answers.
7. If you can rule out even one wrong answer but cannot find the right answer, guess.

TIME LIMIT

The time limits for these tests are very short. Most people finish only half the questions on this type of test. Try to do as many questions as you can.

HOW TO USE THE PRACTICE QUESTIONS

There are practice questions on this and the following pages and more at the end of this book.

• Do the practice questions in this chapter without any time limit.

• Time yourself when you do the practice questions at the end of the book, using the time limit shown there.

Practice Questions

1.

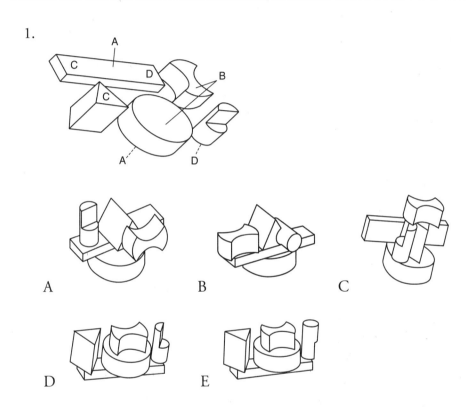

2.

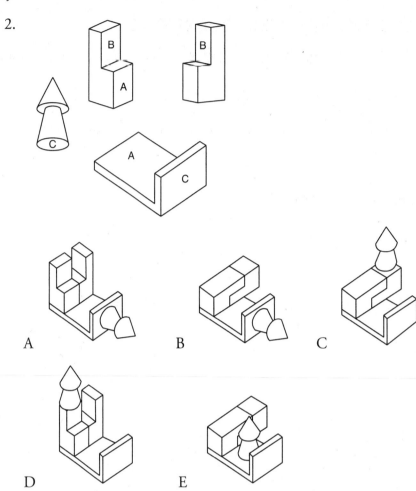

A

B

C

D

E

3.

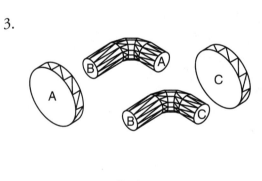

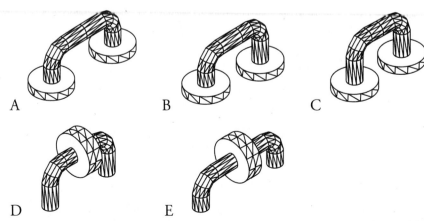

A

B

C

D

E

4.

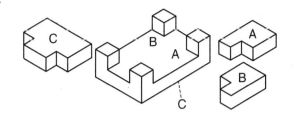

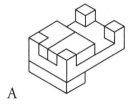 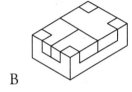 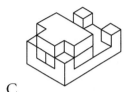

A B C

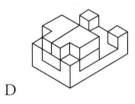 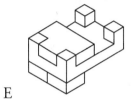

D E

5.

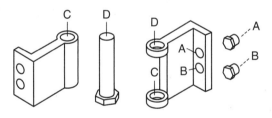

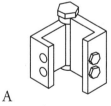 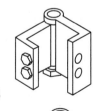 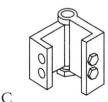

A B C

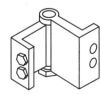 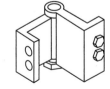

D E

6.

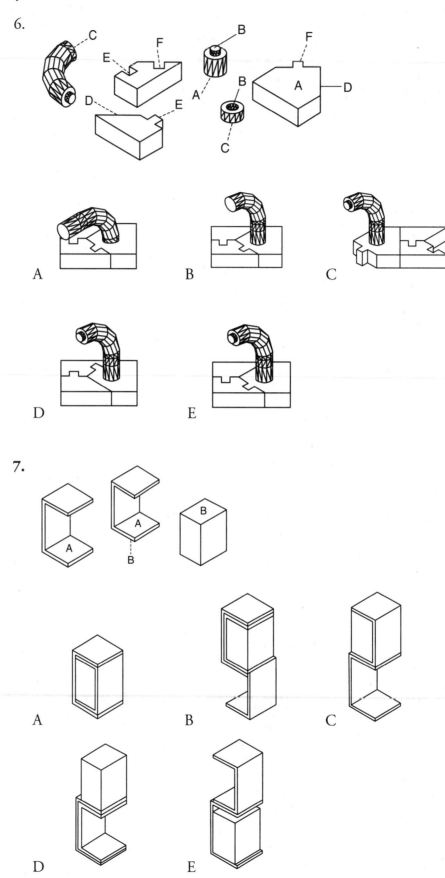

7.

8.

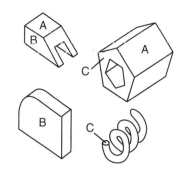

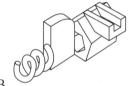

A   B   C

D   E

9.

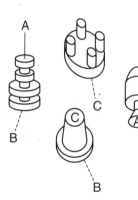

A   B   C

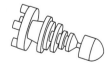

D   E

10.

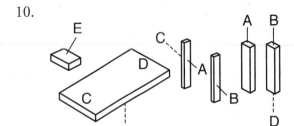

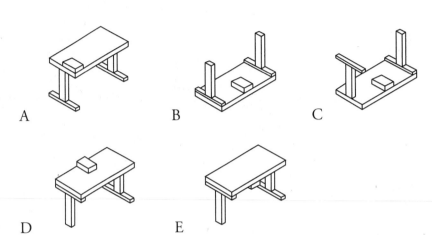

The answers to these questions are at the bottom of this page.
You will find more questions on parts assembly at the end of this book.

ANSWERS TO PRACTICE QUESTIONS: PARTS ASSEMBLY

1. **D**
2. **B**
3. **A**
4. **A**
5. **C**
6. **E**
7. **B**
8. **C**
9. **D**
10. **D**

Practice Tests

This chapter has 18 practice tests, one for each of the test question chapters in this book. These tests give examples of all the most common types of tests and questions, and some of the less common tests and questions.

The 18 tests in this chapter are on the following topics:

- General Mechanical Understanding
- Gears
- Pulleys
- Tools
- Map Reading
- Line Following
- Matching Shapes
- Visual Comparison
- Finding Rotated Shapes
- Cut-Ups
- Jigsaw Puzzles
- Hole Punching
- Hidden Blocks
- Counting Touching Blocks
- Making Rectangular Boxes
- Paper Folding—Shape Known
- Paper Folding—Shape Unknown
- Parts Assembly

On the first page of each practice test is a checklist for using the test, the time limit you should use when timing yourself on the test, and instructions for taking the test. The earlier chapters in this book give tips and suggestions for taking each of these tests.

To get the most out of these practice tests try this:

- Take each practice test as you will take a real test: sitting at a desk with no music and no TV.

- Have someone else time you while you take each practice test.

- If you finish a test before the time limit, practice checking your answers and your answer sheet.

- After you take each test, go over the questions you got wrong or guessed at and learn from them.

- Take each test again after a week or two.

The time and effort you put into preparation will help you earn a higher test score. It is time well spent!

GENERAL MECHANICAL UNDERSTANDING: PRACTICE TEST

To get the most out of this practice test, take it twice.

- First take this test with the time limit shown below, and grade the test.

- Then take this test a second time with no time limit, answering every question. (It is best to wait a full day or even a week or two before taking the test a second time.)

After you take the test both ways, review every question you got wrong or were unsure about. Try to understand why the right answer is right and the other answers are wrong.

You will get the most out of this practice test if you **first read the chapter on General Mechanical Understanding.** That chapter begins on page 13.

CHECKLIST FOR USING THIS PRACTICE TEST

Put a check mark in each box to keep track of your progress on this practice test.

- ❏   Take the test using the time limit.
- ❏   Grade the timed test.
- ❏   Review your performance on the timed test.

- ❏   Take the test a second time with no time limit.
- ❏   Grade the untimed test.

- ❏   Go over each question you got wrong.
- ❏   Go over each question you were not sure about.

Time Limit for This Test: **10 MINUTES**

Instructions: Before you start, carefully tear out the answer sheet on the next page. Practice with an answer sheet is important. You will get the most out of this practice test if you take it the way you will take a real test.

Read each question and choose the correct answer. Then mark your answer on the answer sheet.

If you have extra time, use **all** of it to check your work. Your goal in taking the practice test should be to get the highest score possible. You do not get any credit for finishing early.

When you are ready to start, turn the page and answer questions 1 to 10.

Answer Sheet
PRACTICE TEST

General Mechanical Understanding—Timed Test

Time Limit: 10 minutes

Time Started: _____

Time Ended: _____

Time Spent Taking This Test: _____

1 Ⓐ Ⓑ Ⓒ Ⓓ Ⓔ   6 Ⓐ Ⓑ Ⓒ

2 Ⓐ Ⓑ Ⓒ   7 Ⓐ Ⓑ Ⓒ Ⓓ

3 Ⓐ Ⓑ Ⓒ Ⓓ Ⓔ Ⓕ   8 Ⓐ Ⓑ Ⓒ Ⓓ Ⓔ Ⓕ

4 Ⓐ Ⓑ Ⓒ Ⓓ   9 Ⓐ Ⓑ Ⓒ Ⓓ Ⓔ

5 Ⓐ Ⓑ Ⓒ Ⓓ   10 Ⓐ Ⓑ Ⓒ

General Mechanical Understanding—Untimed Test

1 Ⓐ Ⓑ Ⓒ Ⓓ Ⓔ   6 Ⓐ Ⓑ Ⓒ

2 Ⓐ Ⓑ Ⓒ   7 Ⓐ Ⓑ Ⓒ Ⓓ

3 Ⓐ Ⓑ Ⓒ Ⓓ Ⓔ Ⓕ   8 Ⓐ Ⓑ Ⓒ Ⓓ Ⓔ Ⓕ

4 Ⓐ Ⓑ Ⓒ Ⓓ   9 Ⓐ Ⓑ Ⓒ Ⓓ Ⓔ

5 Ⓐ Ⓑ Ⓒ Ⓓ   10 Ⓐ Ⓑ Ⓒ

GENERAL MECHANICAL UNDERSTANDING: PRACTICE TEST

1. How many switches do you have to close to light up at least one bulb?

   (A) 0
   (B) 1
   (C) 2
   (D) 3
   (E) 4

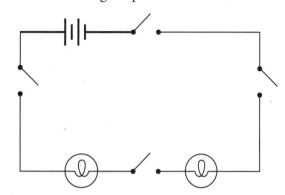

2. Will this bulb light up?

   (A) Yes
   (B) No
   (C) Can't tell

3. How many other pulleys will turn in the same direction of the largest pulley?

   (A) 0
   (B) 1
   (C) 2
   (D) 3
   (E) 4
   (F) 5

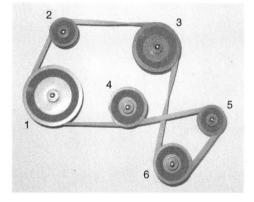

4. You want to lift this pole off the ground and carry it using one hand. Where should you pick it up to be able to carry it most easily?

   (A) A
   (B) B
   (C) C
   (D) It does not make a difference.

5. If you close both switches, how many bulbs will light up?

(A) 0
(B) 1
(C) 2
(D) 3

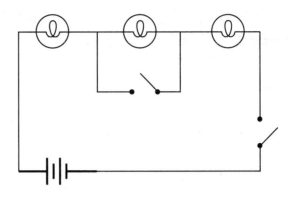

6. In this typical traffic signal, which light is the red one?

(A) A
(B) B
(C) C

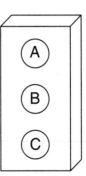

7. If you close the switch, how many bulbs will light up?

(A) None
(B) 1
(C) 2
(D) 3

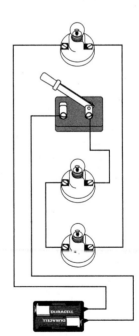

8. How many other pulleys will turn in the same direction of the largest pulley?

(A) 0
(B) 1
(C) 2
(D) 3
(E) 4
(F) 5

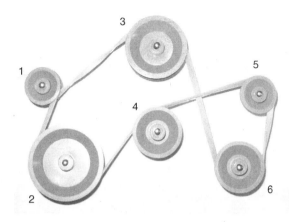

9. If you removed bulb 1 and closed the switch, how many bulbs would go on?

(A) 0
(B) 1
(C) 2
(D) 3
(E) Can't tell

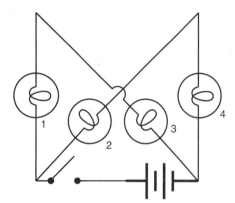

10. The girl wants to swing fast. On which swing can she go faster?

(A) A
(B) B
(C) No difference

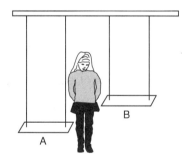

The answers to the practice test questions are on the next page.

Grading and Learning from the Practice Test on General Mechanical Understanding

1. **(E)** This is a series circuit. To have a path for the electricity to go from the battery through the lightbulbs and back to the battery, all the switches need to be closed.

2. **(B)** There is no electricity flowing through the bulb so it will not light up. There is no way for the electricity to flow from one end of the battery to the other.

3. **(D)** Pulleys 2, 3, and 4 will turn in the same direction as pulley 1.

4. **(C)** The pole is a lever. It will be balanced if you lift it in the middle.

5. **(C)** Closing the upper switch causes a path that is a short circuit for the middle bulb. The electricity will go through the switch rather than through the middle bulb.

6. **(A)** The red light is on the top in most traffic signals.

7. **(D)** This is a series circuit. The electricity will flow through all the bulbs.

8. **(B)** Only pulley 3 will turn in the same direction as pulley 2.

9. **(C)** You can trace a path for the electricity from the battery through bulbs 2 and 4 and back to the battery, so they will light up. You cannot do that for bulb 3, so bulb 3 will not light up.

10. **(B)** Short pendulums swing faster than long pendulums.

SUMMARIZE YOUR PERFORMANCE ON THE TIMED TEST

Number of questions you answered in 10 minutes:_____

Number of questions you got right: _____

Number of questions you got wrong: _____

Number of questions you left blank: _____

REVIEW YOUR PERFORMANCE ON THE TIMED TEST

You should try to get a high score on this test. If you got less than a perfect score, take the test a second time with no time limit. An average score on this test is about seven right.

If you answered fewer than 10 questions in 10 minutes, you should try to work faster.

If you finished the test before the time limit and did not get a perfect score, did you use the extra time to review your answers? Try to make it a habit to use any extra time to review your answers and your answer sheet.

GEARS: PRACTICE TEST

To get the most out of this practice test, take it twice.

- First take this test with the time limit shown below, and grade the test.

- Then take this test a second time with no time limit, answering every question. (It is best to wait a full day or even a week or two before taking the test a second time.)

After you take the test both ways, review every question you got wrong or were unsure about. Try to understand why the right answer is right and the other answers are wrong.

You will get the most out of this practice test if you **first read the chapter on Gears.** That chapter begins on page 49.

CHECKLIST FOR USING THIS PRACTICE TEST

Put a check mark in each box to keep track of your progress on this practice test.

- ❏ Take the test using the time limit.
- ❏ Grade the timed test.
- ❏ Review your performance on the timed test.

- ❏ Take the test a second time with no time limit.
- ❏ Grade the untimed test.

- ❏ Go over each question you got wrong.
- ❏ Go over each question you were not sure about.

Time Limit for This Test: 10 MINUTES

Instructions: Before you start, carefully tear out the answer sheet on the next page. Practice with an answer sheet is important. You will get the most out of this practice test if you take it the way you will take a real test.

Read each question and choose the correct answer. Then mark your answer on the answer sheet.

If you have extra time, use **all** of it to check your work. Your goal in taking the practice test should be to get the highest score possible. You do not get any credit for finishing early.

When you are ready to start, turn the page and answer questions 1 to 10.

Gears

Answer Sheet
PRACTICE TEST

Gears—Timed Test

Time Limit: 10 minutes

Time Started: _____

Time Ended: _____

Time Spent Taking This Test: _____

1 (A) (B) (C) (D) (E)   6 (A) (B) (C) (D) (E)

2 (A) (B) (C) (D) (E)   7 (A) (B) (C) (D)

3 (A) (B) (C) (D) (E)   8 (A) (B) (C) (D) (E)

4 (A) (B) (C) (D) (E)   9 (A) (B) (C) (D) (E)

5 (A) (B) (C) (D)   10 (A) (B) (C)

Gears—Untimed Test

1 (A) (B) (C) (D) (E)   6 (A) (B) (C) (D) (E)

2 (A) (B) (C) (D) (E)   7 (A) (B) (C) (D)

3 (A) (B) (C) (D) (E)   8 (A) (B) (C) (D) (E)

4 (A) (B) (C) (D) (E)   9 (A) (B) (C) (D) (E)

5 (A) (B) (C) (D)   10 (A) (B) (C)

GEARS: PRACTICE TEST

1. Which gear will turn fastest?

   (A) Gear A
   (B) Gear B
   (C) Gear D
   (D) Gear E
   (E) Can't tell

2. If gear B turns twice, gear A will turn _____ times.

   (A) 1
   (B) 2
   (C) 3
   (D) 4
   (E) 5

3. If A turns clockwise 20 times a second, then C turns

   (A) clockwise 20 times a second.
   (B) counterclockwise 20 times a second.
   (C) clockwise 10 times a second.
   (D) counterclockwise 10 times a second.
   (E) Can't tell

4. How many gears will turn faster than gear G?

(A) 1
(B) 2
(C) 4
(D) 6
(E) Can't tell

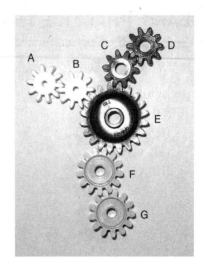

5. If gear C turns 10 times a minute, then gear D turns

(A) more than 10 times a minute.
(B) 10 times a minute.
(C) fewer than 10 times a minute.
(D) Can't tell

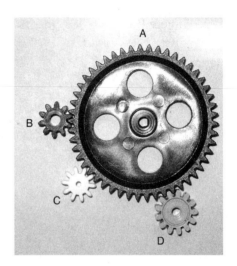

6. If the largest gear moves counterclockwise, how many other gears will turn counterclockwise?

(A) 0
(B) 1
(C) 3
(D) 5
(E) 6

7. Which gear will turn fastest?

   (A) A
   (B) B
   (C) C
   (D) Can't tell

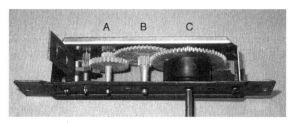

8. If gear D is turned as shown, how many other gears will turn in the same direction as D?

   (A) 0
   (B) 1
   (C) 2
   (D) 3
   (E) 4

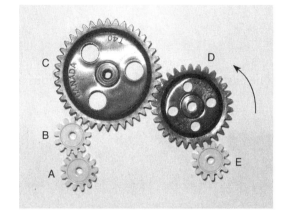

9. If the top gear turns 100 times a second, how many other gears will turn at the same speed?

   (A) 6
   (B) 7
   (C) 9
   (D) 11
   (E) Can't tell

10. If the bottom gear is turning as shown, which way will the top gear turn?

(A) A
(B) B
(C) Can't tell

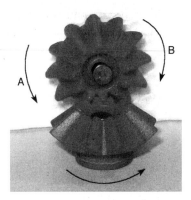

The answers to the practice test questions are on the next page.

Grading and Learning from the Practice Test on Gears

1. **(B)** The gear with the fewest teeth will turn fastest.

2. **(D)** Counting teeth shows that gear A has 10 and gear B has 20. So gear A turns twice as often as gear B. Two times 2 is 4.

3. **(A)** Connected gears with the same number of teeth turn at the same speed. Every other gear turns in the same direction.

4. **(C)** Gears A, B, C, and D all have 10 teeth so they will turn faster than gear G, which has 13 teeth.

5. **(C)** Gear D has 13 teeth, so it turns slower than gear A which has 10 teeth.

6. **(C)** Every gear next to the large gear turns clockwise, and every gear next to those gears turns counterclockwise.

7. **(A)** In each case a small gear is next to a large gear. The first small gear will turn fastest.

8. **(B)** Every other gear will turn in the same direction as D, so gears A, C, and E turn in the opposite direction, and B turns in the same direction as D.

9. **(A)** Connected gears the same size will turn at the same speed.

10. **(B)** Imagine the bottom gear turning very slowly and think about how the top gear would have to turn.

SUMMARIZE YOUR PERFORMANCE ON THE TIMED TEST

Number of questions you answered in 10 minutes:_____

Number of questions you got right: _____

Number of questions you got wrong: _____

Number of questions you left blank: _____

REVIEW YOUR PERFORMANCE ON THE TIMED TEST

You should try to get a high score on this test. If you got less than a perfect score, take the test a second time with no time limit. An average score on this test is about seven right.

If you answered fewer than 10 questions in 10 minutes, you should try to work faster.

If you finished the test before the time limit and did not get a perfect score, did you use the extra time to review your answers? Try to make it a habit to use any extra time to review your answers and your answer sheet.

Gears

PULLEYS: PRACTICE TEST

To get the most out of this practice test, take it twice.

- First take this test with the time limit shown below, and grade the test.

- Then take this test a second time with no time limit, answering every question. (It is best to wait a full day or even a week or two before taking the test a second time.)

After you take the test both ways, review every question you got wrong or were unsure about. Try to understand why the right answer is right and the other answers are wrong.

You will get the most out of this practice test if you **first read the chapter on Pulleys.** That chapter begins on page 67.

CHECKLIST FOR USING THIS PRACTICE TEST

Put a check mark in each box to keep track of your progress on this practice test.

- ❏ Take the test using the time limit.
- ❏ Grade the timed test.
- ❏ Review your performance on the timed test.

- ❏ Take the test a second time with no time limit.
- ❏ Grade the untimed test.

- ❏ Go over each question you got wrong.
- ❏ Go over each question you were not sure about.

Time Limit for This Test: 3 MINUTES

Instructions: Before you start, carefully tear out the answer sheet on the next page. Practice with an answer sheet is important. You will get the most out of this practice test if you take it the way you will take a real test.

Read each question and choose the correct answer. Then mark your answer on the answer sheet.

When you are ready to start, turn the page and answer questions 1 to 10.

Answer Sheet
PRACTICE TEST

Pulleys–Timed Test

Time Limit: 3 minutes

Time Started: _____

Time Ended: _____

Time Spent Taking This Test: _____

1 (A) (B) (C) (D) (E)   6 (A) (B) (C) (D) (E)

2 (A) (B) (C) (D) (E)   7 (A) (B) (C)

3 (A) (B) (C) (D) (E)   8 (A) (B) (C) (D) (E)

4 (A) (B) (C) (D) (E)   9 (A) (B) (C)

5 (A) (B) (C) (D)   10 (A) (B) (C) (D) (E)

Pulleys–Untimed Test

1 (A) (B) (C) (D) (E)   6 (A) (B) (C) (D) (E)

2 (A) (B) (C) (D) (E)   7 (A) (B) (C)

3 (A) (B) (C) (D) (E)   8 (A) (B) (C) (D) (E)

4 (A) (B) (C) (D) (E)   9 (A) (B) (C)

5 (A) (B) (C) (D)   10 (A) (B) (C) (D) (E)

PULLEYS

1. To lift the 150-pound weight you need to pull with a force of about _____ pounds.

    (A) 15
    (B) 75
    (C) 100
    (D) 150
    (E) 300

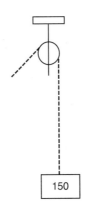

2. To lift the weight you need to pull with a force of about _____ pounds.

    (A) 20
    (B) 50
    (C) 100
    (D) 200
    (E) 400

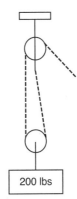

3. To lift the 200-pound weight you need to pull with a force of about _____ pounds.

    (A) 20
    (B) 50
    (C) 100
    (D) 150
    (E) 200

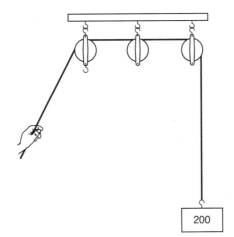

4. One end of the rope is attached to a wall and you are lifting on the other end. To lift the weight you need to pull with a force of about _____ pounds.

    (A) 25
    (B) 50
    (C) 75
    (D) 100
    (E) 200

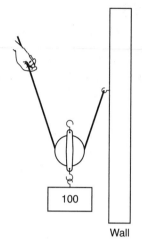

Wall

5. In these two drawings, the pulleys, the ropes, and the weights are all the same size. Which needs more force to lift the weight?

    (A) Drawing A
    (B) Drawing B
    (C) No difference

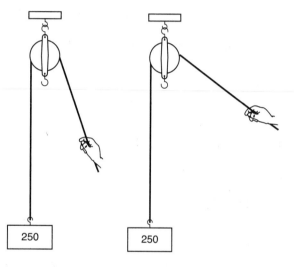

6. To lift the weight you need to pull with a force of about _____ pounds.

    (A) 30
    (B) 60
    (C) 90
    (D) 100
    (E) 300

7. Which way would take more force to lift the weight?

    (A) Drawing A
    (B) Drawing B
    (C) No difference

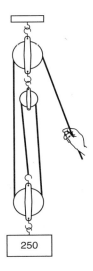
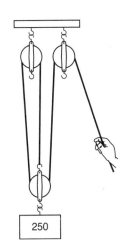

8. To lift the weight you need to pull with a force of about _____ pounds.

    (A) 20
    (B) 30
    (C) 60
    (D) 90
    (E) 120

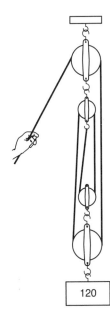

9. Is this stable?

   (A) Yes
   (B) No
   (C) Can't tell

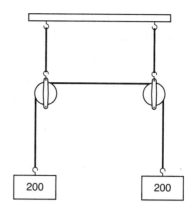

10. To lift the weight you need to pull
    with a force of about _____ pounds.

    (A) 50
    (B) 75
    (C) 125
    (D) 250
    (E) 500

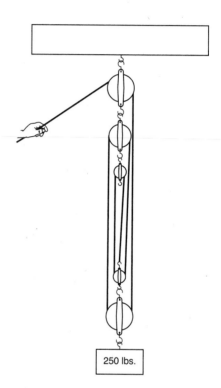

The answers to the practice test questions are on the next page.

Grading and Learning from the Practice Test on Pulleys

1. (**D**)
2. (**C**)
3. (**E**)
4. (**B**)
5. (**C**)
6. (**D**)
7. (**C**)
8. (**B**)
9. (**B**)
10. (**A**)

SUMMARIZE YOUR PERFORMANCE ON THE TIMED TEST

Number of questions you answered in three minutes:_____

Number of questions you got right: _____

Number of questions you got wrong: _____

Number of questions you left blank: _____

REVIEW YOUR PERFORMANCE ON THE TIMED TEST

You should try to get a high score on this test. If you got less than a perfect score, take the test a second time with no time limit. An average score on this test is about seven right.

If you answered fewer than 10 questions in three minutes, you should try to work faster.

If you finished the test before the time limit and did not get a perfect score, did you use the extra time to review your answers? Try to make it a habit to use any extra time to review your answers and your answer sheet.

TOOLS: PRACTICE TEST

To get the most out of this practice test, take it twice.

- First take this test with the time limit shown below, and grade the test.

- Then take this test a second time with no time limit, answering every question. (It is best to wait a full day or even a week or two before taking the test a second time.)

After you take the test both ways, review every question you got wrong or were unsure about. Try to understand why the right answer is right and the other answers are wrong.

You will get the most out of this practice test if you **first read the chapter on Tools.** That chapter begins on page 85.

CHECKLIST FOR USING THIS PRACTICE TEST

Put a check mark in each box to keep track of your progress on this practice test.

- ❏ Take the test using the time limit.
- ❏ Grade the timed test.
- ❏ Review your performance on the timed test.

- ❏ Take the test a second time with no time limit.
- ❏ Grade the untimed test.

- ❏ Go over each question you got wrong.
- ❏ Go over each question you were not sure about.

Time Limit for This Test: 4 MINUTES

Instructions: Before you start, carefully tear out the answer sheet on the next page. Practice with an answer sheet is important. You will get the most out of this practice test if you take it the way you will take a real test.

Read each question and choose the correct answer. Then mark your answer on the answer sheet.

When you are ready to start, turn the page and answer questions 1 to 10.

Answer Sheet
PRACTICE TEST

Tools—Timed Test

Time Limit: 4 minutes

Time Started: _____

Time Ended: _____

Time Spent Taking This Test: _____

1 Ⓐ Ⓑ Ⓒ Ⓓ   6 Ⓐ Ⓑ Ⓒ Ⓓ

2 Ⓐ Ⓑ Ⓒ Ⓓ   7 Ⓐ Ⓑ Ⓒ Ⓓ

3 Ⓐ Ⓑ Ⓒ Ⓓ   8 Ⓐ Ⓑ Ⓒ Ⓓ

4 Ⓐ Ⓑ Ⓒ Ⓓ   9 Ⓐ Ⓑ Ⓒ

5 Ⓐ Ⓑ Ⓒ Ⓓ   10 Ⓐ Ⓑ Ⓒ Ⓓ

Tools—Untimed Test

1 Ⓐ Ⓑ Ⓒ Ⓓ   6 Ⓐ Ⓑ Ⓒ Ⓓ

2 Ⓐ Ⓑ Ⓒ Ⓓ   7 Ⓐ Ⓑ Ⓒ Ⓓ

3 Ⓐ Ⓑ Ⓒ Ⓓ   8 Ⓐ Ⓑ Ⓒ Ⓓ

4 Ⓐ Ⓑ Ⓒ Ⓓ   9 Ⓐ Ⓑ Ⓒ

5 Ⓐ Ⓑ Ⓒ Ⓓ   10 Ⓐ Ⓑ Ⓒ Ⓓ

TOOLS: PRACTICE TEST

1. The letter A is next to the
   _____ part of this wrench.

   (A) open end
   (B) box
   (C) combination
   (D) crescent

2. What type of hammer is this?

   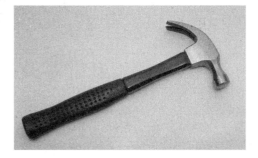

   (A) Ball peen
   (B) Claw
   (C) Sledge
   (D) Mallet

3. Which type of wrench is adjustable?

   (A) Box
   (B) Open end
   (C) Combination
   (D) Crescent

4. Which type of pliers is most often used in electrical work?

   (A) Slip-joint
   (B) Vise-grip®
   (C) Needle-nose
   (D) Channel-lock

5. What word is used for this?

   (A) Blade
   (B) Phillips
   (C) Cross-cut
   (D) Stilson

6. The name for these pliers is:

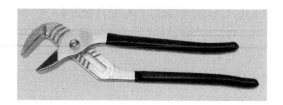

   (A) channel-lock.
   (B) needle-nose.
   (C) slip-joint.
   (D) Vise-grip®

7. Which part is the peen?

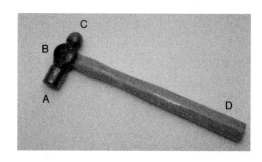

   (A) A
   (B) B
   (C) C
   (D) D

8. Which of these pliers usually has long handles?

   (A) Slip-joint
   (B) Vise-grip®
   (C) Channel-lock
   (D) Needle-nose

9. This wrench is made to be used on:

   (A) pipes.
   (B) bolts.
   (C) both pipe and bolts.

10. To cut a curve at the end of a flat piece of wood it is best to use a:

   (A) wood saw.
   (B) saber saw.
   (C) hacksaw.
   (D) circular saw.

The answers to the practice test questions are on the next page.

Grading and Learning from the Practice Test on Tools

1. (**B**)
2. (**B**)
3. (**D**)
4. (**C**)
5. (**B**)
6. (**A**)
7. (**C**)
8. (**C**)
9. (**A**)
10. (**B**)

SUMMARIZE YOUR PERFORMANCE ON THE TIMED TEST

Number of questions you answered in four minutes:_____

Number of questions you got right: _____

Number of questions you got wrong: _____

Number of questions you left blank: _____

REVIEW YOUR PERFORMANCE ON THE TIMED TEST

You should try to get a high score on this test. If you got less than a perfect score, take the test a second time with no time limit. An average score on this test is about nine right.

If you answered fewer than 10 questions in four minutes, you should try to work faster.

MAP READING: PRACTICE TEST

To get the most out of this practice test, take it twice.

- First take this test with the time limit shown below, and grade the test.

- Then take this test a second time with no time limit, answering every question. (It is best to wait a full day or even a week or two before taking the test a second time.)

After you take the test both ways, review every question you got wrong or were unsure about. Try to understand why the right answer is right and the other answers are wrong.

You will get the most out of this practice test if you **first read the chapter on Map Reading.** That chapter begins on page 101.

CHECKLIST FOR USING THIS PRACTICE TEST

Put a check mark in each box to keep track of your progress on this practice test.

- ❏ Take the test using the time limit.
- ❏ Grade the timed test.
- ❏ Review your performance on the timed test.

- ❏ Take the test a second time with no time limit.
- ❏ Grade the untimed test.

- ❏ Go over each question you got wrong.
- ❏ Go over each question you were not sure about.

Time Limit for This Test: **15 MINUTES**

Before You Start

Before you start, carefully tear out the answer sheet on the next page. Practice with an answer sheet is important. You will get the most out of this practice test if you take it the way you will take a real test.

Answer Sheet
PRACTICE TEST

Map Reading—Timed Test

Time Limit: 15 minutes

Time Started: _____

Time Ended: _____

Time Spent Taking This Test: _____

1 Ⓐ Ⓑ Ⓒ Ⓓ Ⓔ   6 Ⓐ Ⓑ Ⓒ Ⓓ Ⓔ

2 Ⓐ Ⓑ Ⓒ Ⓓ Ⓔ   7 Ⓐ Ⓑ Ⓒ Ⓓ Ⓔ

3 Ⓐ Ⓑ Ⓒ Ⓓ Ⓔ   8 Ⓐ Ⓑ Ⓒ Ⓓ Ⓔ

4 Ⓐ Ⓑ Ⓒ Ⓓ Ⓔ   9 Ⓐ Ⓑ Ⓒ Ⓓ Ⓔ

5 Ⓐ Ⓑ Ⓒ Ⓓ Ⓔ   10 Ⓐ Ⓑ Ⓒ Ⓓ Ⓔ

Map Reading—Untimed Test

1 Ⓐ Ⓑ Ⓒ Ⓓ Ⓔ   6 Ⓐ Ⓑ Ⓒ Ⓓ Ⓔ

2 Ⓐ Ⓑ Ⓒ Ⓓ Ⓔ   7 Ⓐ Ⓑ Ⓒ Ⓓ Ⓔ

3 Ⓐ Ⓑ Ⓒ Ⓓ Ⓔ   8 Ⓐ Ⓑ Ⓒ Ⓓ Ⓔ

4 Ⓐ Ⓑ Ⓒ Ⓓ Ⓔ   9 Ⓐ Ⓑ Ⓒ Ⓓ Ⓔ

5 Ⓐ Ⓑ Ⓒ Ⓓ Ⓔ   10 Ⓐ Ⓑ Ⓒ Ⓓ Ⓔ

Instructions: Use the map on page 326 to answer the questions. One-way streets are marked with arrows. Streets that are not marked are two-way. Follow traffic laws when answering the questions. Buildings are numbered like this: 1500–1599 between 15th St. and 16th St., 1600–1699 between 16th St. and 17th St., and so on. When you count blocks, count one whenever you get to a cross street, whether the cross street is on the left or the right or both, and whatever the size or shape of the block.

If you have extra time, check your answers.

When you are ready to start, turn the page and answer questions 1 to 10.

USE THIS MAP TO HELP ANSWER THE QUESTIONS

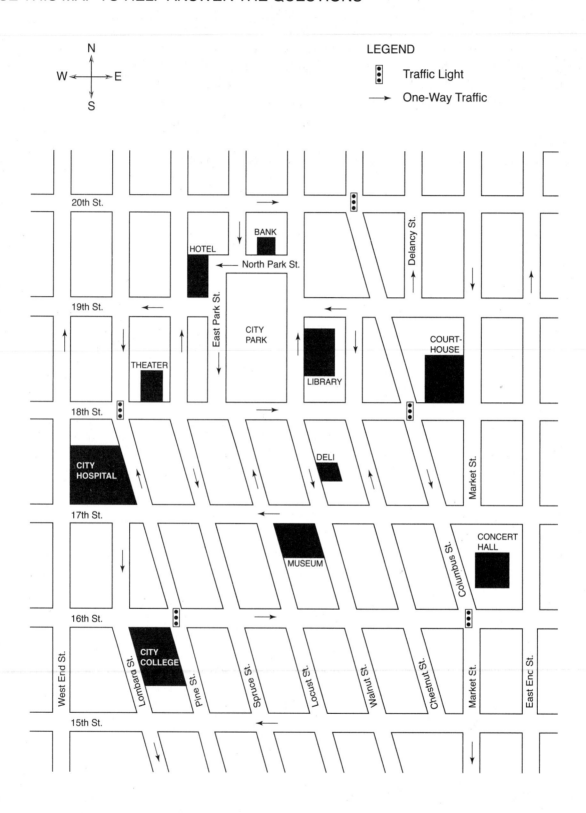

MAP READING: PRACTICE TEST

1. You are at the intersection of 16th St. and Spruce St. You walk two blocks east, two blocks northwest, three blocks east, one block south, and five blocks west. You are now at:

   (A) 20th St. and Walnut St.
   (B) 16th St. and Pine St.
   (C) 17th and Spruce St.
   (D) the museum.
   (E) the city hospital.

2. You are driving on 17th St. What is the next street you would come to after crossing Market St.?

   (A) East End St.
   (B) Columbus St.
   (C) Chestnut St.
   (D) 18th St.
   (E) 16th St.

3. You are parked in front of the library and want to go to the theater. Which of the following is the shortest way to drive there?

   (A) North on Walnut St., west on 20th St., south on Pine St., east on 18th St.
   (B) South on Walnut St., west on 18th St.
   (C) North on Walnut St., west on North Park St., south on East Park St., west on 18th St.
   (D) North on Walnut St., west on North Park St., south on East Park St., west on 19th St., south on Pine St., east on 18th St.
   (E) North on Walnut St., east on 19th St., south on Chestnut St., West on 18th St.

4. You are parked on East Park St. in front of the Hotel. Which of the following is the shortest route to drive to the deli?

   (A) South on East Park St., turn right on 18th St., turn right on Columbus St., turn left on 17th St., turn right on Walnut St.
   (B) South on East Park St., turn right on 18th St., turn right on Chestnut St., turn left on 17th St., turn right on Walnut St.
   (C) South on East Park St., turn right on 18th St., then right on Walnut St.
   (D) South on East Park St., turn left on 18th St., turn right on Chestnut St., turn right on 17th St., turn right on Walnut St.
   (E) South on East Park St., turn left on 18th St., then right on Walnut St.

USE THIS MAP TO HELP ANSWER THE QUESTIONS

The map is repeated here so you do not have to turn back when answering the questions.

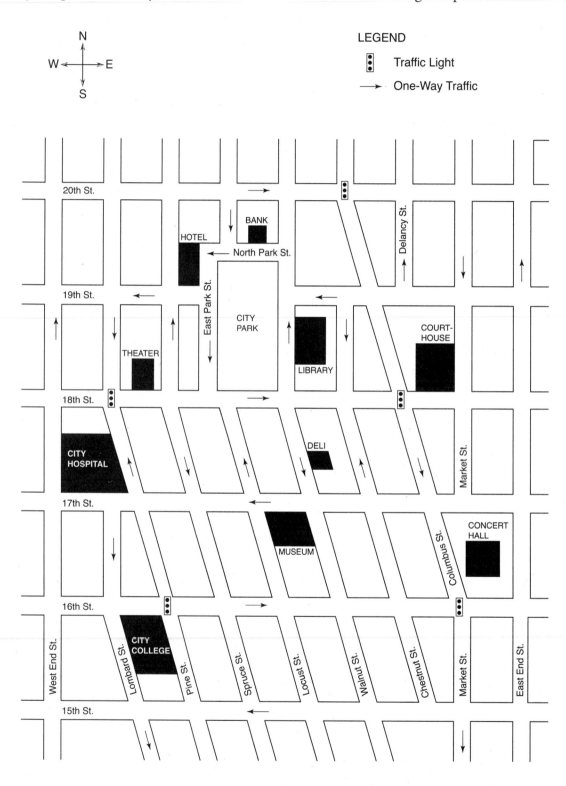

5. There has been an accident at 1723 Market St. An ambulance leaves the hospital and travels south on Lombard St. Which is the best route to the scene of the accident?

   (A) East on 16th St., northwest on Chestnut St., east on 18th St., south on Market St.

   (B) East on 16th St., northwest on Market St., east on 17th St., north on Market St.

   (C) East on 16th St., north on East End St., west on 18th St., south on Market St.

   (D) East on 17th St., north on Market St.

   (E) East on 16th St., north on East End St., west on 19th St., south on Market St.

6. The address of your favorite restaurant is 1615 Spruce St. The restaurant is on:

   (A) 16th St. between Spruce St. and Locust St.

   (B) 16th St. between Pine St. and Spruce St.

   (C) Spruce St. between Pine St. and Locust St.

   (D) Spruce St. between 16th St. and 17th St.

   (E) Spruce St. between 15th St. and 16th St.

7. Tomorrow there will be a street fair on Walnut St. between 15th St. and North Park St. That section of Walnut St. will be closed to traffic between 7 A.M. and 7 P.M. At 2 P.M. tomorrow you must drive from the 16th St. side of City College to the 18th St. side of the courthouse. Of the following, the most direct way for you to go is to:

   (A) travel east on 16th St., turn left on Chestnut St., turn right on 18th St.

   (B) travel east on 16th St., turn left on Pine St., turn right on 18th St.

   (C) travel east on 16th St., go northwest on Pine St., turn right on 18th St., turn left on Spruce St., turn right on 20th St., turn right on Columbus St., turn left on 18th St.

   (D) travel east on 16th St., go northwest on Pine St., turn right on 18th St., turn left on Spruce St., turn right on 20th St., turn right on Columbus St., turn right on 18th St.

   (E) travel east on 16th St., turn left on Pine St., turn right on 20th St., turn right on Columbus St., turn left on 18th St.

8. You are at the intersection of 19th St. and Market St. You walk one block south, three blocks west, one block southeast, three blocks west, one block northwest, one block east, and one block north. You are now closest to:

   (A) the hotel

   (B) city hospital

   (C) the library

   (D) 19th St. and Pine St.

   (E) 19th St. and Market St.

USE THIS MAP TO HELP ANSWER THE QUESTIONS

The map is repeated here so you do not have to turn back when answering the questions.

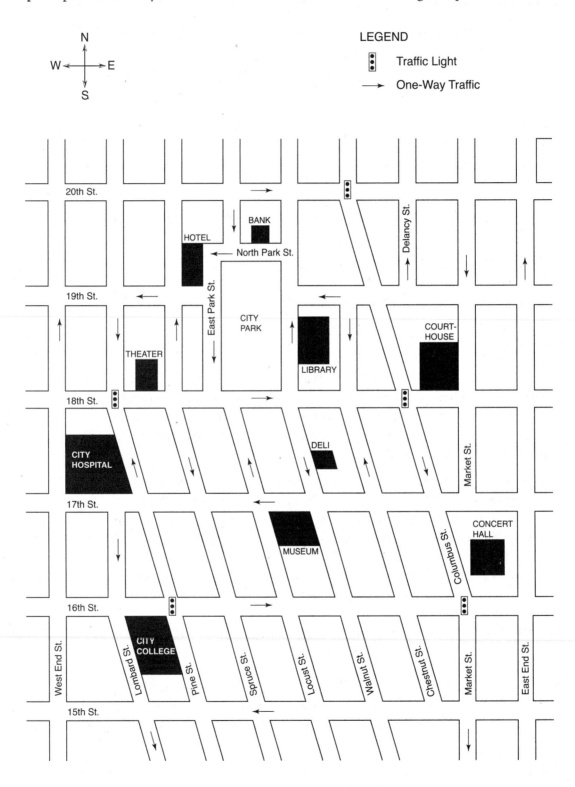

9. Your car is parked in front of the bank. If you take the first possible left and then the first possible right you will be near the:

   (A) hotel.
   (B) city hospital.
   (C) courthouse.
   (D) museum.
   (E) theater.

10. You drive by the most direct route from the bank to the entrance of City College on Pine St. How many traffic lights do you pass on the way?

    (A) 0
    (B) 1
    (C) 2
    (D) 3
    (E) 4

The answers to the practice test questions are on the next page.

Map Reading

Grading and Learning from the Practice Test on Map Reading

1. **(C)**

2. **(B)**

3. **(D)**

4. **(E)**

5. **(A)**

6. **(D)**

7. **(C)**

8. **(A)**

9. **(A)**

10. **(B)**

SUMMARIZE YOUR PERFORMANCE ON THE TIMED TEST

Number of questions you answered in 15 minutes:_____

Number of questions you got right: _____

Number of questions you got wrong: _____

Number of questions you left blank: _____

REVIEW YOUR PERFORMANCE ON THE TIMED TEST

You should try to get a very high score on this test. If you got less than a perfect score, take the test a second time with no time limit. An average score on this test is about six right.

If you answered fewer than 10 questions in 15 minutes, you should try to work faster.

If you finished the test before the time limit and did not get a perfect score, did you use the extra time to review your answers? Try to make it a habit to use any extra time to review your answers and your answer sheet.

LINE FOLLOWING: PRACTICE TEST

To get the most out of this practice test, take it twice.

- First take this test with the time limit shown below, and grade the test.

- Then take this test a second time with no time limit, answering every question. (It is best to wait a full day or even a week or two before taking the test a second time.)

After you take the test both ways, review every question you got wrong or were unsure about. Try to understand why the right answer is right and the other answers are wrong.

You will get the most out of this practice test if you **first read the chapter on Line Following.** That chapter begins on page 121.

CHECKLIST FOR USING THIS PRACTICE TEST

Put a check mark in each box to keep track of your progress on this practice test.

- ❏ Take the test using the time limit.
- ❏ Grade the timed test.
- ❏ Review your performance on the timed test.

- ❏ Take the test a second time with no time limit.
- ❏ Grade the untimed test.

- ❏ Go over each question you got wrong.
- ❏ Go over each question you were not sure about.

Time Limit for This Test: 3½ MINUTES

Instructions: Before you start, carefully tear out the answer sheet on the next page. Practice with an answer sheet is important, especially for tests like this one with short time limits.

The test has 20 numbered boxes. Trace the line leading from each numbered box until it comes to a letter. Mark that letter on your answer sheet.

When you are ready to start, turn the page and answer questions 1 to 20.

Answer Sheet
PRACTICE TEST

Line Following—Timed Test

Time Limit: 3½ minutes

Time Started: _____

Time Ended: _____

Time Spent Taking This Test: _____

1 ⒶⒷⒸⒹⒺ 6 ⒶⒷⒸⒹⒺ 11 ⒶⒷⒸⒹⒺ 16 ⒶⒷⒸⒹⒺ

2 ⒶⒷⒸⒹⒺ 7 ⒶⒷⒸⒹⒺ 12 ⒶⒷⒸⒹⒺ 17 ⒶⒷⒸⒹⒺ

3 ⒶⒷⒸⒹⒺ 8 ⒶⒷⒸⒹⒺ 13 ⒶⒷⒸⒹⒺ 18 ⒶⒷⒸⒹⒺ

4 ⒶⒷⒸⒹⒺ 9 ⒶⒷⒸⒹⒺ 14 ⒶⒷⒸⒹⒺ 19 ⒶⒷⒸⒹⒺ

5 ⒶⒷⒸⒹⒺ 10 ⒶⒷⒸⒹⒺ 15 ⒶⒷⒸⒹⒺ 20 ⒶⒷⒸⒹⒺ

Line Following—Untimed Test

1 ⒶⒷⒸⒹⒺ 6 ⒶⒷⒸⒹⒺ 11 ⒶⒷⒸⒹⒺ 16 ⒶⒷⒸⒹⒺ

2 ⒶⒷⒸⒹⒺ 7 ⒶⒷⒸⒹⒺ 12 ⒶⒷⒸⒹⒺ 17 ⒶⒷⒸⒹⒺ

3 ⒶⒷⒸⒹⒺ 8 ⒶⒷⒸⒹⒺ 13 ⒶⒷⒸⒹⒺ 18 ⒶⒷⒸⒹⒺ

4 ⒶⒷⒸⒹⒺ 9 ⒶⒷⒸⒹⒺ 14 ⒶⒷⒸⒹⒺ 19 ⒶⒷⒸⒹⒺ

5 ⒶⒷⒸⒹⒺ 10 ⒶⒷⒸⒹⒺ 15 ⒶⒷⒸⒹⒺ 20 ⒶⒷⒸⒹⒺ

LINE FOLLOWING: PRACTICE TEST

For each numbered box, follow the line to a lettered box.

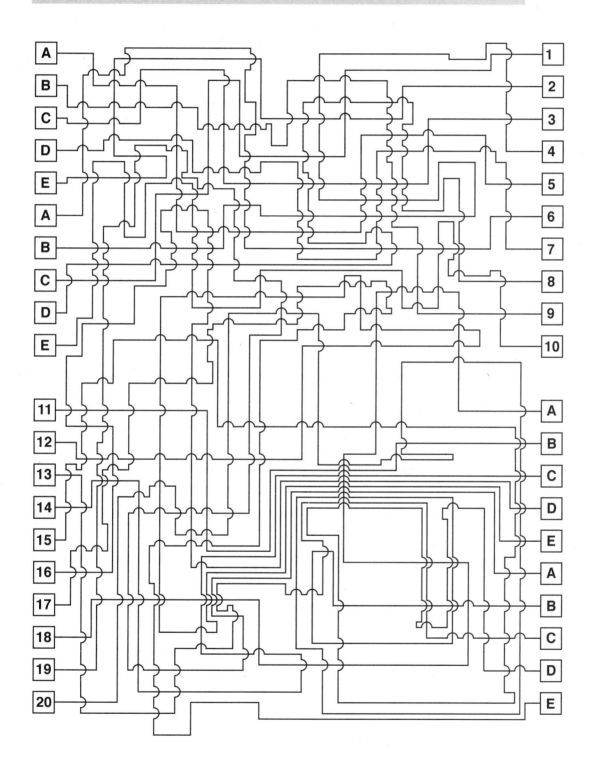

The answers to the practice test questions are on the next page.

Grading and Learning from the Practice Test on Line Following

1. (C)	11. (B)
2. (E)	12. (E)
3. (C)	13. (C)
4. (B)	14. (C)
5. (A)	15. (D)
6. (A)	16. (D)
7. (D)	17. (E)
8. (D)	18. (A)
9. (B)	19. (A)
10. (E)	20. (B)

SUMMARIZE YOUR PERFORMANCE ON THE TIMED TEST

Number of questions you answered in 3½ minutes:_____

Number of questions you got right: _____

Number of questions you got wrong: _____

Number of questions you left blank: _____

REVIEW YOUR PERFORMANCE ON THE TIMED TEST

You should try to get a high score on this test. If you got less than a perfect score, take the test a second time with no time limit. An average score on this test is about 11 right.

If you answered fewer than 12 questions in 3½ minutes, you should try to work faster.

MATCHING SHAPES: PRACTICE TEST

To get the most out of this practice test, take it twice.

- First take this test with the time limit shown below, and grade the test.

- Then take this test a second time with no time limit, answering every question. (It is best to wait a full day or even a week or two before taking the test a second time.)

After you take the test both ways, review every question you got wrong or were unsure about. Try to understand why the right answer is right and the other answers are wrong.

You will get the most out of this practice test if you **first read the chapter on Matching Shapes.** That chapter begins on page 127.

> ## CHECKLIST FOR USING THIS PRACTICE TEST
>
> Put a check mark in each box to keep track of your progress on this practice test.
>
> ❏ Take the test using the time limit.
> ❏ Grade the timed test.
> ❏ Review your performance on the timed test.
>
> ❏ Take the test a second time with no time limit.
> ❏ Grade the untimed test.
>
> ❏ Go over each question you got wrong.
> ❏ Go over each question you were not sure about.

Time Limit for This Test: **4 MINUTES**

Instructions: Before you start, carefully tear out the answer sheet on the next page. Practice with an answer sheet is important, and especially for tests like this one with short time limits.

Look at each numbered shape on the top half of the page, and find the lettered shape on the bottom half of the page that is exactly the same. Then mark your answer on the answer sheet.

When you are ready to start, turn the page and answer questions 1 to 30.

Answer Sheet
PRACTICE TEST

Matching Shapes—Timed Test

Time Limit: 4 minutes

Time Started: _____

Time Ended: _____

Time Spent Taking This Test: _____

	D F G I L	Q R T BB DD		B E H J K	M O S U AA
1	○ ○ ○ ○ ○	○ ○ ○ ○ ○	16	○ ○ ○ ○ ○	○ ○ ○ ○ ○
	D F G I L	Q R T BB DD		A C N P V	W X Y Z CC
2	○ ○ ○ ○ ○	○ ○ ○ ○ ○	17	○ ○ ○ ○ ○	○ ○ ○ ○ ○
	A C N P V	W X Y Z CC		B E H J K	M O S U AA
3	○ ○ ○ ○ ○	○ ○ ○ ○ ○	18	○ ○ ○ ○ ○	○ ○ ○ ○ ○
	D F G I L	Q R T BB DD		D F G I L	Q R T BB DD
4	○ ○ ○ ○ ○	○ ○ ○ ○ ○	19	○ ○ ○ ○ ○	○ ○ ○ ○ ○
	A C N P V	W X Y Z CC		B E H J K	M O S U AA
5	○ ○ ○ ○ ○	○ ○ ○ ○ ○	20	○ ○ ○ ○ ○	○ ○ ○ ○ ○
	B E H J K	M O S U AA		D F G I L	Q R T BB DD
6	○ ○ ○ ○ ○	○ ○ ○ ○ ○	21	○ ○ ○ ○ ○	○ ○ ○ ○ ○
	D F G I L	Q R T BB DD		B E H J K	M O S U AA
7	○ ○ ○ ○ ○	○ ○ ○ ○ ○	22	○ ○ ○ ○ ○	○ ○ ○ ○ ○
	B E H J K	M O S U AA		A C N P V	W X Y Z CC
8	○ ○ ○ ○ ○	○ ○ ○ ○ ○	23	○ ○ ○ ○ ○	○ ○ ○ ○ ○
	A C N P V	W X Y Z CC		D F G I L	Q R T BB DD
9	○ ○ ○ ○ ○	○ ○ ○ ○ ○	24	○ ○ ○ ○ ○	○ ○ ○ ○ ○
	B E H J K	M O S U AA		A C N P V	W X Y Z CC
10	○ ○ ○ ○ ○	○ ○ ○ ○ ○	25	○ ○ ○ ○ ○	○ ○ ○ ○ ○
	B E H J K	M O S U AA		A C N P V	W X Y Z CC
11	○ ○ ○ ○ ○	○ ○ ○ ○ ○	26	○ ○ ○ ○ ○	○ ○ ○ ○ ○
	A C N P V	W X Y Z CC		B E H J K	M O S U AA
12	○ ○ ○ ○ ○	○ ○ ○ ○ ○	27	○ ○ ○ ○ ○	○ ○ ○ ○ ○
	A C N P V	W X Y Z CC		D F G I L	Q R T BB DD
13	○ ○ ○ ○ ○	○ ○ ○ ○ ○	28	○ ○ ○ ○ ○	○ ○ ○ ○ ○
	B E H J K	M O S U AA		D F G I L	Q R T BB DD
14	○ ○ ○ ○ ○	○ ○ ○ ○ ○	29	○ ○ ○ ○ ○	○ ○ ○ ○ ○
	D F G I L	Q R T BB DD		A C N P V	W X Y Z CC
15	○ ○ ○ ○ ○	○ ○ ○ ○ ○	30	○ ○ ○ ○ ○	○ ○ ○ ○ ○

Answer Sheet
PRACTICE TEST

Matching Shapes—Untimed Test

	D F G I L	Q R T BB DD			B E H J K	M O S U AA
1	○ ○ ○ ○ ○	○ ○ ○ ○ ○	16	○ ○ ○ ○ ○	○ ○ ○ ○ ○
2	D F G I L ○ ○ ○ ○ ○	Q R T BB DD ○ ○ ○ ○ ○	17	A C N P V ○ ○ ○ ○ ○	W X Y Z CC ○ ○ ○ ○ ○
3	A C N P V ○ ○ ○ ○ ○	W X Y Z CC ○ ○ ○ ○ ○	18	B E H J K ○ ○ ○ ○ ○	M O S U AA ○ ○ ○ ○ ○
4	D F G I L ○ ○ ○ ○ ○	Q R T BB DD ○ ○ ○ ○ ○	19	D F G I L ○ ○ ○ ○ ○	Q R T BB DD ○ ○ ○ ○ ○
5	A C N P V ○ ○ ○ ○ ○	W X Y Z CC ○ ○ ○ ○ ○	20	B E H J K ○ ○ ○ ○ ○	M O S U AA ○ ○ ○ ○ ○
6	B E H J K ○ ○ ○ ○ ○	M O S U AA ○ ○ ○ ○ ○	21	D F G I L ○ ○ ○ ○ ○	Q R T BB DD ○ ○ ○ ○ ○
7	D F G I L ○ ○ ○ ○ ○	Q R T BB DD ○ ○ ○ ○ ○	22	B E H J K ○ ○ ○ ○ ○	M O S U AA ○ ○ ○ ○ ○
8	B E H J K ○ ○ ○ ○ ○	M O S U AA ○ ○ ○ ○ ○	23	A C N P V ○ ○ ○ ○ ○	W X Y Z CC ○ ○ ○ ○ ○
9	A C N P V ○ ○ ○ ○ ○	W X Y Z CC ○ ○ ○ ○ ○	24	D F G I L ○ ○ ○ ○ ○	Q R T BB DD ○ ○ ○ ○ ○
10	B E H J K ○ ○ ○ ○ ○	M O S U AA ○ ○ ○ ○ ○	25	A C N P V ○ ○ ○ ○ ○	W X Y Z CC ○ ○ ○ ○ ○
11	B E H J K ○ ○ ○ ○ ○	M O S U AA ○ ○ ○ ○ ○	26	A C N P V ○ ○ ○ ○ ○	W X Y Z CC ○ ○ ○ ○ ○
12	A C N P V ○ ○ ○ ○ ○	W X Y Z CC ○ ○ ○ ○ ○	27	B E H J K ○ ○ ○ ○ ○	M O S U AA ○ ○ ○ ○ ○
13	A C N P V ○ ○ ○ ○ ○	W X Y Z CC ○ ○ ○ ○ ○	28	D F G I L ○ ○ ○ ○ ○	Q R T BB DD ○ ○ ○ ○ ○
14	B E H J K ○ ○ ○ ○ ○	M O S U AA ○ ○ ○ ○ ○	29	D F G I L ○ ○ ○ ○ ○	Q R T BB DD ○ ○ ○ ○ ○
15	D F G I L ○ ○ ○ ○ ○	Q R T BB DD ○ ○ ○ ○ ○	30	A C N P V ○ ○ ○ ○ ○	W X Y Z CC ○ ○ ○ ○ ○

MATCHING SHAPES: PRACTICE TEST

The answers to the practice test questions are on the next page.

Grading and Learning from the Practice Test on Matching Shapes

Matching Shapes

Answer Key
PRACTICE TEST

Matching Shapes

#	Answer	#	Answer
1	D F G I **L** · Q R T BB DD	16	B E H J K · M O S U **AA**
2	D F G I L · Q R T BB **DD**	17	A **C** N P V · W X Y Z CC
3	A C N **P** V · W X Y Z CC	18	B E H **J** K · M O S U AA
4	D F G I L · **Q** R T BB DD	19	**D** F G I L · Q R T BB DD
5	A C N P V · W X Y Z **CC**	20	B E H J K · **M** O S U AA
6	B E H J **K** · M O S U AA	21	D F G I L · Q **R** T BB DD
7	D F G I L · Q R **T** BB DD	22	**B** E H J K · M O S U AA
8	B E H J K · M **O** S U AA	23	**A** C N P V · W X Y Z CC
9	A C N P V · W **X** Y Z CC	24	D F **G** I L · Q R T BB DD
10	B E **H** J K · M O S U AA	25	A C N P V · W X **Y** Z CC
11	B E H J K · M O S **U** AA	26	A C N P **V** · W X Y Z CC
12	A C **N** P V · W X Y Z CC	27	B E H J K · M O **S** U AA
13	A C N P V · **W** X Y Z CC	28	D F G I L · Q R T **BB** DD
14	B **E** H J K · M O S U AA	29	D **F** G I L · Q R T BB DD
15	**D** F G I L · Q R T BB DD	30	A C N P V · W X Y **Z** CC

SUMMARIZE YOUR PERFORMANCE ON THE TIMED TEST

Number of questions you answered in four minutes:_____

Number of questions you got right: _____

Number of questions you got wrong: _____

Number of questions you left blank: _____

REVIEW YOUR PERFORMANCE ON THE TIMED TEST

You should try to get a high score on this test. If you got less than a perfect score, take the test a second time with no time limit. An average score on this test is about 12 right.

If you answered fewer than 17 questions in four minutes, you should try to work faster.

VISUAL COMPARISON: PRACTICE TEST

To get the most out of this practice test, take it twice.

- First take this test with the time limit shown below, and grade the test.

- Then take this test a second time with no time limit, answering every question.

After you take the test both ways, review every question you got wrong or were unsure about. Try to understand why the right answer is right and the other answers are wrong.

You will get the most out of this practice test if you **first read the chapter on Visual Comparison.** That chapter begins on page 135.

CHECKLIST FOR USING THIS PRACTICE TEST

Put a check mark in each box to keep track of your progress on this practice test.

- ❏ Take the test using the time limit.
- ❏ Grade the timed test.
- ❏ Review your performance on the timed test.

- ❏ Take the test a second time with no time limit.
- ❏ Grade the untimed test.

- ❏ Go over each question you got wrong.
- ❏ Go over each question you were not sure about.

Time Limit for This Test: 3 MINUTES

Instructions: Before you start, carefully tear out the answer sheet for this test. Practice with an answer sheet is important, especially for tests like this one with short time limits.

For each question, choose the two drawings that are exactly the same. Then fill in the two bubbles on the answer sheet for these two choices. The answer sheet has a sample answer that shows you how to do this.

When you are ready to start, turn the page and answer questions 1 to 10.

Answer Sheet
PRACTICE TEST

Visual Comparison—Timed Test

Time Limit: 3 minutes

Sample Answer
If you decide choices A and D are exactly the same, you should fill in your answer sheet like this:

● Ⓑ Ⓒ ● Ⓔ

Time Started: _____

Time Ended: _____

Time Spent Taking This Test: _____

1 Ⓐ Ⓑ Ⓒ Ⓓ Ⓔ   6 Ⓐ Ⓑ Ⓒ Ⓓ Ⓔ

2 Ⓐ Ⓑ Ⓒ Ⓓ Ⓔ   7 Ⓐ Ⓑ Ⓒ Ⓓ Ⓔ

3 Ⓐ Ⓑ Ⓒ Ⓓ Ⓔ   8 Ⓐ Ⓑ Ⓒ Ⓓ Ⓔ

4 Ⓐ Ⓑ Ⓒ Ⓓ Ⓔ   9 Ⓐ Ⓑ Ⓒ Ⓓ Ⓔ

5 Ⓐ Ⓑ Ⓒ Ⓓ Ⓔ   10 Ⓐ Ⓑ Ⓒ Ⓓ Ⓔ

Visual Comparison—Untimed Test

1 Ⓐ Ⓑ Ⓒ Ⓓ Ⓔ   6 Ⓐ Ⓑ Ⓒ Ⓓ Ⓔ

2 Ⓐ Ⓑ Ⓒ Ⓓ Ⓔ   7 Ⓐ Ⓑ Ⓒ Ⓓ Ⓔ

3 Ⓐ Ⓑ Ⓒ Ⓓ Ⓔ   8 Ⓐ Ⓑ Ⓒ Ⓓ Ⓔ

4 Ⓐ Ⓑ Ⓒ Ⓓ Ⓔ   9 Ⓐ Ⓑ Ⓒ Ⓓ Ⓔ

5 Ⓐ Ⓑ Ⓒ Ⓓ Ⓔ   10 Ⓐ Ⓑ Ⓒ Ⓓ Ⓔ

VISUAL COMPARISON: PRACTICE TEST

For each question on this page, find the two choices that are exactly the same.

1.

   A   B   C   D   E

2.

   A   B   C   D   E

3.

   A   B   C   D   E

4.

   A   B   C   D   E

5.

   A   B   C   D   E

6.

   A   B   C   D   E

7.

   A   B   C   D   E

Visual Comparison

8.

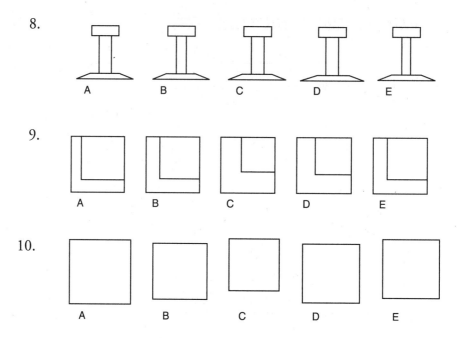

9.

10.

The answers to the practice test questions are on the next page.

Grading and Learning from the Practice Test on Visual Comparison

1. **(A)**, **(B)**

2. **(C)**, **(E)**

3. **(A)**, **(E)**

4. **(A)**, **(D)**

5. **(A)**, **(C)**

6. **(A)**, **(E)**

7. **(C)**, **(D)**

8. **(A)**, **(C)**

9. **(B)**, **(E)**

10. **(D)**, **(E)**

SUMMARIZE YOUR PERFORMANCE ON THE TIMED TEST

Number of questions you answered in three minutes:_____

Number of questions you got right: _____

Number of questions you got wrong: _____

Number of questions you left blank: _____

REVIEW YOUR PERFORMANCE ON THE TIMED TEST

You should try to get a high score on this test. If you got less than a perfect score, take the test a second time with no time limit. An average score on this test is about five right.

If you answered fewer than nine questions in three minutes, you should try to work faster.

Visual Comparison

FINDING ROTATED SHAPES: PRACTICE TEST

To get the most out of this practice test, take it twice.

- First take this test with the time limit shown below, and grade the test.

- Then take this test a second time with no time limit, answering every question. (It is best to wait a full day or even a week or two before taking the test a second time.)

After you take the test both ways, review every question you got wrong or were unsure about. Try to understand why the right answer is right and the other answers are wrong.

You will get the most out of this practice test if you **first read the chapter on Finding Rotated Shapes.** That chapter begins on page 141.

CHECKLIST FOR USING THIS PRACTICE TEST

Put a check mark in each box to keep track of your progress on this practice test.

- ❏ Take the test using the time limit.
- ❏ Grade the timed test.
- ❏ Review your performance on the timed test.

- ❏ Take the test a second time with no time limit.
- ❏ Grade the untimed test.

- ❏ Go over each question you got wrong.
- ❏ Go over each question you were not sure about.

Time Limit for This Test: 2½ MINUTES

Instructions: Before you start, carefully tear out the answer sheet for this test on the next page. Practice with an answer sheet is important, especially for tests like this one with short time limits.

For each numbered shape, choose the letter of the shape that is exactly the same and not flipped over. Then mark your answer on the answer sheet.

When you are ready to start, turn the page and answer questions 1 to 10.

Answer Sheet
PRACTICE TEST

Finding Rotated Shapes—Timed Test

Time Limit: 2½ minutes

Time Started: _____

Time Ended: _____

Time Spent Taking This Test: _____

1 Ⓐ Ⓑ Ⓒ Ⓓ Ⓔ   6 Ⓐ Ⓑ Ⓒ Ⓓ Ⓔ

2 Ⓐ Ⓑ Ⓒ Ⓓ Ⓔ   7 Ⓐ Ⓑ Ⓒ Ⓓ Ⓔ

3 Ⓐ Ⓑ Ⓒ Ⓓ Ⓔ   8 Ⓐ Ⓑ Ⓒ Ⓓ Ⓔ

4 Ⓐ Ⓑ Ⓒ Ⓓ Ⓔ   9 Ⓐ Ⓑ Ⓒ Ⓓ Ⓔ

5 Ⓐ Ⓑ Ⓒ Ⓓ Ⓔ   10 Ⓐ Ⓑ Ⓒ Ⓓ Ⓔ

Finding Rotated Shapes—Untimed Test

1 Ⓐ Ⓑ Ⓒ Ⓓ Ⓔ   6 Ⓐ Ⓑ Ⓒ Ⓓ Ⓔ

2 Ⓐ Ⓑ Ⓒ Ⓓ Ⓔ   7 Ⓐ Ⓑ Ⓒ Ⓓ Ⓔ

3 Ⓐ Ⓑ Ⓒ Ⓓ Ⓔ   8 Ⓐ Ⓑ Ⓒ Ⓓ Ⓔ

4 Ⓐ Ⓑ Ⓒ Ⓓ Ⓔ   9 Ⓐ Ⓑ Ⓒ Ⓓ Ⓔ

5 Ⓐ Ⓑ Ⓒ Ⓓ Ⓔ   10 Ⓐ Ⓑ Ⓒ Ⓓ Ⓔ

FINDING ROTATED SHAPES: PRACTICE TEST

1.
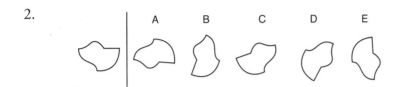

2.
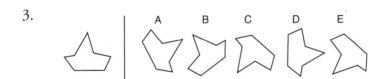

3.
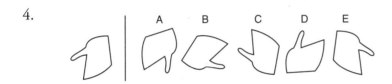

4.
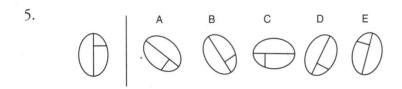

5.
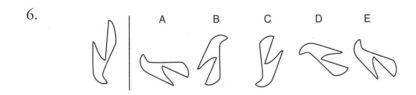

6.

7.

8.

9.

10.

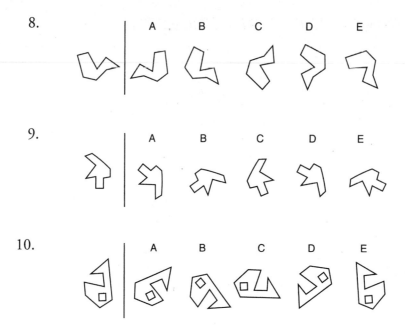

The answers to the practice test questions are on the next page.

Grading and Learning from the Practice Test on Finding Rotated Shapes

1. **(B)**

2. **(D)**

3. **(E)**

4. **(B)**

5. **(A)**

6. **(D)**

7. **(C)**

8. **(B)**

9. **(E)**

10. **(C)**

SUMMARIZE YOUR PERFORMANCE ON THE TIMED TEST

Number of questions you answered in 2½ minutes:_____

Number of questions you got right: _____

Number of questions you got wrong: _____

Number of questions you left blank: _____

REVIEW YOUR PERFORMANCE ON THE TIMED TEST

You should try to get a high score on this test. If you got less than a perfect score, take the test a second time with no time limit. An average score on this test is about five right.

If you answered fewer than seven questions in 2½ minutes, you should try to work faster.

CUT-UPS: PRACTICE TEST

To get the most out of this practice test, take it twice.

- First take this test with the time limit shown below, and grade the test.

- Then take this test a second time with no time limit, answering every question. (It is best to wait a full day or even a week or two before taking the test a second time.)

After you take the test both ways, review every question you got wrong or were unsure about. Try to understand why the right answer is right and the other answers are wrong.

You will get the most out of this practice test if you **first read the chapter on Cut-Ups.** That chapter begins on page 149.

CHECKLIST FOR USING THIS PRACTICE TEST

Put a check mark in each box to keep track of your progress on this practice test.

- ❏ Take the test using the time limit.
- ❏ Grade the timed test.
- ❏ Review your performance on the timed test.

- ❏ Take the test a second time with no time limit.
- ❏ Grade the untimed test.

- ❏ Go over each question you got wrong.
- ❏ Go over each question you were not sure about.

Time Limit for This Test: 8 MINUTES

Instructions: Before you start, carefully tear out the answer sheet for this test on the next page. Practice with an answer sheet is important, especially for tests like this one with short time limits.

Read each question and choose the correct answer. Then mark your answer on the answer sheet.

If you have extra time, check your work. Your goal is to get the highest possible score, not to put down your pencil as soon as possible.

When you are ready to start, turn the page and answer questions 1 to 10.

Answer Sheet
PRACTICE TEST

Cut-Ups—Timed Test

Time Limit: 8 minutes

Time Started: _____

Time Ended: _____

Time Spent Taking This Test: _____

1 Ⓐ Ⓑ Ⓒ Ⓓ   6 Ⓐ Ⓑ Ⓒ Ⓓ

2 Ⓐ Ⓑ Ⓒ Ⓓ   7 Ⓐ Ⓑ Ⓒ Ⓓ

3 Ⓐ Ⓑ Ⓒ Ⓓ   8 Ⓐ Ⓑ Ⓒ Ⓓ

4 Ⓐ Ⓑ Ⓒ Ⓓ   9 Ⓐ Ⓑ Ⓒ Ⓓ

5 Ⓐ Ⓑ Ⓒ Ⓓ   10 Ⓐ Ⓑ Ⓒ Ⓓ

Cut-Ups—Untimed Test

1 Ⓐ Ⓑ Ⓒ Ⓓ   6 Ⓐ Ⓑ Ⓒ Ⓓ

2 Ⓐ Ⓑ Ⓒ Ⓓ   7 Ⓐ Ⓑ Ⓒ Ⓓ

3 Ⓐ Ⓑ Ⓒ Ⓓ   8 Ⓐ Ⓑ Ⓒ Ⓓ

4 Ⓐ Ⓑ Ⓒ Ⓓ   9 Ⓐ Ⓑ Ⓒ Ⓓ

5 Ⓐ Ⓑ Ⓒ Ⓓ   10 Ⓐ Ⓑ Ⓒ Ⓓ

CUT-UPS: PRACTICE TEST

Use these answer choices to answer the questions on this page.

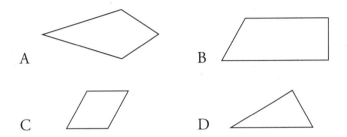

A   B   C   D

1. Which one of the four answer choices above can you make from these pieces?

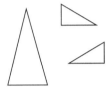

2. Which one of the four answer choices above can you make from these pieces?

3. Which one of the four answer choices above can you make from these pieces?

4. Which one of the 4 answer choices above can you make from these pieces?

5. Which one of the four answer choices above can you make from these pieces?

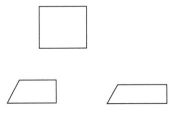

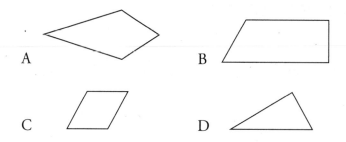

A   B   C   D

6. Which one of the four answer choices above can you make from these pieces?

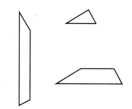

7. Which one of the four answer choices above can you make from these pieces?

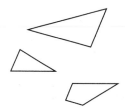

8. Which one of the four answer choices above can you make from these pieces?

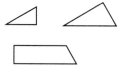

9. Which one of the four answer choices above can you make from these pieces?

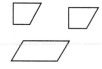

10. Which one of the four answer choices above can you make from these pieces?

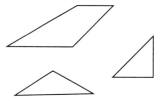

The answers to the practice test questions are on the next page.

Grading and Learning from the Practice Test on Cut-Ups

1. **(A)**

2. **(B)**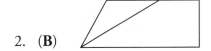

3. **(C)**

4. **(C)**

5. **(B)**

6. **(D)**

7. **(A)**

8. **(D)**

9. **(C)**

10. **(B)**

SUMMARIZE YOUR PERFORMANCE ON THE TIMED TEST

Number of questions you answered in eight minutes:_____

Number of questions you got right: _____

Number of questions you got wrong: _____

Number of questions you left blank: _____

REVIEW YOUR PERFORMANCE ON THE TIMED TEST

You should try to get a high score on this test. If you got less than a perfect score, take the test a second time with no time limit. An average score on this test is about six right.

If you answered fewer than 10 questions in eight minutes, you should try to work faster.

If you finished the test before the time limit and did not get a perfect score, did you use the extra time to review your answers? Try to make it a habit to use any extra time to review your answers and your answer sheet.

JIGSAW PUZZLES: PRACTICE TEST

To get the most out of this practice test, take it twice.

- First take this test with the time limit shown below, and grade the test.

- Then take this test a second time with no time limit, answering every question. (It is best to wait a full day or even a week or two before taking the test a second time.)

After you take the test both ways, review every question you got wrong or were unsure about. Try to understand why the right answer is right and the other answers are wrong.

You will get the most out of this practice test if you **first read the chapter on Jigsaw Puzzles.** That chapter begins on page 161.

CHECKLIST FOR USING THIS PRACTICE TEST

Put a check mark in each box to keep track of your progress on this practice test.

- ❏ Take the test using the time limit.
- ❏ Grade the timed test.
- ❏ Review your performance on the timed test.

- ❏ Take the test a second time with no time limit.
- ❏ Grade the untimed test.

- ❏ Go over each question you got wrong.
- ❏ Go over each question you were not sure about.

Time Limit for This Test: 4 MINUTES

Instructions: Before you start, carefully tear out the answer sheet for this test on the next page. Practice with an answer sheet is important, especially for tests like this one with short time limits.

For each question, pick the lettered shape that can be made from the pieces in the upper left hand corner. Then mark your answer on the answer sheet.

If you have extra time, check your work. Your goal is to get the highest possible score, not to finish as quickly as possible.

When you are ready to start, turn the page and answer questions 1 to 10.

Jigsaw Puzzles

Answer Sheet
PRACTICE TEST

Jigsaw Puzzles—Timed Test

Time Limit: 4 minutes

Time Started: _____

Time Ended: _____

Time Spent Taking This Test: _____

1 Ⓐ Ⓑ Ⓒ Ⓓ Ⓔ   6 Ⓐ Ⓑ Ⓒ Ⓓ Ⓔ

2 Ⓐ Ⓑ Ⓒ Ⓓ Ⓔ   7 Ⓐ Ⓑ Ⓒ Ⓓ Ⓔ

3 Ⓐ Ⓑ Ⓒ Ⓓ Ⓔ   8 Ⓐ Ⓑ Ⓒ Ⓓ Ⓔ

4 Ⓐ Ⓑ Ⓒ Ⓓ Ⓔ   9 Ⓐ Ⓑ Ⓒ Ⓓ Ⓔ

5 Ⓐ Ⓑ Ⓒ Ⓓ Ⓔ   10 Ⓐ Ⓑ Ⓒ Ⓓ Ⓔ

Jigsaw Puzzles—Untimed Test

1 Ⓐ Ⓑ Ⓒ Ⓓ Ⓔ   6 Ⓐ Ⓑ Ⓒ Ⓓ Ⓔ

2 Ⓐ Ⓑ Ⓒ Ⓓ Ⓔ   7 Ⓐ Ⓑ Ⓒ Ⓓ Ⓔ

3 Ⓐ Ⓑ Ⓒ Ⓓ Ⓔ   8 Ⓐ Ⓑ Ⓒ Ⓓ Ⓔ

4 Ⓐ Ⓑ Ⓒ Ⓓ Ⓔ   9 Ⓐ Ⓑ Ⓒ Ⓓ Ⓔ

5 Ⓐ Ⓑ Ⓒ Ⓓ Ⓔ   10 Ⓐ Ⓑ Ⓒ Ⓓ Ⓔ

JIGSAW PUZZLES: PRACTICE TEST

For each question, you should pick the shape that can be made from the pieces in the upper left-hand corner.

1.

A

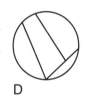
B

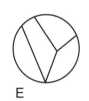
C

D

E

2.

A

B

C

D

E

3.

A

B

C

D

E

4.

A

B

C

D

E

5.

6.

7.

8.

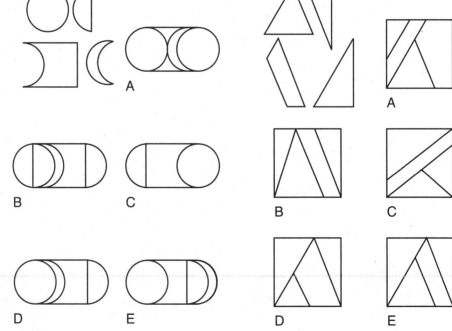

9.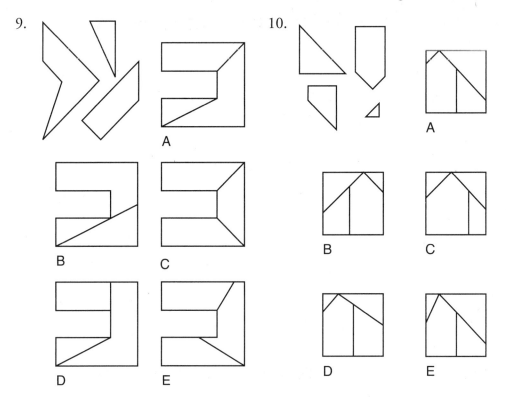

The answers to the practice test questions are on the next page.

Grading and Learning from the Practice Test on Jigsaw Puzzles

1. (**E**)

2. (**B**)

3. (**D**)

4. (**D**)

5. (**A**)

6. (**D**)

7. (**B**)

8. (**E**)

9. (**A**)

10. (**A**)

SUMMARIZE YOUR PERFORMANCE ON THE TIMED TEST

Number of questions you answered in four minutes:_____

Number of questions you got right: _____

Number of questions you got wrong: _____

Number of questions you left blank: _____

REVIEW YOUR PERFORMANCE ON THE TIMED TEST

You should try to get a high score on this test. If you got less than a perfect score, take the test a second time with no time limit. An average score on this test is about four or five right.

If you answered fewer than six questions in four minutes, you should try to work faster.

HOLE PUNCHING: PRACTICE TEST

To get the most out of this practice test, take it twice.

- First take this test with the time limit shown below, and grade the test.

- Then take this test a second time with no time limit, answering every question. (It is best to wait a full day or even a week or two before taking the test a second time.)

After you take the test both ways, review every question you got wrong or were unsure about. Try to understand why the right answer is right and the other answers are wrong.

You will get the most out of this practice test if you **first read the chapter on Hole Punching.** That chapter begins on page 177.

CHECKLIST FOR USING THIS PRACTICE TEST

Put a check mark in each box to keep track of your progress on this practice test.

- ❏ Take the test using the time limit.
- ❏ Grade the timed test.
- ❏ Review your performance on the timed test.

- ❏ Take the test a second time with no time limit.
- ❏ Grade the untimed test.

- ❏ Go over each question you got wrong.
- ❏ Go over each question you were not sure about.

Time Limit for This Test: 9 MINUTES

Instructions: Read the first three pages of the chapter on hole punching to learn how to take this test. Otherwise, the test questions will not make any sense to you.

Mark your answers next to each question. There is no separate answer sheet for this test.

When you are ready to start, turn the page and answer questions 1 to 10.

HOLE PUNCHING: PRACTICE TEST (TIMED)

Time Limit: 9 minutes

Time Started: _____   Time Ended: _____   Time Spent Taking Test: _____

1.

2.

3.

4.

5.

6.

7.

8.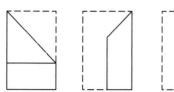

9.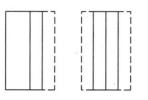

10.

HOLE PUNCHING: PRACTICE TEST (UNTIMED)

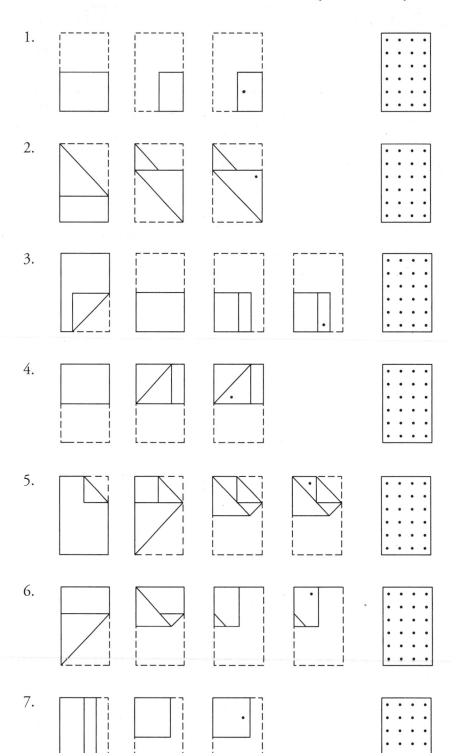

8.

9.

10.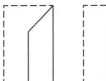

Grading and Learning from the Practice Test on Hole Punching

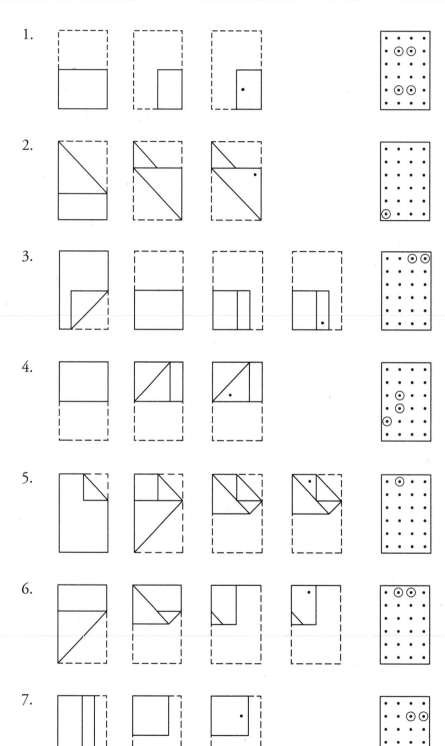

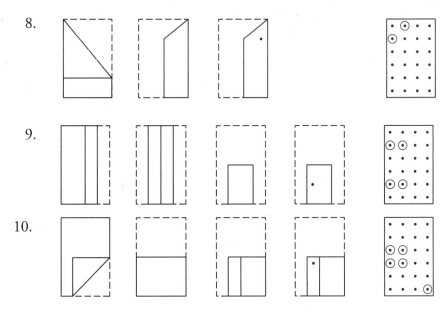

SUMMARIZE YOUR PERFORMANCE ON THE TIMED TEST

Number of questions you answered in nine minutes:_____

Number of questions you got right: _____

Number of questions you got wrong: _____

Number of questions you left blank: _____

REVIEW YOUR PERFORMANCE ON THE TIMED TEST

You should try to get a high score on this test. If you got less than a perfect score, take the test a second time with no time limit. An average score on this test is about five right.

If you answered fewer than nine questions in nine minutes, you should try to work faster.

HIDDEN BLOCKS: PRACTICE TEST

To get the most out of this practice test, take it twice.

- First take this test with the time limit shown below, and grade the test.

- Then take this test a second time with no time limit, answering every question. (It is best to wait a full day or even a week or two before taking the test a second time.)

After you take the test both ways, review every question you got wrong or were unsure about. Try to understand why the right answer is right and the other answers are wrong.

You will get the most out of this practice test if you **first read the chapter on Hidden Blocks.** That chapter begins on page 189.

CHECKLIST FOR USING THIS PRACTICE TEST

Put a check mark in each box to keep track of your progress on this practice test.

- ❏ Take the test using the time limit.
- ❏ Grade the timed test.
- ❏ Review your performance on the timed test.

- ❏ Take the test a second time with no time limit.
- ❏ Grade the untimed test.

- ❏ Go over each question you got wrong.
- ❏ Go over each question you were not sure about.

Time Limit for This Test: 3 MINUTES

Instructions: Before you start, carefully tear out the answer sheet for this test on the next page. Practice with an answer sheet is important, especially for tests like this one with short time limits.

For each question, count the number of blocks in the pile. In each pile there will be some blocks that you cannot see, but they must be there to hold up other blocks. You should count the hidden blocks as well as the blocks you can see. The blocks in these questions are all the same size and shape.

For each question, write in the number in the boxes above the bubbles and then fill in the bubbles. An example of how to fill in the answer sheet is given on the answer sheet.

If you have extra time, check your work. Your goal is to get the highest possible score, not to finish as quickly as possible.

When you are ready to start, turn the page and answer questions 1 to 10.

Answer Sheet
PRACTICE TEST

Hidden Blocks—Timed Test

Answer Sheet Instructions

If you counted 17 blocks, you should mark your answer sheet like this

1	7
0	0
●	1
2	2
3	3
4	4
5	5
6	6
7	●
8	8
9	9

Time Limit: 3 minutes

Time Started: _____

Time Ended: _____

Time Spent Taking This Test: _____

1 2 3 4 5 6 7 8 9 10

Hidden Blocks—Untimed Test

1 2 3 4 5 6 7 8 9 10

HIDDEN BLOCKS: PRACTICE TEST

1. All the blocks are the same size and shape. How many blocks are there?

    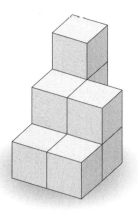

2. All the blocks are the same size and shape. How many blocks are there?

    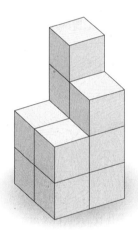

3. All the blocks are the same size and shape. How many blocks are there?

    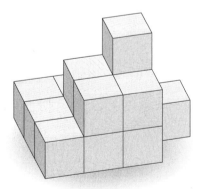

4. All the blocks are the same size and shape. How many blocks are there?

5. All the blocks are the same size and shape. How many blocks are there?

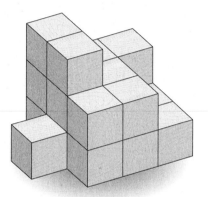

6. All the blocks are the same size and shape. How many blocks are there?

7. All the blocks are the same size and shape. How many blocks are there?

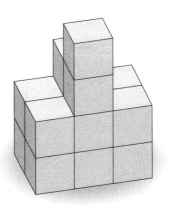

8. All the blocks are the same size and shape. How many blocks are there?

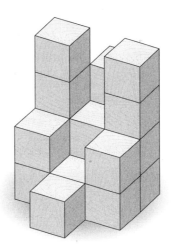

9. All the blocks are the same size and shape. How many blocks are there?

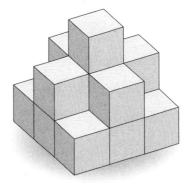

10. All the blocks are the same size and shape. How many blocks are there?

The answers to the practice test questions are on the next page.

Grading and Learning from the Practice Test on Hidden Blocks

1. **9**

2. **11**

3. **14**

4. **18**

5. **19**

6. **20**

7. **15**

8. **19**

9. **14**

10. **27**

SUMMARIZE YOUR PERFORMANCE ON THE TIMED TEST

Number of questions you answered in three minutes: _____

Number of questions you got right: _____

Number of questions you got wrong: _____

Number of questions you left blank: _____

REVIEW YOUR PERFORMANCE ON THE TIMED TEST

You should try to get a high score on this test. If you got less than a perfect score, take the test a second time with no time limit. An average score on this test is about six right.

If you answered fewer than seven questions in three minutes, you should try to work faster.

COUNTING TOUCHING BLOCKS: PRACTICE TEST

To get the most out of this practice test, take it twice.

- First take this test with the time limit shown below, and grade the test.

- Then take this test a second time with no time limit, answering every question. (It is best to wait a full day or even a week or two before taking the test a second time.)

After you take the test both ways, review every question you got wrong or were unsure about. Try to understand why the right answer is right and the other answers are wrong.

You will get the most out of this practice test if you **first read the chapter on Counting Touching Blocks.** That chapter begins on page 203.

CHECKLIST FOR USING THIS PRACTICE TEST

Put a check mark in each box to keep track of your progress on this practice test.

- ❏ Take the test using the time limit.
- ❏ Grade the timed test.
- ❏ Review your performance on the timed test.

- ❏ Take the test a second time with no time limit.
- ❏ Grade the untimed test.

- ❏ Go over each question you got wrong.
- ❏ Go over each question you were not sure about.

Time Limit for This Test: 4 MINUTES

Instructions: Before you start, carefully tear out the answer sheet for this test on the next page. Practice with an answer sheet is important, especially for tests like this one with short time limits.

For each question, count the number of blocks touching the block that has a letter on it. Count blocks as touching only if a flat side of one block is next to a flat side of another block. The blocks in these questions are all the same size and shape.

Follow the instructions on the answer sheet for marking your answers.

If you have extra time, check your work. Your goal is to get the highest possible score, not to finish as quickly as possible.

When you are ready to start, turn the page and answer questions 1 to 20.

Answer Sheet
PRACTICE TEST

Counting Touching Blocks—Timed Test

Time Limit: 4 minutes

Time Started: _____

Time Ended: _____

Time Spent Taking This Test: _____

Answer Sheet Instructions
Mark your answer by shading in a numbered bubble. For example, if you counted 5 blocks, you should mark your answer sheet like this:

① ② ③ ④ ● ⑥ ⑦ ⑧ ⑨

1 ① ② ③ ④ ⑤ ⑥ ⑦ ⑧ ⑨
2 ① ② ③ ④ ⑤ ⑥ ⑦ ⑧ ⑨
3 ① ② ③ ④ ⑤ ⑥ ⑦ ⑧ ⑨
4 ① ② ③ ④ ⑤ ⑥ ⑦ ⑧ ⑨
5 ① ② ③ ④ ⑤ ⑥ ⑦ ⑧ ⑨

6 ① ② ③ ④ ⑤ ⑥ ⑦ ⑧ ⑨
7 ① ② ③ ④ ⑤ ⑥ ⑦ ⑧ ⑨
8 ① ② ③ ④ ⑤ ⑥ ⑦ ⑧ ⑨
9 ① ② ③ ④ ⑤ ⑥ ⑦ ⑧ ⑨
10 ① ② ③ ④ ⑤ ⑥ ⑦ ⑧ ⑨

11 ① ② ③ ④ ⑤ ⑥ ⑦ ⑧ ⑨
12 ① ② ③ ④ ⑤ ⑥ ⑦ ⑧ ⑨
13 ① ② ③ ④ ⑤ ⑥ ⑦ ⑧ ⑨
14 ① ② ③ ④ ⑤ ⑥ ⑦ ⑧ ⑨
15 ① ② ③ ④ ⑤ ⑥ ⑦ ⑧ ⑨

16 ① ② ③ ④ ⑤ ⑥ ⑦ ⑧ ⑨
17 ① ② ③ ④ ⑤ ⑥ ⑦ ⑧ ⑨
18 ① ② ③ ④ ⑤ ⑥ ⑦ ⑧ ⑨
19 ① ② ③ ④ ⑤ ⑥ ⑦ ⑧ ⑨
20 ① ② ③ ④ ⑤ ⑥ ⑦ ⑧ ⑨

Counting Touching Blocks—Untimed Test

1 ① ② ③ ④ ⑤ ⑥ ⑦ ⑧ ⑨
2 ① ② ③ ④ ⑤ ⑥ ⑦ ⑧ ⑨
3 ① ② ③ ④ ⑤ ⑥ ⑦ ⑧ ⑨
4 ① ② ③ ④ ⑤ ⑥ ⑦ ⑧ ⑨
5 ① ② ③ ④ ⑤ ⑥ ⑦ ⑧ ⑨

6 ① ② ③ ④ ⑤ ⑥ ⑦ ⑧ ⑨
7 ① ② ③ ④ ⑤ ⑥ ⑦ ⑧ ⑨
8 ① ② ③ ④ ⑤ ⑥ ⑦ ⑧ ⑨
9 ① ② ③ ④ ⑤ ⑥ ⑦ ⑧ ⑨
10 ① ② ③ ④ ⑤ ⑥ ⑦ ⑧ ⑨

11 ① ② ③ ④ ⑤ ⑥ ⑦ ⑧ ⑨
12 ① ② ③ ④ ⑤ ⑥ ⑦ ⑧ ⑨
13 ① ② ③ ④ ⑤ ⑥ ⑦ ⑧ ⑨
14 ① ② ③ ④ ⑤ ⑥ ⑦ ⑧ ⑨
15 ① ② ③ ④ ⑤ ⑥ ⑦ ⑧ ⑨

16 ① ② ③ ④ ⑤ ⑥ ⑦ ⑧ ⑨
17 ① ② ③ ④ ⑤ ⑥ ⑦ ⑧ ⑨
18 ① ② ③ ④ ⑤ ⑥ ⑦ ⑧ ⑨
19 ① ② ③ ④ ⑤ ⑥ ⑦ ⑧ ⑨
20 ① ② ③ ④ ⑤ ⑥ ⑦ ⑧ ⑨

COUNTING TOUCHING BLOCKS: PRACTICE TEST

1. How many blocks is block A touching?

2. How many blocks is block B touching?

3. How many blocks is block C touching?

4. How many blocks is block D touching?

5. How many blocks is block E touching?

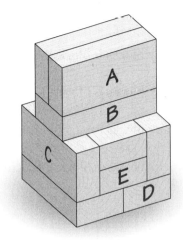

6. How many blocks is block A touching?

7. How many blocks is block B touching?

8. How many blocks is block C touching?

9. How many blocks is block D touching?

10. How many blocks is block E touching?

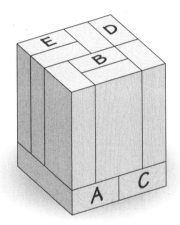

11. How many blocks is block A touching?

12. How many blocks is block B touching?

13. How many blocks is block C touching?

14. How many blocks is block D touching?

15. How many blocks is block E touching?

Counting Touching Blocks

16. How many blocks is block A touching?

17. How many blocks is block B touching?

18. How many blocks is block C touching?

19. How many blocks is block D touching?

20. How many blocks is block E touching?

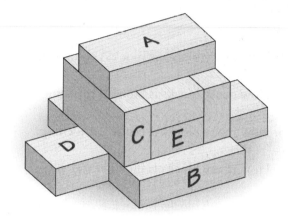

The answers to the practice test questions are on the next page.

Grading and Learning from the Practice Test on Counting Touching Blocks

1. **2**	6. **6**	11. **5**	16. **3**
2. **5**	7. **7**	12. **3**	17. **5**
3. **4**	8. **6**	13. **5**	18. **6**
4. **3**	9. **3**	14. **5**	19. **5**
5. **5**	10. **3**	15. **5**	20. **7**

SUMMARIZE YOUR PERFORMANCE ON THE TIMED TEST

Number of questions you answered in four minutes: _____

Number of questions you got right: _____

Number of questions you got wrong: _____

Number of questions you left blank: _____

REVIEW YOUR PERFORMANCE ON THE TIMED TEST

You should try to get a high score on this test. If you got less than a perfect score, take the test a second time with no time limit. An average score on this test is about 10 right.

If you answered fewer than 13 questions in four minutes, you should try to work faster.

Counting Touching Blocks

MAKING RECTANGULAR BOXES: PRACTICE TEST

To get the most out of this practice test, take it twice.

- First take this test with the time limit shown below, and grade the test.

- Then take this test a second time with no time limit, answering every question. (It is best to wait a full day or even a week or two before taking the test a second time.)

After you take the test both ways, review every question you got wrong or were unsure about. Try to understand why the right answer is right and the other answers are wrong.

You will get the most out of this practice test if you **first read the chapter on Making Rectangular Boxes.** That chapter begins on page 211.

CHECKLIST FOR USING THIS PRACTICE TEST

Put a check mark in each box to keep track of your progress on this practice test.

- ❏ Take the test using the time limit.
- ❏ Grade the timed test.
- ❏ Review your performance on the timed test.

- ❏ Take the test a second time with no time limit.
- ❏ Grade the untimed test.

- ❏ Go over each question you got wrong.
- ❏ Go over each question you were not sure about.

Time Limit for This Test: 10 MINUTES

Instructions: Before you start, carefully tear out the answer sheet on the next page. Practice with an answer sheet is important, especially for tests like this one with short time limits.

There is a pattern at the top of each test page. For each question, choose the box that can be made from the pattern. If none of the boxes can be made from the pattern, choose E. Mark your answers on the answer sheet.

If you have extra time, use it to check your work. Your goal in taking the practice test should be to get the highest score possible. You do not get any credit for finishing early.

When you are ready to start, turn the page and answer questions 1 to 10.

Answer Sheet
PRACTICE TEST

Making Rectangular Boxes—Timed Test

Time Limit: 10 minutes

Time Started: _____

Time Ended: _____

Time Spent Taking This Test: _____

1 Ⓐ Ⓑ Ⓒ Ⓓ Ⓔ   6 Ⓐ Ⓑ Ⓒ Ⓓ Ⓔ

2 Ⓐ Ⓑ Ⓒ Ⓓ Ⓔ   7 Ⓐ Ⓑ Ⓒ Ⓓ Ⓔ

3 Ⓐ Ⓑ Ⓒ Ⓓ Ⓔ   8 Ⓐ Ⓑ Ⓒ Ⓓ Ⓔ

4 Ⓐ Ⓑ Ⓒ Ⓓ Ⓔ   9 Ⓐ Ⓑ Ⓒ Ⓓ Ⓔ

5 Ⓐ Ⓑ Ⓒ Ⓓ Ⓔ   10 Ⓐ Ⓑ Ⓒ Ⓓ Ⓔ

Making Rectangular Boxes—Untimed Test

1 Ⓐ Ⓑ Ⓒ Ⓓ Ⓔ   6 Ⓐ Ⓑ Ⓒ Ⓓ Ⓔ

2 Ⓐ Ⓑ Ⓒ Ⓓ Ⓔ   7 Ⓐ Ⓑ Ⓒ Ⓓ Ⓔ

3 Ⓐ Ⓑ Ⓒ Ⓓ Ⓔ   8 Ⓐ Ⓑ Ⓒ Ⓓ Ⓔ

4 Ⓐ Ⓑ Ⓒ Ⓓ Ⓔ   9 Ⓐ Ⓑ Ⓒ Ⓓ Ⓔ

5 Ⓐ Ⓑ Ⓒ Ⓓ Ⓔ   10 Ⓐ Ⓑ Ⓒ Ⓓ Ⓔ

MAKING RECTANGULAR BOXES: PRACTICE TEST

For each line of boxes below, answer this question:

Which box can be made from this pattern? If none of the boxes can be made from the pattern, choose E.

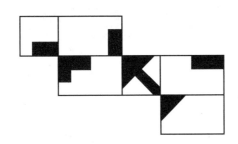

1.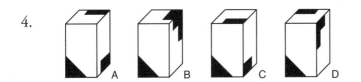

2.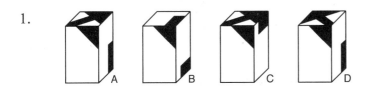

3.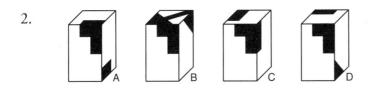

4.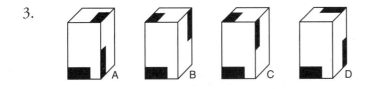

5.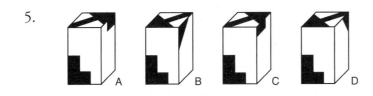

For each line of boxes below, answer this question:

Which box can be made from this pattern? If none of the boxes can be made from the pattern, choose E.

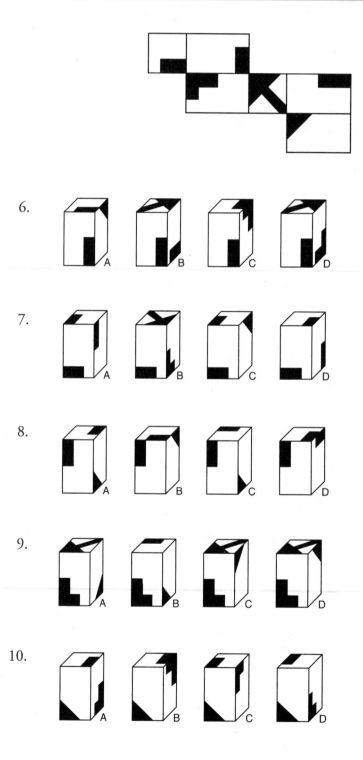

6.

7.

8.

9.

10.

The answers to the practice test questions are on the next page.

Grading and Learning from the Practice Test on Making Rectangular Boxes

1. (**D**)

2. (**A**)

3. (**C**)

4. (**B**)

5. (**D**)

6. (**E**)

7. (**A**)

8. (**C**)

9. (**D**)

10. (**B**)

SUMMARIZE YOUR PERFORMANCE ON THE TIMED TEST

Number of questions you answered in 10 minutes: _____

Number of questions you got right: _____

Number of questions you got wrong: _____

Number of questions you left blank: _____

REVIEW YOUR PERFORMANCE ON THE TIMED TEST

You should try to get a high score on this test. If you got less than a perfect score, take the test a second time with no time limit. An average score on this test is about five right.

If you answered fewer than 10 questions in 10 minutes, you should try to work faster.

If you finished the test before the time limit and did not get a perfect score, did you use the extra time to review your answers? Try to make it a habit to use any extra time to review your answers and your answer sheet.

PAPER FOLDING—SHAPE KNOWN: PRACTICE TEST

To get the most out of this practice test, take it twice.

- First take this test with the time limit shown below, and grade the test.

- Then take this test a second time with no time limit, answering every question. (It is best to wait a full day or even a week or two before taking the test a second time.)

After you take the test both ways, review every question you got wrong or were unsure about. Try to understand why the right answer is right and the other answers are wrong.

You will get the most out of this practice test if you **first read the chapter on Paper Folding—Shape Known.** That chapter begins on page 223.

CHECKLIST FOR USING THIS PRACTICE TEST

Put a check mark in each box to keep track of your progress on this practice test.

- ❏ Take the test using the time limit.
- ❏ Grade the timed test.
- ❏ Review your performance on the timed test.

- ❏ Take the test a second time with no time limit.
- ❏ Grade the untimed test.

- ❏ Go over each question you got wrong.
- ❏ Go over each question you were not sure about.

Time Limit for This Test: 6 MINUTES

Instructions: Before you start, carefully tear out the answer sheet on the next page. Practice with an answer sheet is important. You will get the most out of this practice test if you take it the way you will take a real test.

For each question, choose the object that can be made from the pattern shown. Then mark your answer on the answer sheet.

If you have time left over, review your answers, just as you would when taking a real test.

When you are ready to start, turn the page and answer questions 1 to 10.

Answer Sheet
PRACTICE TEST

Paper Folding–Shape Known–Timed Test

Time Limit: 6 minutes

Time Started: _____

Time Ended: _____

Time Spent Taking This Test: _____

1 Ⓐ Ⓑ Ⓒ Ⓓ Ⓔ   6 Ⓐ Ⓑ Ⓒ Ⓓ Ⓔ

2 Ⓐ Ⓑ Ⓒ Ⓓ Ⓔ   7 Ⓐ Ⓑ Ⓒ Ⓓ Ⓔ

3 Ⓐ Ⓑ Ⓒ Ⓓ Ⓔ   8 Ⓐ Ⓑ Ⓒ Ⓓ Ⓔ

4 Ⓐ Ⓑ Ⓒ Ⓓ Ⓔ   9 Ⓐ Ⓑ Ⓒ Ⓓ Ⓔ

5 Ⓐ Ⓑ Ⓒ Ⓓ Ⓔ   10 Ⓐ Ⓑ Ⓒ Ⓓ Ⓔ

Paper Folding–Shape Known–Untimed Test

1 Ⓐ Ⓑ Ⓒ Ⓓ Ⓔ   6 Ⓐ Ⓑ Ⓒ Ⓓ Ⓔ

2 Ⓐ Ⓑ Ⓒ Ⓓ Ⓔ   7 Ⓐ Ⓑ Ⓒ Ⓓ Ⓔ

3 Ⓐ Ⓑ Ⓒ Ⓓ Ⓔ   8 Ⓐ Ⓑ Ⓒ Ⓓ Ⓔ

4 Ⓐ Ⓑ Ⓒ Ⓓ Ⓔ   9 Ⓐ Ⓑ Ⓒ Ⓓ Ⓔ

5 Ⓐ Ⓑ Ⓒ Ⓓ Ⓔ   10 Ⓐ Ⓑ Ⓒ Ⓓ Ⓔ

PAPER FOLDING—SHAPE KNOWN: PRACTICE TEST

For each question, choose the object that can be made from the pattern shown.

1.

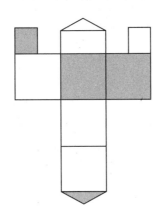

A	B	C	D	E

2.

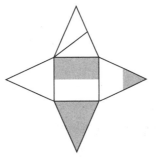

A	B	C	D	E

3.

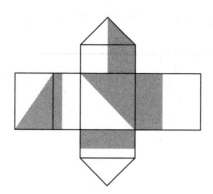

A B C D E

4.

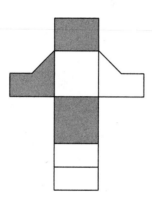

A B C D E

5.

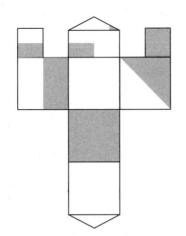

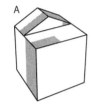 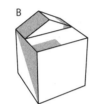 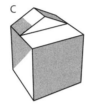  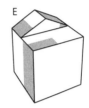

A   B   C   D   E

6.

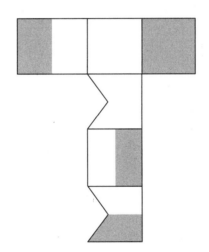

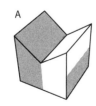 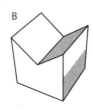 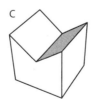 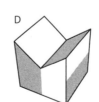

A   B   C   D   E

7.

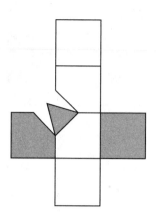

A B C D E

8.

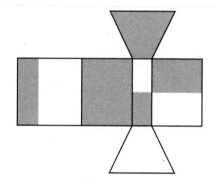

A B C D E

9.

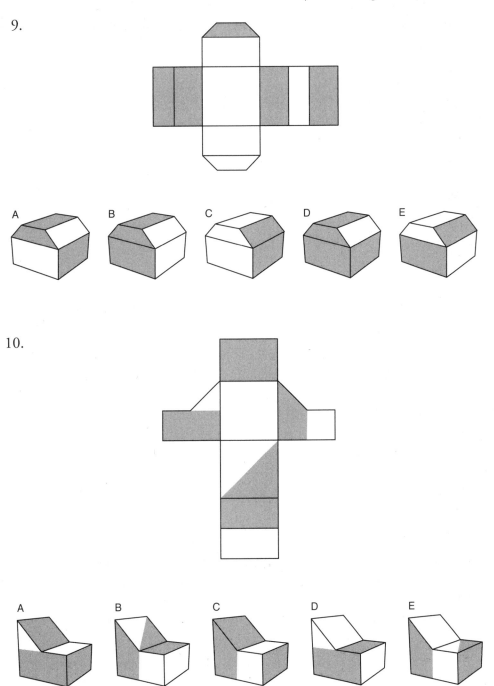

10.

The answers to the practice test questions are on the next page.

Grading and Learning from the Practice Test on Paper Folding—Shape Known

1. **(C)**
2. **(E)**
3. **(A)**
4. **(D)**
5. **(E)**
6. **(D)**
7. **(B)**
8. **(E)**
9. **(A)**
10. **(C)**

SUMMARIZE YOUR PERFORMANCE ON THE TIMED TEST

Number of questions you answered in six minutes: _____

Number of questions you got right: _____

Number of questions you got wrong: _____

Number of questions you left blank: _____

REVIEW YOUR PERFORMANCE ON THE TIMED TEST

You should try to get a high score on this test. If you got less than a perfect score, take the test a second time with no time limit. An average score on this test is about six right.

If you answered fewer than eight questions in six minutes, you should try to work faster.

PAPER FOLDING—SHAPE UNKNOWN: PRACTICE TEST

To get the most out of this practice test, take it twice.

- First take this test with the time limit shown below, and grade the test.

- Then take this test a second time with no time limit, answering every question. (It is best to wait a full day or even a week or two before taking the test a second time.)

After you take the test both ways, review every question you got wrong or were unsure about. Try to understand why the right answer is right and the other answers are wrong.

You will get the most out of this practice test if you **first read the chapter on Paper Folding—Shape Unknown.** That chapter begins on page 239.

CHECKLIST FOR USING THIS PRACTICE TEST

Put a check mark in each box to keep track of your progress on this practice test.

- ❏ Take the test using the time limit.
- ❏ Grade the timed test.
- ❏ Review your performance on the timed test.

- ❏ Take the test a second time with no time limit.
- ❏ Grade the untimed test.

- ❏ Go over each question you got wrong.
- ❏ Go over each question you were not sure about.

Time Limit for This Test: **6 MINUTES**

Instructions: Before you start, carefully tear out the answer sheet for this test on the next page. Practice with an answer sheet is important, especially for tests like this one with short time limits.

For each question, choose the object that can be made from the pattern shown. Then mark your answer on the answer sheet.

When you are ready to start, turn the page and answer questions 1 to 10.

Answer Sheet
PRACTICE TEST

Paper Folding–Shape Unknown–Timed Test

Time Limit: 6 minutes

Time Started: _____

Time Ended: _____

Time Spent Taking This Test: _____

1 Ⓐ Ⓑ Ⓒ Ⓓ   6 Ⓐ Ⓑ Ⓒ Ⓓ

2 Ⓐ Ⓑ Ⓒ Ⓓ   7 Ⓐ Ⓑ Ⓒ Ⓓ

3 Ⓐ Ⓑ Ⓒ Ⓓ   8 Ⓐ Ⓑ Ⓒ Ⓓ

4 Ⓐ Ⓑ Ⓒ Ⓓ   9 Ⓐ Ⓑ Ⓒ Ⓓ

5 Ⓐ Ⓑ Ⓒ Ⓓ   10 Ⓐ Ⓑ Ⓒ Ⓓ

Paper Folding–Shape Unknown–Untimed Test

1 Ⓐ Ⓑ Ⓒ Ⓓ   6 Ⓐ Ⓑ Ⓒ Ⓓ

2 Ⓐ Ⓑ Ⓒ Ⓓ   7 Ⓐ Ⓑ Ⓒ Ⓓ

3 Ⓐ Ⓑ Ⓒ Ⓓ   8 Ⓐ Ⓑ Ⓒ Ⓓ

4 Ⓐ Ⓑ Ⓒ Ⓓ   9 Ⓐ Ⓑ Ⓒ Ⓓ

5 Ⓐ Ⓑ Ⓒ Ⓓ   10 Ⓐ Ⓑ Ⓒ Ⓓ

PAPER FOLDING—SHAPE UNKNOWN: PRACTICE TEST

For each question, choose the object that can be made from the pattern shown.

1.

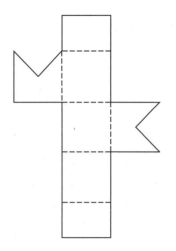

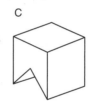

A B C D

2.

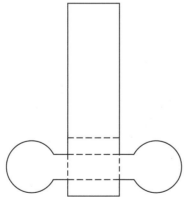

A B C D

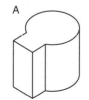

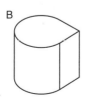

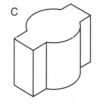

3.

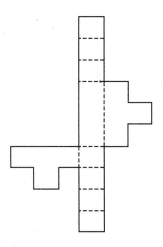

A   B   C   D

4.

A 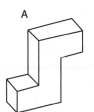   B 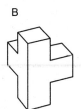   C    D

5.

6.

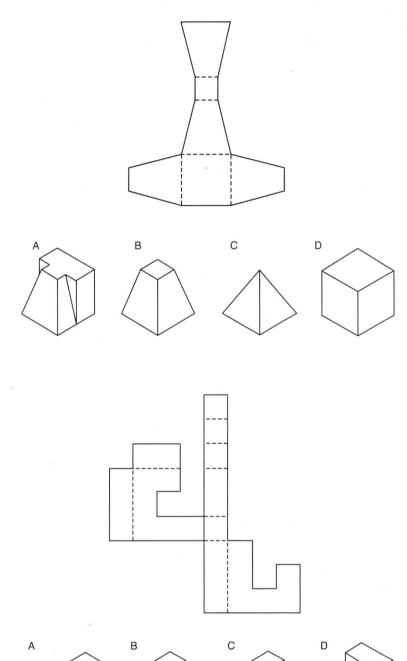

7.

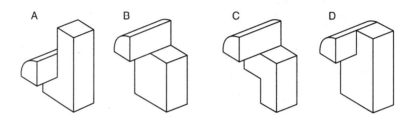

8.

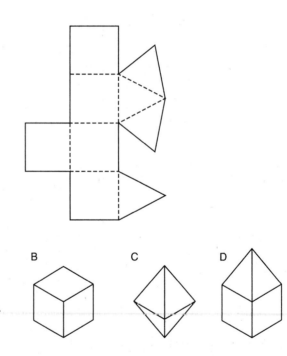

9.

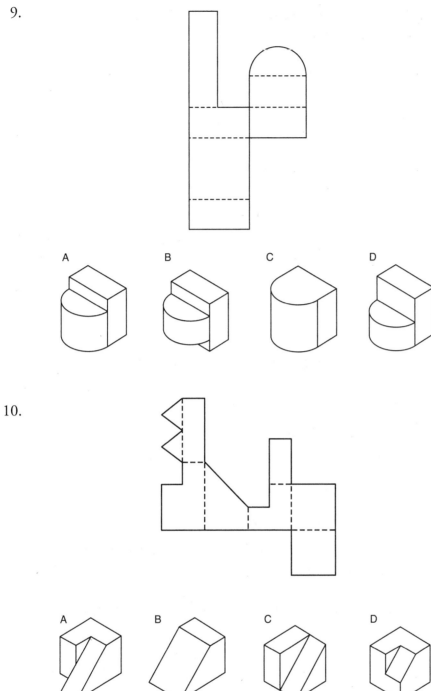

10.

The answers to the practice test questions are on the next page.

Grading and Learning from the Practice Test on Paper Folding—Shape Unknown

1. **(C)**
2. **(A)**
3. **(A)**
4. **(C)**
5. **(B)**
6. **(C)**
7. **(B)**
8. **(D)**
9. **(D)**
10. **(A)**

SUMMARIZE YOUR PERFORMANCE ON THE TIMED TEST

Number of questions you answered in six minutes: _____

Number of questions you got right: _____

Number of questions you got wrong: _____

Number of questions you left blank: _____

REVIEW YOUR PERFORMANCE ON THE TIMED TEST

You should try to get a high score on this test. If you got less than a perfect score, take the test a second time with no time limit. An average score on this test is about five right.

If you answered fewer than eight questions in six minutes, you should try to work faster.

PARTS ASSEMBLY: PRACTICE TEST

To get the most out of this practice test, take it twice.

- First take this test with the time limit shown below, and grade the test.

- Then take this test a second time with no time limit, answering every question. (It is best to wait a full day or even a week or two before taking the test a second time.)

After you take the test both ways, review every question you got wrong or were unsure about. Try to understand why the right answer is right and the other answers are wrong.

You will get the most out of this practice test if you **first read the chapter on Parts Assembly.** That chapter begins on page 271.

CHECKLIST FOR USING THIS PRACTICE TEST

Put a check mark in each box to keep track of your progress on this practice test.

- ❑ Take the test using the time limit.
- ❑ Grade the timed test.
- ❑ Review your performance on the timed test.

- ❑ Take the test a second time with no time limit.
- ❑ Grade the untimed test.

- ❑ Go over each question you got wrong.
- ❑ Go over each question you were not sure about.

Time Limit for This Test: **5 MINUTES**

Instructions: Before you start, carefully tear out the answer sheet on the next page. Practice with an answer sheet is important, especially for tests like this one with short time limits.

For each question, choose the object that can be made from the parts shown. Then mark your answer on the answer sheet.

When you are ready to start, turn the page and answer questions 1 to 10.

Parts Assembly

Answer Sheet
PRACTICE TEST

Parts Assembly—Timed Test

Time Limit: 5 minutes

Time Started: _____

Time Ended: _____

Time Spent Taking This Test: _____

1 Ⓐ Ⓑ Ⓒ Ⓓ Ⓔ   6 Ⓐ Ⓑ Ⓒ Ⓓ Ⓔ

2 Ⓐ Ⓑ Ⓒ Ⓓ Ⓔ   7 Ⓐ Ⓑ Ⓒ Ⓓ Ⓔ

3 Ⓐ Ⓑ Ⓒ Ⓓ Ⓔ   8 Ⓐ Ⓑ Ⓒ Ⓓ Ⓔ

4 Ⓐ Ⓑ Ⓒ Ⓓ Ⓔ   9 Ⓐ Ⓑ Ⓒ Ⓓ Ⓔ

5 Ⓐ Ⓑ Ⓒ Ⓓ Ⓔ   10 Ⓐ Ⓑ Ⓒ Ⓓ Ⓔ

Parts Assembly—Untimed Test

1 Ⓐ Ⓑ Ⓒ Ⓓ Ⓔ   6 Ⓐ Ⓑ Ⓒ Ⓓ Ⓔ

2 Ⓐ Ⓑ Ⓒ Ⓓ Ⓔ   7 Ⓐ Ⓑ Ⓒ Ⓓ Ⓔ

3 Ⓐ Ⓑ Ⓒ Ⓓ Ⓔ   8 Ⓐ Ⓑ Ⓒ Ⓓ Ⓔ

4 Ⓐ Ⓑ Ⓒ Ⓓ Ⓔ   9 Ⓐ Ⓑ Ⓒ Ⓓ Ⓔ

5 Ⓐ Ⓑ Ⓒ Ⓓ Ⓔ   10 Ⓐ Ⓑ Ⓒ Ⓓ Ⓔ

PARTS ASSEMBLY: PRACTICE TEST

Choose the object that can be made from the parts shown in the numbered box.

1.

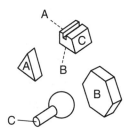

A B

C

2.

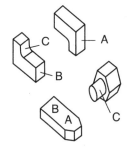
A

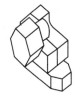
B C

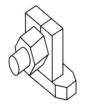
D E

3.

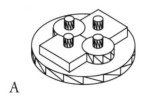

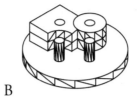

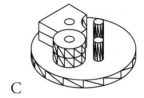

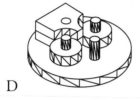

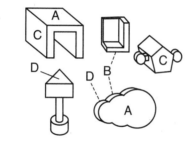

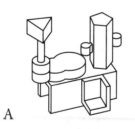

A

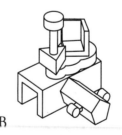

B

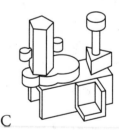

C

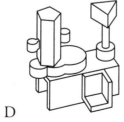

D

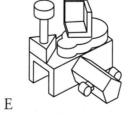

E

4.

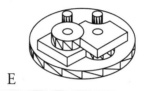

A

B

C

D

E

5.

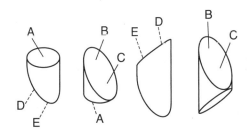

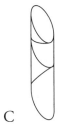

A

B

C

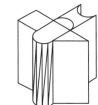

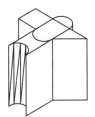

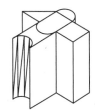

D

E

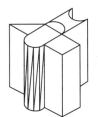

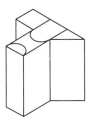

6.

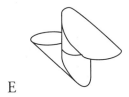

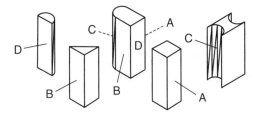

A

B

C

D

E

7.

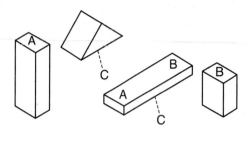

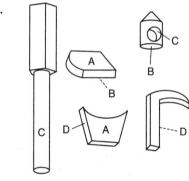

A

B

C

D

E

8.

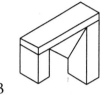

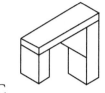

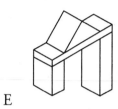

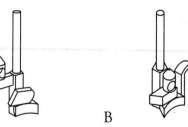

A

B

C

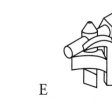

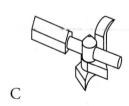

D

E

9.

10.

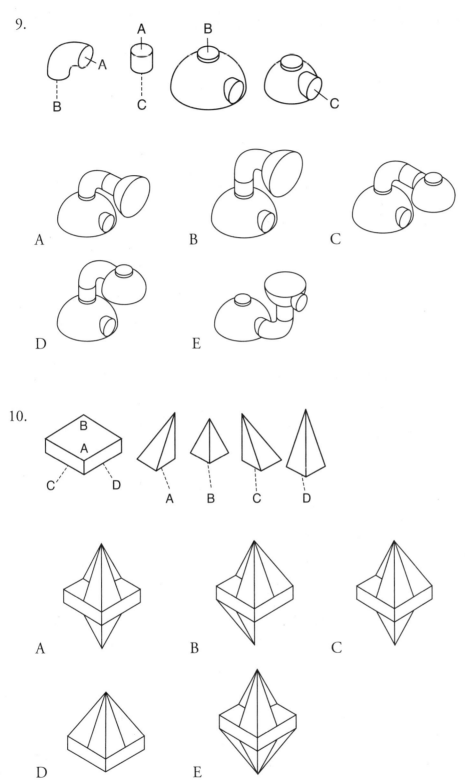

The answers to the practice test questions are on the next page.

Grading and Learning from the Practice Test on Parts Assembly

1. **(A)**
2. **(D)**
3. **(C)**
4. **(B)**
5. **(A)**
6. **(B)**
7. **(E)**
8. **(D)**
9. **(C)**
10. **(E)**

SUMMARIZE YOUR PERFORMANCE ON THE TIMED TEST

Number of questions you answered in five minutes: _____

Number of questions you got right: _____

Number of questions you got wrong: _____

Number of questions you left blank: _____

REVIEW YOUR PERFORMANCE ON THE TIMED TEST

You should try to get a high score on this test. If you got less than a perfect score, take the test a second time with no time limit. An average score on this test is about six right.

If you answered fewer than eight questions in five minutes, you should try to work faster.

The Different Types of Computer-Based Tests

APPENDIX A

This chapter tells you about a few different types of computer-based tests and some differences between taking a computer-based test and a paper-and-pencil test. The chapter explains how the computer-based tests work. It will help you decide if you know enough about computers to feel comfortable taking a computer-based test, and gives helpful hints if you don't know much about computers. There is one type of computer-based test that uses videos. That type is covered in the next chapter.

WHAT DO THESE TESTS LOOK LIKE?

Many computer-based tests use the same type of questions as paper-and-pencil tests. Some computer-based tests show both the questions and the answers on a computer screen. Others show an answer sheet on the computer screen and show the questions in a paper test booklet. A few computer-based tests use fill-in-the-blank questions, especially when the answers are numbers. Usually paper-and-pencil tests avoid fill-in-the-blank questions because they are harder to grade.

FILL-IN-THE-BLANK QUESTIONS

Unlike multiple-choice questions where you choose answer A, B, C, D, or E, fill-in-the-blank questions ask you to write in your answer without giving you any choices. For these questions, you will need to click inside a text box on the screen and type your answer.

Example: A tool used to drive a screw into a piece of wood is a _____.

Computer-based tests may give full credit for a few different spellings of the correct answer. For example, the correct answer for the question above is:

screwdriver.

But a computer-based test may give full credit for other answers like:

Screwdriver

screw driver

screw-driver.

So don't panic if you are not a great speller. Of course, you should do your best to spell words correctly, to capitalize words only if they're supposed to be capitalized, and to use spaces correctly, but don't stress out about these things. Just do your best and move on.

Note: Do NOT use abbreviations for answers to fill-in-the-blank questions unless you are told to do that.

The Five Ways Computer-Based Tests Are Set Up

There are five different ways computer-based tests are usually set up:

1. Computer-based test with paper test booklet
2. Paperless computer-based test with all the questions on one page
3. Paperless computer-based test with one question per page
4. Computer-Adaptive tests
5. Speed tests.

COMPUTER-BASED TEST WITH PAPER TEST BOOKLET

A computer-based test with a paper test booklet will show all the questions in a paper booklet and an answer sheet on the computer screen.

Usually on these tests, answer bubbles for all the questions will be on one screen. So it is easy to skip questions, change answers, and review your answers if you have time left at the end of the test. (This is just like a paper answer sheet.)

For this type of computer-based test, there will be a button somewhere on the screen (usually at the very bottom) that says something like "Submit" or "Finished." Do NOT click this button until you are sure you have answered every question to the best of your ability. Once you click this button, you will not be able to go back and change your answers.

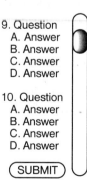

PAPERLESS COMPUTER-BASED TEST: ALL THE QUESTIONS ON ONE PAGE

On this type of computer-based test, all questions and answer choices will be on the screen at the same time. You can see every question, each followed by its answer choices, just by scrolling up and down. So you can skip questions you want to come back to later, change answers, and review your answers if you have time left at the end of the test.

For this kind of test, there will be a button somewhere on the screen (usually at the bottom) that says something like "Submit" or "Finished." Do NOT click this button till you are sure you have answered every question and are ready to hand in the test. Once you click this button, you will not be able to go back to change your answers.

PAPERLESS COMPUTER-BASED TEST: ONE QUESTION PER PAGE

On this type of computer-based test, only one question is on the screen at a time. Sometimes you may see a small group of questions and their answer options on the screen.

Once you've answered the question or questions on the screen, one of two things will happen:

1. The computer will automatically move to another screen with a different question or set of questions.
2. You will have to click a button on the screen that says something like "Done" or "Submit" or "Go on" or "Next."

Pay careful attention to the directions before you start the test. You will be told whether you can go back to old questions to change your answers after you've moved on to new questions.

If you can go back to change your answers, the directions will tell you exactly how to do this. Usually, you will have to click a button on the screen. This button will say something like "Back" or "Previous Question," or it will display a picture of an arrow pointing left.

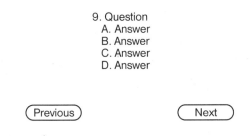

9. Question
   A. Answer
   B. Answer
   C. Answer
   D. Answer

Previous   Next

> **HINT**
>
> Be very careful typing your name and any ID number.

COMPUTER-ADAPTIVE TESTS

Computer-adaptive tests are very different from paper-and-pencil tests. Usually a computer-adaptive test has fewer questions than a paper-and-pencil test, and not everyone gets the same questions. On a computer-adaptive test, the first question you see will be of medium difficulty. If you answer correctly, the computer will give you a slightly harder question. If you answer wrong, the computer will give you a slightly easier question.

Once the computer thinks it knows your level, it will stop asking you questions. Be careful with each question, since the test can stop at any time. Don't make any careless mistakes on a computer-adaptive test, and don't skip any questions. Also, once you move on to the next question, you cannot go back.

SPEED TESTS

A speed test is a special kind of paperless computer-based test on multiple pages. When you take a speed test, you see only one question and its answer options at any given time on the screen. These answer options are the same for every question.

The directions for a speed test might look like this:

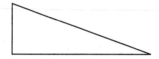

Look at the shape shown above. When you start this test, you will see a new shape. If the new shape is the mirror image of the shape shown above, press the K key on your keyboard. This is what the mirror image looks like:

If the new picture is **not** the mirror image, press the D key on your keyboard.

Immediately after you make your choice, a new picture will appear. Again, press K if the shape is the same, or press D if the shape is the mirror image.

This is a test of speed. So you should make your choice for each question as quickly as possible. Press any key to begin the test.

For this kind of test, it is best to hold one finger over one answer key and another finger over the other answer key (D and K, in the example above). You will not be able to go back to change your answers. You should answer as fast as you can without making mistakes. Remember, the faster you answer, the better your score, if you answer correctly. This type of test has a short time limit.

Review Your Answers at the End of the Test

Some tests let you "flag" questions you're not sure about. (Flagging a question just means marking it to help you remember that you want to go back to it later.) After you've answered the last question, you can choose to go back through the flagged questions to change your answers. Be careful about using the flagging feature too much, since you might have little or no time at the end of the test.

Even if there is no flagging feature, some tests will let you check your answers if you have time. Use all the time you are given; do not turn in your test early. After you finish checking your answers, you will have to click a button on the screen that says "Submit" or "Finished" or something like that.

Do I Know Enough About Computers to Take a Computer-Based Test?

This section gives two computer exercises and shows some important computer keys. If you are comfortable doing the exercises and you have a good idea of what the keys do, you should have no trouble taking a computer-based test.

COMPUTER EXERCISES

See if you can do these quickly and easily.

1. Open an Internet browser:
   a. Go to a webpage (like barronstestprep.com) by typing its address in the right field.
   b. Once you've gone to a new webpage, use your browser's "back" and "forward" buttons to move between pages.
   c. Now do a web search for a topic that interests you.
   d. After you do a web search, scroll down the page to see all the results on that page.

2. Open a word processor:
   a. Type a few sentences.
   b. Make a few typing errors and correct them.
   c. Use the mouse to highlight, copy, and paste a few words of the text.

> **HINT**
>
> If the screen is blank and you do not see a red or green light, the computer might not be turned on.

KEYS TO KNOW

Look at the name of each of the computer keys listed below. Do you know what each key looks like and does?

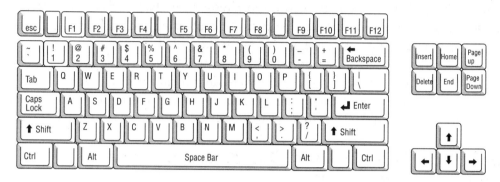

If you can do the two exercises described above, and if you already know the keys listed (shown) above, you have the computer skills you need to take a computer-based test.

If you're not so comfortable with the exercises and the keys, don't worry. The next section will give some suggestions to help you take a computer-based test even if you are not very comfortable around computers.

I DON'T OWN A COMPUTER. HOW CAN I GET MORE PRACTICE USING ONE?

If you don't own a computer, but you want to practice using one, here are some things you could do:

1. Find a friend or family member who does own a computer, and ask if that person would show you how to do some basic things with it. You might ask the person to help you:
   a. Turn the computer on and off.
   b. Go online and visit a webpage.
   c. Open a word processor and type a few sentences.

2. Go to your local library and use the public computers there to:
   a. Find a book on test-taking or gardening or baseball or any subject that interests you. Learning to use the library's online book catalogue is a great way to become comfortable using a computer.
   b. Go online and visit a webpage. If you don't know any webpages, ask the librarian how to "search the web" to find whatever topic interests you. For example, if you're really interested in baseball, you could say, "Could you please show me how to do a web search for the Baseball Hall of Fame?"

Remember, if you need help with anything while using the library computers, a librarian will be happy to help you.

What if I've Never Used a Computer Before?

If you've never used a computer before and don't have time to learn, here is some advice. First, don't get too nervous. Get to the test room early, and let the person in charge know that you don't know how to use a computer. Ask if you can get some time to practice or some extra help with the instructions. Then listen to all the instructions very carefully. After you've heard the instructions, if you're still not sure about something, raise your hand and ask questions.

WHAT KINDS OF QUESTIONS WOULD I ASK?

Asking questions about how to use a computer doesn't have to be hard. You don't need to use any technical terms, just everyday English. Here are some examples of ways you might ask questions:

1. Do I need to turn on the computer? How do I do that?
2. Could you help me find the page where the test starts?
3. How do I move from one question to the next?
4. What should I do if I push the wrong button?
5. How will I know when the test is over?

Remember, if you have a question about how to use the computer at any time during the test, raise your hand to get the attention of the person in charge.

Of course, it is best to learn something about computers before the test day. Look at the **Computer Exercises** and the **Keys to Know** sections above for suggestions about what you should try to learn about computers.

> **TIP**
>
> If you are not comfortable with computers, tell the person in charge of the testing **before** the test starts.

HOW DO I KNOW IF SOMETHING IS WRONG WITH MY COMPUTER?

Something might be wrong with your computer if:

1. It freezes. When a computer freezes, it no longer works. Nothing you type shows up on the screen, and the cursor does not move, no matter what you do.
2. The computer beeps at you every time you press a key.
3. The computer is really slow. Sometimes when the computer is trying to do too many things at once, you'll see a small hourglass or a spinning wheel on the screen. If this lasts for more than a minute, there's a problem.

HOW DO I GET HELP?

Remember, when you're at the testing center and need help using the computer, raise your hand and tell the person in charge what's wrong. Always, always ask questions if you're unsure, and don't worry about using computer terms; just describe the problem you are having.

What Not to Do When Taking a Computer-Based Test

No matter how much you know about computers, there are some things you should **never do** when taking a computer-based test.

> **HINT**
>
> Do not press keys randomly. Do not press CTRL (Control), ALT (Alternate), and ESC (Escape) at the same time.

- Never turn anything on or off without being asked to do so.

- Don't press any combination of keys you are not asked to press, especially any marked CTRL (for Control), ALT (for Alternate), or ESC (for Escape).

- Don't play with the computer. Just use it to take the test.

The computer-based tests described in this chapter are made so that it is easy to take the test. The questions may be hard, but answering them using a computer should be easy.

The computer-based tests we have looked at in this chapter use questions that look as though they could be printed in a paper test book. There is another type of computer-based test that asks you to watch short videos and then answer questions about what you've seen. That type of test is described in the next chapter.

Taking a Video-Based Test

This chapter is about video-based tests of mechanical aptitude and spatial relations. With this type of test, you watch a video and answer questions, both on a computer. Some of the questions are the same as, or similar to, questions in earlier chapters. Some of the questions are very different, and involve learning about machines in a factory setting. For some hints on how to use a computer to answer questions and how to learn about other kinds of computer-based tests, turn to Appendix A, "The Different Types of Computer-Based Tests."

WHAT DO THESE QUESTIONS ASK ABOUT?

You'll be asked questions about how mechanical objects, or machines, work together and how they move. There are two basic types of questions on the test:

Type 1: General mechanical aptitude questions

Type 2: Operation of a model factory questions.

The general mechanical aptitude questions may be set in the factory, but you don't need to know how the factory works to answer these questions.

Before you are asked any questions about the model factory, you will be shown a video about how the factory works. You will have to learn and remember how each of the machines in the factory works, and how they work together. The questions on this type of test will ask if any of the machines in the model factory are not working correctly, and about what is going wrong.

WHAT DO THESE TESTS LOOK LIKE?

The whole test is on a video that stops after each question so you can answer. The video is a high-quality cartoon that first shows a factory with several machines working, one after another, to make a finished product. The machines are set up so the output of one machine is sent to the next machine to be worked on more. When you take this test, first you'll watch a video that shows how the entire factory works from start to finish. Then you'll watch shorter videos about different parts of what you've just seen. You'll answer one multiple choice question after each of the shorter videos. Here are two sample questions, one like each of the two types you'll see on the test.

Sample General Mechanical Aptitude Question

In the picture to the right, if gear A is turning clockwise. Which way will gear C turn?

☐ Clockwise

☐ Counterclockwise

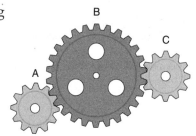

ANSWER AND EXPLANATION

The correct answer is Clockwise. When gear A turns clockwise, gear B will turn counterclockwise. Then when gear B moves counterclockwise, gear C will move clockwise. To read more about how gears work, read Chapter 4 of this book, called "Gears."

Sample Model Factory Question

This chapter can't show you a video, but here is an example of what you might see in the video. This drawing shows a factory that makes chocolate candies.

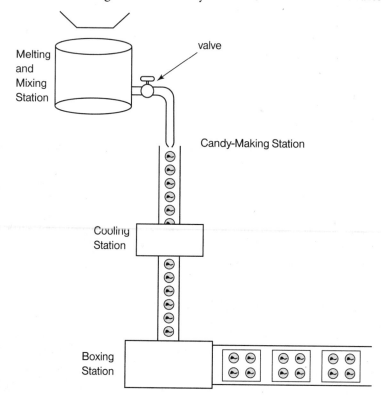

The first machine is the Melting and Mixing Station where the chocolate is mixed. From here, the chocolate mixture goes through a pipe to a Candy-Making Station where the chocolate candies are made. The candies all are round. The Boxing Station puts the candies in boxes of four.

Here is the same factory. Do you notice a problem at any of the stations?

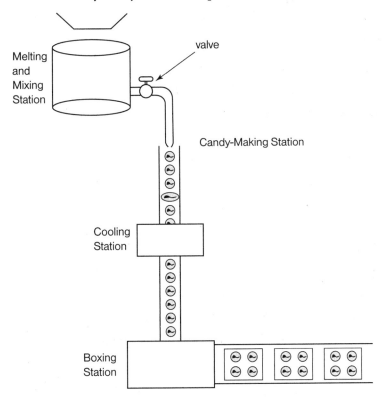

Which station is not working correctly?

(A) Melting and Mixing Station
(B) Candy-Making Station
(C) Cooling Station
(D) Boxing Station
(E) Everything Is Working Normally.

ANSWER AND EXPLANATION

The correct answer is B. Did you notice that one of the chocolates is the wrong shape (in between the Candy-Making Station and the Cooling Station)? It's the only difference between the first drawing and the second, and it shows a problem. On the real test, this question would be a little trickier since you wouldn't have still pictures like these to look at while answering the question. Instead, you would see a video showing the whole factory, one workstation at a time, in motion and working correctly. Then you would see another video showing exactly the same thing, except that this time one of the chocolate candies would be the wrong shape.

WHAT DO THESE QUESTIONS MEASURE?

These questions measure your mechanical knowledge by asking about mechanical objects and about mechanical and physical principles. They also test your ability to recognize problems in complicated mechanical systems. They test your ability to solve problems that require you to think about:

- simple machines such as:

    pulleys

    levers

    inclined planes

    wedges

    wheels and axles

    screws

- gears

- electrical circuits

- the working of machines in a model factory setting, including:

    how the machines work alone and together

    which machine is not working correctly

    what might be causing the machine(s) to work wrong.

For a general overview of the basic mechanics and physics of everyday objects and of the way many simple machines, gears, and electrical circuits work, read Chapter 3, "General Mechanical Understanding."

WHAT THIS CHAPTER COVERS

This rest of this chapter talks more about the format of the video test and the kinds of questions you can expect to see. It does not talk about the mechanical principles you need to know to answer the questions, like the way that gears or pulleys works (look at Chapters 4, 5, and 6 of this book). This chapter gives some helpful test-taking strategies for taking a video test. At the end of the chapter, you'll find information about a practice test you can order to take on a computer in your home (or at a library, if you do not own a computer).

If you haven't used computers much or at all, see Appendix A, "The Different Types of Computer-Based Tests," which talks about what you need to know to take a computer-based test.

Video Test Introduction

The test begins with an introduction that will last a few minutes. You will see this introduction only once, so **pay attention to it!** The introduction may start by showing a very large room in a factory with a few machines. The video will tell you what kind of factory you are in and what it makes (it might make chocolate candies, for example). The video may also give you some helpful tips on taking the test. Pay attention to what the speaker says.

After giving you a general overview of the factory, the video will walk you step-by-step through the factory from beginning to end, explaining each machine or work-station and what happens at that workstation. For example, in a chocolate candy factory, one station melts and mixes the chocolate, another pours out a little of the hot liquid chocolate to make a round candy, another station cools the new candy, and the last one packs the candy in boxes.

At some point, the video will take you into the control room. In the control room, there are some controls for each workstation. For each set of controls, there are dis-plays that show whether the workstation is working correctly.

The Questions

Now the questions begin. Very few questions on this test will take more than sixty seconds to answer, and that includes the time it takes to watch whatever video goes with the question. The questions are divided into two different types.

TYPE 1: GENERAL QUESTIONS

General Questions are set in the factory, but you don't have to know how the whole factory works to answer each question. You can answer these questions without knowing any of the things you were shown in the introduction. General Questions test your knowledge of simple machines (e.g., levers, pulleys), gears, and electrical circuits.

Here are two examples of this type of question.

Sample Question

Gear C can turn but cannot move to the left or right. The flat gears A and B can move to the left and right.

If gear C turns clockwise, in which direction will A and B go?

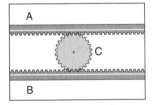

A   **B**   **C**

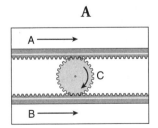
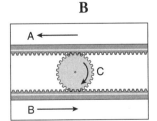
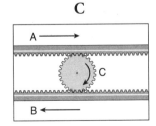

ANSWER AND EXPLANATION

The correct answer is C. When the round gear turns clockwise, the teeth at the top move to the right and the teeth at the bottom move to the left.

Sample Question

Which way can you move the handle on this valve?

(A) Pull the handle towards you.
(B) Push the handle away from you.
(C) Either pull or push the handle.

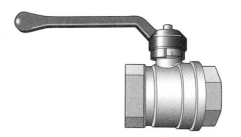

ANSWER AND EXPLANATION

The correct answer is B. There is a little square piece of metal on the valve which will stop the handle from moving if you try to pull it towards you. Look at the photo until you see this little square piece of metal. It is touching the bottom of the black handle.

LISTEN CAREFULLY

Before each question, you will see a short video. Then the speaker will ask a question. The question will not show up on the screen as text. So pay attention to what the speaker asks and to the video.

DECIDE WHICH DETAILS ARE IMPORTANT

You will have to decide which details are important and which are not. For example, if you are asked "What is the best way to lift a wooden box with a lever?" probably it does not matter that the box is made of wood. The only thing that matters is where you put the lever. On the other hand, if the question shows you a picture of four screws and asks which is the best one for attaching a thin metal sign to a wooden box, the material of the box does matter since you have to choose the best screw for screwing into wood.

MARKING YOUR ANSWER

> **TIP**
>
> You'll have about 10 seconds to answer a question. Time 10 seconds on your watch to see how long that is.

After the speaker asks a question, you will see the answer choices, perhaps next to pictures of the choices. For example, if you're asked what screw is best for attaching a thin metal sign to a wooden box, you might see pictures of four different kinds of screws marked A, B, C, and D. Somewhere on the screen you'll be able to click the option you want: A, B, C, or D. Click the one you think is best. After you mark the answer you think is best, you may have to click another button, with a label like "Answer," to tell the computer you've selected your final answer. You'll have only about 10 seconds to answer. So think before you mark, but make sure you answer the question before the time is up. You will not be able to go back and review your answers.

DIAGRAMS

Some of the questions may involve diagrams. If you see one on the test, don't panic. Just stop and ask yourself what the question is asking you and what you really need to know to find the answer. Once you've figured this out, you'll be able to see what information in the diagram you need and what information you can ignore.

In the sample question below, there's a paragraph for you to read before looking at the diagram. On the real test, you might not have a paragraph like this to read. Instead, the speaker will tell you about what's going on in the factory and then ask you a question. That means you'll have to pay careful attention to what the speaker says since you won't be able to go back and read the question.

Sample Question

You are in a chocolate factory. There are four workstations in this factory, the pouring station, the cooling station, the decorating station, and the wrapping station. As you can see in the diagram below, three switches control the electricity to the workstations. Everything is turned off in this diagram.

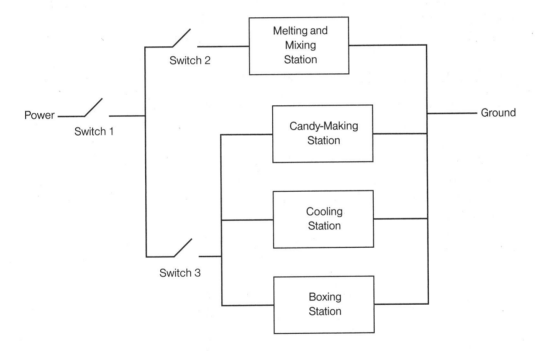

To turn on the Melting and Mixing Station only, what switches should you close?

(A) Switch 1 only
(B) Switches 1 and 2 only
(C) Switches 1 and 3 only
(D) Switches 2 and 3 only
(E) Switches 1, 2, and 3

ANSWER AND EXPLANATION

The correct answer is B. Switch 1 lets power flow to the two other switches. Switch 2 controls the Melting and Mixing Station. To read more about how electrical circuits work, see Chapter 3 of this book.

TYPE 2: FACTORY OPERATION QUESTIONS

For Factory Operation Questions, everything you were shown during the introduction becomes important again. Before each question, you will be shown a short video. After you watch the video, you'll have to decide if there's a problem in the factory and, if so, which workstation has the problem. There are two different videos, a factory machine video and a control room video.

VIDEO 1: FACTORY MACHINE VIDEO

This video takes you step-by-step through the factory (just as the speaker did during the introduction, except that this time, there is no speaker), showing you each workstation in the line for several seconds. Every time you see this video you will see the same workstations in the same order. Then you will be asked to choose the station that has a problem. If you don't think anything is wrong, you should mark the choice that says something like "Everything Is Working Normally." If you don't have a choice like that, then you know there is a problem somewhere.

VIDEO 2: CONTROL ROOM VIDEO

The Control Room Video takes you off the main floor of the factory and into the control room (just as the speaker did during the introduction, except that this time, there is no speaker), showing you the gauge for each workstation. There may be several different types of gauges, but they usually are easy to read. For example, there may be an arrow that points to a scale. The scale may have a "safe" area and a "danger" area. In this drawing, the arrow is pointing to the danger zone. This means there is a problem.

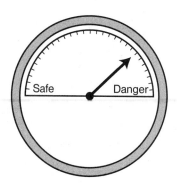

Every time you see the Control Room Series, you will see the same gauges in the same order. At the end, you will be asked to choose which station has a problem. If you don't think anything is wrong, you should mark the choice that says something like "Everything Is Working Normally." If you don't have a choice like that, then you know there is definitely a problem somewhere on the line.

How Do I Decide Which Station Has a Problem?

Deciding which station has a problem is like playing a game of spot-the-difference. When the speaker took you step-by-step through the factory during the introduction, you had the chance to see all the workstations working correctly. Now you have to decide which station looks or sounds different from the first time you saw it. You will be shown each station for several seconds. As you're looking at each station, pay attention to:

1. Strange Noises.

   Some stations have a sound they always make. Others are quiet; so when you're looking at them, you should hear only the steady hum of the factory. If a station sounds different from the first time the speaker took you step-by-step through the factory, that's where the problem is.

   > This is the kind of question you might ask yourself:
   > *Did that gear make a clanking sound the last time I saw it?*

2. Anything New or Missing.

   Try to decide if there is something new in the picture . . .

   > This is the kind of question you might ask yourself:
   > *There's water dripping from that spout. Was there water dripping from that spout before?*

   or if something is missing.

   > This is the kind of question you might ask yourself:
   > *There's nothing on that conveyer belt. Should there be something on that conveyer belt?*

3. Anything Moved or Turned.

   Try to decide if something has changed positions.

   > This is the kind of question you might ask yourself:
   > *Was that hose pulled out of that barrel the last time I saw it?*

4. New Shapes or Sizes.

   Try to decide if anything is the wrong shape or size.

   > This is the kind of question you might ask yourself:
   > *Are those chocolate candies a different shape from the first time I saw them?*

5. Unexpected Colors.

   Try to decide if something has changed color.

Usually color changes, noises, and the like will be obvious, if you pay attention.

How Do I Decide Which Station Has a Problem for a Control Room Video Question?

For a Control Room Video question, often there is a clear problem. Each gauge will show dials or bars. The dials or the bars will point to or show either a "safe" value, which will probably be green, or a "danger" value, which will probably be red. (When the speaker walks you through the control room during the introduction, he/she will tell you about the "safe" and "danger" zones on the gauges.) If something is wrong, at least one dial or bar will be in a danger zone. Since each station has its own gauge in the control room, when you see a gauge with a dial or a bar in the danger zone, you'll know that is the station that is having trouble.

For example, here is a bar gauge that reads in the danger zone.

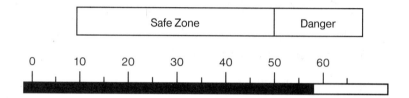

TESTING LOCATIONS

Though you might take the test on-site at the company you're applying to work for, there are also special off-site testing centers that employers sometimes hire to test applicants. Carefully read anything the company gives you about the tests or the test location.

THE ONLINE FIRETEAM PRACTICE TEST

The FireTEAM Practice Test, published by Ergometrics, Inc., gives you a chance to see firsthand what it's like to take a video-based mechanical aptitude test. This practice test is actually made up of several different sections, but the only section that is important for you is the FireTEAM ErgoMechanical Reasoning Video Test. The other sections on the test are for people planning to be firefighters.

How Do I Purchase the Test?

In order to purchase the test, go to the ErgoMetrics FireTEAM website at http://www.ergometricsonline.com/ftt/login.cfm and click "Order Form." This will take you to a webpage where you can order the test using either Visa or MasterCard.

(The author of this Barron's book has no connection with the ErgoMetrics company. At the time this book was written, this was the only practice test available on the web. You might search the web to see if there are others that have come out since this book was written.)

How Is the Practice Test Administered?

There are two versions of the test. Both are taken on a computer, but one is taken online, and the other on a DVD or a CD-ROM. Both have the same content. It is faster to take the online version. You should order only the CD-ROM version if your Internet connection is very slow or you cannot get the online version to work. You will be able to take the test only twice per order, no matter which version you buy.

How Much Does the Practice Test Cost?

At the time this book was written, the test cost about $25.

TIPS FOR TAKING THE PRACTICE TEST

1. Reboot your computer before starting the practice test.
2. Set Windows Media Player as your default media player.
3. Close all windows except the one for Internet Explorer.
4. Turn off firewalls and pop-up blocking software.
5. Set Internet Explorer to accept cookies.
6. Copy and paste your password and user name directly from the e-mail ErgoMetrics sends you into the correct fields on the log-in page. This way you'll avoid typos.
7. If you get disconnected during the test, just log on again. The test will begin where you were cut off.
8. If the test plays the first video but won't advance any further, move the cursor to the lower-right corner of the video screen. There's a button there that will make the test move forward. Be careful, though. If you do this in the middle of a video, it will take you to the next video, and you won't be able to go back.

What Else Can I Do to Prepare?

Preparing for this type of test can be a lot of fun. Here are two ideas.

Take a tour of an actual factory. If you are lucky enough to live near a factory, call and ask if they give tours. You may be able to ask questions on the tour. If so, try asking something like, "who makes repairs to the machines, and what kind of repairs do they make?"

Talk with people who repair anything. Ask them about their job. How do they know what needs to be fixed? How do they know what to do? Ask them to show you examples. If they let you, watch them while they work. Maybe thay will tell you what they are doing as they figure out what is broken or causing the problem.

Index

AC (alternating current)
    electric generator, 19
    power supply, 19
Adjustable wrench, 93–94
Allen wrench, 94

Back diagonal view, 181
Ball-peen hammer, 88
Basic electricity, 15–16
Batteries
    connected wrong, 31–32
    in holder, 19
    in parallel, 20–21
    in series, 20
Battery, 18–19, 23–24, 29
Belt pulleys, 38–39
Belts, 39
Block, 68–69
Bolt, 93
Box wrench, 93–94

C-clamp, 96
Channel-lock® pliers, 89–90
Cheating, 6
Circuit, 15, 21–22
Circular saw, 95
Classes, 11
Claw, 87
Claw hammer, 87, 96
Clockwise, 38, 52, 58–59
Closed circuits, 21–22
Closed position (on), 17
Combination wrench, 93–94, 96
Compass directions, 102–103
Complicated pulleys, 77
Computer-based test. *See also* test
    taking; video-based test

answers, reviewing your, 449
new computer user, 451–452
readiness for, 449–451
set up of, 446–448
what not to do, 452
what tests looked like, 445–446
Conductor, 15
Counterclockwise, 38, 52, 58–59
Counting
    blocks, 190, 194–195
    sides, 242
    touching blocks, 203–211
Crescent® wrench, 86, 94
Crossing lines, 122
Cut-ups, 149–156

Diagonal fold, 179–180
Doing, 10
Double pulley, 72–78
Double spur gear, 57–58
Drawings side by side, 243
Driver/follower, 50–51

East, 103
Electric drill, 95
Electric saber saw, 95
Electrical
    circuit parts, 15–16, 20–21
    hardware on test, 17–21
    load, 27
    path, 16, 22, 26, 29
    switch, 17–18
    symbols, 16, 20

Facedown, 227–228
Fasteners, 92–93
Filament, 22

FireTEAM Practice Test, 462–463
Flat-head screwdriver, 91
Flat shapes, 143–145
Flip, 163, 168
Folding pattern for box, 212–214
Front diagonal view, 181
Fuse, 20
Fuse holder, 20

Gears, 15, 50–61
Gears with missing teeth, 60
Glue gun, 96
Gravity, 32–34
Groove, 38
Ground, 21
Guessing, 6

Hacksaw, 91, 97
Hammer face, 87–88
Hammer head, 87–88
Hammers, 87–88
Hidden blocks, 189–196
Hole punching, 177–183
Horizontal fold, 179–180
Horseshoe magnet, 40

Important words, 13
Incandescent lightbulb, 22–24
Inside out, 227–228, 242
Intent of questions, 13
Internal gear, 59–60

Jigsaw, 95
Jigsaw puzzles, 161–172
Jobs requiring tests, vi
Jumper, 121–122

Knife switch, 17

Legend, 107–108
Level, 88–89
Levers, 35–38
Lightbulb, 22–24
Lightbulb in holder, 17
Line following, 121–123
Load, 15, 20–21
Locking pliers, 90

Machine screw, 92
Magnets, 40
Map
    question rule, 104–106
    reading, 101–113
    symbols, 107
Matching shapes, 127–131
Mating gears, 51–52, 59
Mechanical aptitude, 9–11
Mechanical aptitude test, v, 85,
        453–454
Mechanics of everyday objects, 40–42
Miter gear, 56
Motion, 42
Move, 163, 167

Needle nose pliers, 89–90
Negative pole, 29–30, 32
9-volt battery, 18, 29
Nonadjustable wrench, 93
North, 103, 111
Northeast, 108–110
Northwest, 108–110
Nut, 92–93

On-off knife switch, 17
On-off toggle switch, 18
1½ volt battery, 18, 29
110-volt power, 19
Open circuit, 21–22, 24–25
Open-ended wrench, 93
Open position (off), 17

Paper folding
    shape known, 239–243
    shape unknown, 223–238
Parallel circuit, 23–24, 26, 30–31
Partly hidden blocks, 193–195, 207
Parts assembly, 271–277
Path of electricity, 15, 20–21
Pattern folding, 229
Patterns, 215
Pendulum, 34–35
Phillips screwdriver, 92
Physics of everyday objects, 40–42
Pipe wrench, 94
Pivot point, 35–38

Pliers, 89–90
Positive pole, 29–30, 32
Power source, 16, 20–21
Practice questions, using, 43, 61
Pulleys, 15, 68–70

Reading, 10–11
Rechargeable battery, 95
Rectangular boxes, 211–218
Retractable rule, 88–89
Rotate, 163
Rotated shapes, 141–146
Rotating, 142
Rotations per second, 55
Rubber mallet, 88

Saber saw, 95
Saws, 90–91
Scissors, 37–38
Screwdrivers, 91–92
Screws, 92–93
Series circuit, 23–24, 26–27, 30
Shaft, 51
Short circuit, 27–29
Side view, 193
Single pulley, 68–71, 78
6-volt battery, 19
Sledge hammer, 88
Slip-joint pliers, 89–90
Slotted screwdriver, 91–92
Small electrical power tools, 87, 95
Socket wrench, 94
Solid shapes, 224
Source of electricity, 15
South, 103
Southeast, 108–110
Southwest, 108–110
Spatial ability, 9–11
Spatial aptitude test, v–vi
Speed of gears, 53
Spur gear, 50, 57–58
Square, 88–89
Square gear, 60
Stable, 73–76
Stilson wrench, 94
Supporting block, 189
Switch, 16, 20–21

Teeth, 50, 53–59
Temporary lever, 36–37
Test taking. *See also* computer-based
    test; video-based test
  answer, best, 240–242
  answer sheet, 4–5, 7
  answers, checking your, 7
  practice questions, using, 43, 61, 79,
      97, 113, 123, 131, 138, 146, 156,
      183, 196, 208, 218, 232, 244,
      277
  rules for questions, 104–106, 130,
      150–151, 163–164, 204–205,
      272–273
  suggested approach, 137, 145–146,
      152–155, 165, 180–181, 206,
      217, 231, 274–276
  test, after the, 7
  test, before the, 2–3
  test, day of the, 3
  test, writing on the, 7
  test instructions, 5
  test location, 4
  test-taking strategies, 5–6
  time limit, 6, 43, 61, 78, 97, 112,
      123, 131, 137, 146, 156, 172,
      183, 196, 208, 218, 231, 243,
      276
  tips for questions, 1, 61, 78, 112,
      123, 130, 136, 146, 156, 171,
      182, 196, 208, 218, 231, 276
  week before the test, 3
  what questions ask, 13, 49, 67
  what questions measure, 14–15
  what tests cover, 2
  what tests look like, 14, 49–50,
      67–68, 86, 101–102, 121–122,
      127–129, 135, 141–142,
      149–150, 161–162, 177–178,
      203–204, 211–212, 223–224,
      271–272
  what to bring to test, 3–4
  what to do to prepare, 43, 61, 78,
      97, 112, 123, 137, 146, 156, 171,
      183, 196, 208, 217, 231, 243,
      276

what to learn to do better, 43, 61, 78, 112, 130, 137, 146, 170, 196, 207, 217, 231, 243, 276
Thinking, 11
Three pulleys, 72–73
Toggle switch, 18
Tongue-and-groove pliers, 90
Tools, 85–99
Touching block, 203–211
Turn, 167
Turning over, 142
12-volt battery, 30
Two batteries, 29

Vertical fold, 179–180
Video-based test. *See also* computer-based test; test taking
    control room question, 462
    diagrams, 459–460
    general questions, 457–458
    introduction, 456–457
    mechanical aptitude test, 453–454
    model factory question, 453–455
    on-line FireTEAM Practice Test, 462–463

    problems with station, 461
    questions asked, 453
    test cost, 463
    test location, 462
    test purchase, 462
    tips for taking, 463
    what questions measure, 456
    what tests looked like, 453–454
Vise-grip® pliers, 89–90
Visual comparison, 135–138

Washers, 93
Watching, 9–10
Weight times distance, 36
West, 103
Wheel, 68, 70
Wing nut, 93
Wires making connection, 19
Wires not making connection, 20
Wood saw, 91
Wood screw, 92
Worm gear, 60
Wrenches, 93–94

MOVE TO THE HEAD OF YOUR CLASS
THE EASY WAY!

Barron's presents **THE E-Z SERIES** (formerly THE EASY WAY SERIES)—specially prepared by top educators, it maximizes effective learning while minimizing the time and effort it takes to raise your grades, brush up on the basics, and build your confidence. Comprehensive and full of clear review examples, **THE E-Z SERIES** is your best bet for better grades, quickly!

ISBN 978-0-7641-4256-7	**E-Z Accounting, 5th Ed.**
ISBN 978-0-7641-4257-4	**E-Z Algebra, 5th Ed.**
ISBN 978-0-7641-1973-6	**American History the Easy Way, 3rd Ed.**
ISBN 978-0-7641-3428-9	**American Sign Language the Easy Way, 2nd Ed.**
ISBN 978-0-7641-1979-8	**Anatomy and Physiology the Easy Way, 2nd Ed.**
ISBN 978-0-7641-2913-1	**Arithmetic the Easy Way, 4th Ed.**
ISBN 978-0-7641-4134-8	**E-Z Biology, 4th Ed.**
ISBN 978-0-7641-1079-5	**Bookkeeping the Easy Way, 3rd Ed.**
ISBN 978-0-7641-0314-8	**Business Letters the Easy Way, 3rd Ed.**
ISBN 978-0-7641-4259-8	**E-Z Business Math, 4th Ed.**
ISBN 978-0-7641-2920-9	**Calculus the Easy Way, 4th Ed.**
ISBN 978-0-7641-4128-7	**E-Z Chemistry, 5th Ed.**
ISBN 978-0-7641-2579-9	**Creative Writing the Easy Way**
ISBN 978-0-7641-2146-3	**Earth Science the Easy Way**
ISBN 978-0-7641-1981-1	**Electronics the Easy Way, 4th Ed.**
ISBN 978-0-7641-3736-5	**English for Foreign Language Speakers the Easy Way**
ISBN 978-0-7641-4260-4	**E-Z English, 5th Ed.**
ISBN 978-0-7641-3050-2	**Forensics the Easy Way**
ISBN 978-0-7641-3411-1	**French the Easy Way, 4th Ed.**
ISBN 978-0-7641-2435-8	**French Grammar the Easy Way**
ISBN 978-0-7641-3918-5	**E-Z Geometry, 4th Ed.**
ISBN 978-0-7641-4261-1	**E-Z Grammar, 2nd Ed.**
ISBN 978-0-7641-3413-5	**Italian the Easy Way, 3rd Ed.**
ISBN 978-0-8120-9627-9	**Japanese the Easy Way**
ISBN 978-0-7641-3237-7	**Macroeconomics the Easy Way**
ISBN 978-0-7641-9369-9	**Mandarin Chinese the Easy Way, 2nd Ed.**
ISBN 978-0-7641-4132-4	**E-Z Math, 5th Ed.**
ISBN 978-0-7641-1871-5	**Math Word Problems the Easy Way**
ISBN 978-0-7641-2845-5	**Microbiology the Easy Way**
ISBN 978-0-8120-9601-9	**Microeconomics the Easy Way**
ISBN 978-0-7641-2794-6	**Organic Chemistry the Easy Way**
ISBN 978-0-7641-4126-3	**E-Z Physics, 4th Ed.**
ISBN 978-0-7641-2892-9	**Precalculus the Easy Way**
ISBN 978-0-7641-2393-1	**Psychology the Easy Way**
ISBN 978-0-7641-4129-4	**E-Z Spanish, 5th Ed.**
ISBN 978-0-7641-2263-7	**Spanish Grammar the Easy Way**
ISBN 978-0-8120-9852-5	**Speed Reading the Easy Way**
ISBN 978-0-7641-3410-4	**Spelling the Easy Way, 4th Ed.**
ISBN 978-0-7641-3978-9	**E-Z Statistics, 4th Ed.**
ISBN 978-0-7641-1360-4	**Trigonometry the Easy Way, 3rd Ed.**
ISBN 978-0-8120-9765-8	**World History the Easy Way, Vol. One**
ISBN 978-0-8120-9766-5	**World History the Easy Way, Vol. Two**
ISBN 978-0-7641-1206-5	**Writing the Easy Way, 3rd Ed.**

Available January 2010

ISBN 978-0-7641-4258-1	**E-Z American History, 4th Ed.**
ISBN 978-0-7641-4133-1	**E-Z Bookkeeping, 4th Ed.**
ISBN 978-0-7641-4249-9	**E-Z Spanish Grammar, 2nd Ed.**
ISBN 978-0-7641-4251-2	**E-Z Trigonometry, 4th Ed.**

Please visit
www.barronseduc.com to view
current prices and to order books

Barron's Educational Series, Inc.
250 Wireless Boulevard
Hauppauge, New York 11788

In Canada: Georgetown Book Warehouse
34 Armstrong Avenue
Georgetown, Ontario L7G 4R9

(#45) R6/09

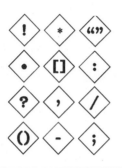

HOW TO USE THIS BOOK

In case you started here at the back, this will help you use this book.

- Flip the pages and find a test you are interested in.
- Read the chapter that teaches about that test.
- Do the practice questions at the end of the chapter.
- Take the timed practice test at the end of the book.
- Read the first three chapters:
    - Introduction
    - The Streetwise Test Taker
    - How to Develop Your Mechanical Aptitude and Spatial Ability